Strategies of
arms control

Political Analyses

This major new series, a flagship for Manchester University Press, will include some of the best new writing across the range of political science subdisciplines. All of them will present exciting new research or provocative syntheses in an accessible style, and will be available in paperback.

Series editors: Bill Jones, Michael Clarke and Michael Moran

Brendan Evans and Andrew Taylor
From Salisbury to Major: continuity and change in Conservative politics

Michael Foley and John E. Owens
Congress and the Presidency: institutional politics in a separated system

E. Franklin Dukes
Resolving public conflict: transforming community and governance

Roland Axtmann
Liberal democracy into the twenty-first century: globalization, integration and the nation state

Strategies of arms control

A history and typology

Stuart Croft

Manchester University Press
Manchester and New York

distributed exclusively in the USA by St. Martin's Press

Published by Manchester University Press
Oxford Road, Manchester M13 9NR, UK
and Room 400, 175 Fifth Avenue, New York, NY 10010, USA

Distributed exclusively in the USA
by St. Martin's Press, Inc., 175 Fifth Avenue, New York, NY 10010, USA

British Library Cataloguing-in-Publication Data
A catalogue record for this book is available from the British Library

Library of Congress Cataloging-in-Publication Data
Croft, Stuart
    Strategies of arms control: a history and typology
  / Stuart Croft.
      p.   cm. — (Political analyses)
      ISBN 0–7190–4877–X — ISBN 0–7190–4878–8 (pbk.)
      1. Arms Control.   2. Arms control—Political aspects.   3. Security International.
    I. Title.
    JX1974.C79   1996
    327.1'74—dc20   96–8349
                                                                                CIP

ISBN 0 7190 4877 X *hardback*
     0 7190 4878 8 *paperback*

First published 1996

00 99 98 97 96   10 9 8 7 6 5 4 3 2 1

Typeset in Great Britain
by Northern Phototypesetting Co, Ltd, Bolton
Printed in Great Britain
by Bell & Bain Ltd, Glasgow

Contents

Foreword

Human activity can in theory take two polar forms: pure anarchy and/or randomness, and rule following. The relations of states have traditionally been regarded as operating more at the anarchic end of this spectrum than through conformity to rules of behaviour. Nowhere has the accuracy of these observations been assumed to be more correct than in the military relationships between states. And yet, as Stuart Croft has been at pains to describe and analyse in this study, polities have sought from their inception to make those relationships both more predictable and less prone to stimulating conflict by embarking upon activities that have been variously labelled arms limitation, arms regulation, disarmament or arms control.

The study seeks to both place such activities in a historical perspective, and to demonstrate that the US–USSR activities that were labelled 'nuclear arms control' in the thirty year period from 1960 to 1990 were not unique, nor solely a product of the advent of nuclear weapon technology. Yet it goes beyond this, for it asks an increasingly significant question: how have these arms control activities changed since the end of the cold war? By implication, this also means asking how past activities were conditioned by the structures and behaviours attendant on the East–West conflict. Answers to these questions are provided not by judgements on whether arms control agreements have been 'successful' or not, but by reference to typologies of the objectives sought by those agreements, and by analysing how both the objectives and scope of those agreements have evolved over time and are still evolving.

Central to this study is the argument that in the post-cold war era, arms control has broadened its scope to encompass the disarmament by international organisations, in particular the UN, of warring factions within states. This emphasises a further key issue: that limitations and constraints on armaments and the actions of military organisations are tools for reinforcing political arrangements between and within states, not ends in themselves. In the period of the cold war, when the US–USSR dialogue on strategic arms limitations was apparently one of the few channels of communications that were open between the two antagonistic armed blocs, this tended to be obscured by the argument that 'jaw, jaw' was better than 'war, war', which gave arms control the appearance of being an end in itself. In the new era, it is useful to be reminded that arms control is merely a facilitator, not an objective.

Stuart Croft has produced a stimulating analysis which can be used in several different ways. It offers a framework for thinking about how arms might be constrained in the future, as well as a very comprehensive description of how they have been constrained in the past. It illuminates how, in the modern world, those anarchic tendencies that may exist have been overlain by webs of overlapping arms control agreements. These webs increasingly demand conformity by all states to accepted rules of behaviour in the area traditionally seen as the epitome of state sovereignty: security policy and military activities. Above all it is a contribution to a task that is now increasingly urgent: to think through the nature of the post-cold war international system; how it differs from the past; and how a secure future international order might be constructed around it.

John Simpson
University of Southampton

Preface

The origin of this book lies in the mid-1980s. At that time, arms control was the subject of great political and academic debate. With no arms control negotiations between the superpowers from the end of 1983 to 1985, massive peace movements (broadly hostile to arms control) in many countries, and the Reagan administration apparently being convinced that security could be found through a unilateral build up of weapons rather than through arms control, the whole debate over the management of arms was perhaps more vital than it had ever been.

In the midst of this debate, Lawrence Freedman published a short monograph entitled 'Why is Arms Control So Boring?'[1] This came as a great surprise for not only had it not really occurred that arms control could be boring, but also because the animated nature of the public and academic debate seemed to imply the opposite. Freedman's critique was that there was an inevitable tendency to become caught in the detail of arms control and this was, to most people, boring. But he also argued that:

> My own view is that the most effective work may also be the most scholarly. Rather than seeking to second guess policy-makers or provide expert backing for political campaigns, the most important contributions may be those that affect the overall conceptual framework within which these issues are considered and discussed.[2]

This call to reconsider the conceptual framework of arms control has at root motivated the writing of this book. With the end of the cold war, and the publication of various critiques of the whole enterprise of arms control, the need for a re-evaluation seemed, if anything, that much greater. There is a large and growing literature on arms control, reflecting the fact that, particularly since the mid-1980s, there has been a tremendous amount of arms

---

[1] Lawrence Freedman 'Why is Arms Control So Boring?' *Faraday Discussion Paper* No.9, London: Council for Arms Control, 1987.
[2] *Ibid.*, p. 5.

control activity between states. Drawing on Freedman's call, this book seeks to add to that literature, but to do so in a novel fashion. The mass of arms control agreements that have been negotiated and signed have rarely been categorised. It is this process of developing a typology that forms the central task of this book. Categorisation is important not simply for itself, but in order to broaden our interpretation (and, therefore, to deepen our understanding) of arms control.

Too often, arms control is defined in a very narrow fashion. Both supporters of arms control and opponents have argued that arms control has sought to reduce the likelihood of war, and in the cold war East–West relationship, to do so by underpinning nuclear deterrence. Of course, this is so. This book, however, will broaden the definition of arms control beyond this, and will thereby produce a more cosmopolitan approach to arms control than that derived from the theoretical framework designed by Thomas Schelling, Morton Halperin, Hedley Bull and others in the late 1950s and early 1960s. Arms control in the 1990s, as before, is also about influencing the nature of relations between polities that are between war and peace. There is no scope for arms control during a bloody conflict; neither is there any scope for arms control when states are genuinely at peace, in the sense in which Canada and the United States, for example, have been at peace since before the Second World War. However, many states – and their premodern equivalents – operate in a state of non-war; where cooperation is at least as important as competition, and where recourse to arms control may be not only to make war less likely, but also to enhance the political position of one state over another, or to affect the nature of government within a target state. Thus, the broader definition of arms control must include not only agreements such as START (Strategic Arms Reduction Treaty) and the NPT (Non-Proliferation Treaty) within its parameters, but also the Geneva Conventions, and United Nations disarmament activity in Somalia and Mozambique. Of course, arms control affects strategic issues in very important ways. However, security is essentially a political phenomenon and, consequently, arms control has been a fundamentally political behavioural pattern, one that the political leaders of many different polities have repeatedly utilised over time. It is this political essence, this pattern of political behaviour, that is at the core of this book.

In order to make the case that arms control must be seen in a broader sense, it is important to see arms control in its true historical setting, a context which can be traced back to the years before Christ. It may seem strange that, in a book which largely focuses upon the arms control agreements of the post-cold war era, a whole chapter is devoted to arms control history. However, this history is vital, for it will be argued that arms control was not invented at a particular point in time, be it 1960, or 1920; rather, a behavioural pattern of arms control has evolved. Only by tracing that evolution can we understand the breadth of arms control in the 1990s and beyond, and only through comprehension of that evolution can the significance of relatively new developments in arms control, such as the greater emphasis in the twentieth century on its depth (defined here as the level of detail, the nature of the verification provisions, and the commitment to regime formation or maintenance) be assessed.

This book produces a typology of arms control, one derived from the text of treaties. For many of the post-cold war treaties, texts have been located in a variety of places, as indicated in the present volume. However, sources of pre-1990 arms control texts are rather more limited. In this book there has been a reliance on seven essential sources of these treaty texts: Richard D. Burns (editor) *Encyclopedia of Arms Control and Disarmament* New York: Charles Scribner 1992; Leon Friedman (editor) *The Law of War: A Documentary History* New York: Random House 1972; Trevor Dupuy and Gay Hammerman *A Documentary History of Arms Control and Disarmament* New York and London: R. R. Bowker and Co., 1973; Geoffrey Symcox *War, Diplomacy, and Imperialism, 1618–1763: Selected Documents* London: Macmillan 1974; United States Arms Control and Disarmament Agency *Arms Control and Disarmament Agreements* London: Transaction Books, 1984; Jozef Goldblat *Agreements for Arms Control* London: Taylor and Francis for SIPRI (Stockholm International Peace Research Institute), 1982; and SIPRI *Arms Control: A Survey and Appraisal of Multilateral Agreements* London: Taylor and Francis, 1978. Within this, the US Arms Control and Disarmament Agency, Goldblat and SIPRI concentrate on the period from the very late nineteenth century, and largely on the cold war period. The other four sources reproduce treaties from a much longer historical perspective.

It will be seen in the text, in particular of Chapter One, that Dupuy and Hammerman, Friedman and Symcox have been widely referenced as sources of the texts of treaties. Quotations used are directly from those volumes, with translations (where appropriate) taken directly from those reproduced by the editors. However, of particular use as a source of treaty texts was Richard D. Burns *Encyclopedia of Arms Control and Disarmament*. This is an extraordinary work, contained within three volumes. The third volume is dedicated to some five hundred pages of treaty texts.

However, the typology advanced in this book is not derived from any of the above. Some are limited by time-reference (for example, Goldblat and Symcox), while others by scope (such as Friedman). The closest typology, perhaps, is that provided by Burns, and it is to this work that further acknowledgement is due. Burns divides arms control agreements into six: limitations of weapons and personnel; demilitarisation, denuclearisation and neutralisation; regulating and outlawing weapons and war; controlling arms manufacture and traffic; rules of war; and stabilising the international environment. However, no justification is provided for this division. As will be seen, in this book greater effort is made to substantiate a categorisation of arms control. Acknowledgement must be made to these sources, without which the arguments of Chapter 1, in particular, would have been much more difficult to support.

Much of the documentary material for this book from Chapters 1 to 6 is drawn from the arms control agreements of the post-cold war era. Dating the emergence of the post-cold war world could be a controversial issue. However, it is not an important one for this book. For the sake of the analysis, it is suggested that the cold war era came to an end in the period between 1988 and 1991 – from the rise of *glasnost* to the fall of the Soviet Union. Agreements reached in this period are examined in this book, for one of the issues is the singular nature of arms control agreements reached at the end of major conflicts. The cold war, as will be seen in the text, is deemed to be a major conflict that ended, uniquely, without violence.

However, the Preface to a work is not the place for a thorough theoretical examination of the nature of the book that is to follow. The themes briefly introduced here will form the core of the argument and structure of the analysis in the book. These themes will be explicitly addressed in the Conclusion.

In a conceptual work of this kind, the author inevitably develops a series of intellectual debts. I would like to take this opportunity to acknowledge mine. In no particular order, I would like to thank: Michael Clarke, David H. Dunn, David Armstrong, Theo Farrell, Michael E. Brown and Colin McInnes for trenchant comments on manuscripts; David Nicholls and Andrew M. Dorman for forcing me to clarify obscure remarks, and to incorporate arguments and material that had originally escaped me; Jane Usherwood, for reading through many drafts, and for patiently improving my grammar; and Shahin Malik and Stephen Hill, for helping me to trace useful material. However, as usual, responsibility for errors and misjudgements rest solely with the author.

Stuart Croft
Birmingham, England
September 1995

Tables

Abbreviations

ABM	Anti-Ballistic Missile
ACV	Armoured Combat Vehicle
AIFV	Armoured Infantry Fighting Vehicle
ALCM	Air-Launched Cruise Missile
APC	Armoured Personnel Carrier
BMD	Ballistic Missile Defence
CBW	Chemical and Biological Weapons/Warfare
CFC	Ceasefire Commission
CFE	Conventional Forces in Europe
CIS	Commonwealth of Independent States
CoCom	Coordinating Committee
CSBM	Confidence- and Security-Building Measures
CSCE	Conference on Security and Cooperation in Europe
CTBT	Comprehensive Test Ban Treaty
CWC	Chemical Weapons Convention
EURATOM	European Atomic Energy Commission
GCD	General and Complete Disarmament
GLCM	Ground-Launched Cruise Missile
HACV	Heavy Armoured Combat Vehicle
IAEA	International Atomic Energy Agency
ICBM	Inter-Continental Ballistic Missile
INF	Intermediate Nuclear Forces
MAD	Mutually Assured Destruction
MD	Military District
MIRV	Multiple Independently-targetable Re-entry Vehicle
MBFR	Mutual and Balanced Force Reductions
MTCR	Missile Technology Control Regime
NAM	Non-Aligned Movement
NATO	North Atlantic Treaty Organisation
NPT	Non-Proliferation Treaty

OPCW	Organisation for the Prohibition of Chemical Weapons
ONOMOZ	United Nations Operation in Mozambique
OAS	Organisation of American States
P5	Permanent Five Members of the UN Security Council
PNE	Peaceful Nuclear Explosions
PTBT	Partial Test Ban Treaty
SALT	Strategic Arms Limitation Treaty
SDI	Strategic Defence Initiative
SIPRI	Stockholm International Peace Research Institute
SLBM	Submarine-Launched Ballistic Missile
SLCM	Submarine-Launched Cruise Missile
SRAM	Short Range Attack Missile
START	Strategic Arms Reduction Treaty
TLE	Treaty Limited Equipment
TTBT	Threshold Test Ban Treaty
UNAMIC	United Nations Advanced Mission in Cambodia
UNOSOM	United Nations Operation in Somalia
UNPROFOR	United Nations Protection Force
UNSCOM	United Nations Special Commission
UNTAC	United Nations Transitional Authority in Cambodia

Introduction

The arms control debate

The subject of arms control became one of the core sub-fields of strategic studies during the last thirty years of the cold war. In this period, arms control theory and practice was developed as a means of regulating and explaining tensions and relations between the superpowers. Brilliant innovative contributions were made on the subject by renowned analysts such as Thomas Schelling, Morton Halperin, Hedley Bull, Donald Brennan and Louis Henkin.[1] For these authors, arms control agreements could be reached in the interests of all antagonistic states, for in the nuclear age, it was in the common interest to avoid war. For the arms control scholars, war was not only caused by deliberate attack. It could be caused as a result of the interaction of powerful forces, described by the term 'security dilemma'. Instabilities, particularly in bilateral relations, could lead one state to calculate that it could best limit damage to itself by attacking first in a situation where war was seen to be inevitable. Thus, by minimising crisis and arms race instability in the interests of all rivals, arms control would develop an adversarial partnership between hostile states, and reduce the likelihood of conflict.

Yet arms control was always controversial, for many critics argued that these notions of arms control were flawed in both theory and practice. Indeed, by the late 1970s it was possible to identify *two* broad schools of thought hostile to arms control. The first school, largely based on the political right in the United States, suggested that totalitarian states such as the USSR would always have an advantage in negotiating arms control agreements, for they would not be subject to public scrutiny and the democratic process, while once agreements had been reached, totalitarian states would not hesitate to covertly breach agreed limits. The second school, largely based on the political left in Western Europe and the northeast of the United States, and in the government statements in much of the developing world, suggested that arms control was a sham, an example of great power condominium designed to legitimise the arms race. These arguments were important not only intellectually, but also in terms of political practice in the 1980s. The conservative arguments provided a major platform for the first Reagan Administration's approach to security matters, while the leftist perspective provided a significant part of the intellectual core of the Western peace movements.

The conservative perspective suggested that arms control is flawed whenever there are negotiations and agreements between democratic countries and totalitarian states. In such arms control arrangements, the totalitarian state always has the advantage. During negotiations, the totalitarian state can propose almost anything without facing domestic problems, while the proposals of the democratic state will be subject to domestic scrutiny by the legislature, the media and, in certain circumstances, public opinion. In addition, the proposals of democratic states tend to be the products of political negotiations within government, between and within foreign and defence ministries and other governmental bodies. Thus, totalitarian states have a major negotiating advantage, which prevents any truly equitable agreements from being reached. Once an agreement is reached, totalitarian countries tend to cheat on the terms and, given the lack of freedom within their societies, tend not to get caught. Cheating, however, is not an option for democracies given the power and freedom of the media. Further, even if the democratic state catches the totalitarian country cheating, little will be done, for arms control has a deadening effect upon democracies, who assume that the strategic problem has been solved by the political agreement. In summary, asymmetric political structures produce advantages for non-democrats.[2] Some scholars would go further and suggest that great benefit would be derived from recognising that arms races as such are not a problem, and that unilateral measures would enhance national security more effectively than any arms control option. Instead of managing weapons stocks through explicit agreements, implicit arrangements through unilateral changes would be the most effective strategy. This concept was, perhaps, most widely applied to arguments in favour of deploying technologies associated with SDI (the Strategic Defence Initiative) in the United States during the 1980s.[3]

The leftist perspective suggested that arms control has, largely, been a sham. It has not affected the arms race in any decisive fashion, and has proved to be a way for the great powers to ignore pressures for disarmament. Arms control has been a tool of the major powers in maintaining dangerous and threatening military postures, and those states have cooperated over arms control rather than face the real problem: the competition in arms which could in itself lead to warfare. Arms control has, therefore, been a conservative tool, fooling the gullible, and preventing a reorientation of national and international security policies. Arms control should be rejected therefore, in favour of the logic of disarmament.[4]

With the end of the cold war, the arguments of the critics of arms control seemed to gain an advantage in the debate over the validity of arms control. However, it has largely been the conservatives who have been to the fore. The major disarmament provisions contained in treaties such as START and the CFE (Conventional Forces in Europe) Treaty may not have been deep enough for some on the left; however, they made it extremely difficult for such analysts to argue that there was a distinction between arms control and disarmament in such a stark manner as they had argued had been the case with the SALT (Strategic Arms Limitation Treaty) treaties. Indeed, arguably from the signing of the INF (Intermediate Nuclear Forces) Treaty in 1987, much of the intellectual force of the leftist argument against arms control in general, as opposed to arguments against particular treaties, lost momentum. In contrast, the conservative critique of arms control continued into the post-cold war period unabated. Not only was arms control flawed, but in addition some analysts have interpreted arms control agreements such as START and CFE as representing an end to arms control as it has been conceived in contemporary intellectual history.[5] Arms control, in this sense, was a cold war creation – and failure – which has even less applicability following the collapse of cold war political structures.

There may be much validity in many of the above arguments. And this approach seemed in accordance with a general view that arms control would be marginalised, given the end of the cold war.[6] However, they are not relevant to the central thesis of this book. This study is not concerned with the success or failure of arms control, in theory or in practice. Despite all the above reservations, arms control practice has continued. Further, records of such practice can be traced back to the ancient world. States and polities in very different political and geopolitical circumstances have, over time, regularly turned to the diplomatic and strategic tool of arms control. If this practice has been so common, should not some attention be paid to understanding its breadth and complexity, to the range of issues that have been subjected to arms control solutions?

A central assumption of this book is that the post-cold war critics of arms control have not developed a damning indictment of arms control. They have not succeeded in invalidating the study of arms control. Essentially, this has been because arms control has been defined in too narrow a fashion. This is not only a fault on the part of the critics of arms control. The emphasis on policy relevance in the strategic studies literature of the cold war has led to a definition of arms control that seems, in historical perspective, to have been something of an aberration. For in order to evaluate the role of arms control in the post-cold war world, it is important to understand the development of arms control from the earliest recorded examples. Although at the end of the twentieth century notions of arms control have been understood very much in terms of the nuclear arms control experiences, arms control was a commonly used tool in relations between states long before the advent of nuclear weapons, and indeed well before the creation of strategic, and later, security, studies.

Arms control has a long history, as will be argued in Chapter One. It is highly probable that throughout that long history, arms control has been an extremely controversial activity. Statesmen and women, military leaders and scholars have almost certainly faced a variety of options and differing opinions leading to, at times, heated political argument with many highly critical of the purpose and outcomes of arms control. This book is not concerned with arguing either that arms control theory, by which it is usually meant the 'golden age' of theorising from the late 1950s to the late 1960s, or more generally arms control practice, have been uniformly beneficial or successful. The argument of this book is that arms control has been, and continues to be, a much broader activity than is usually taken to be the case. This Introduction will attempt to locate that argument in the more critical literature on arms control. The purpose is not to refute the arguments put forward in this literature, nor to put forward a glowing endorsement for arms control. Rather, the argument that will be developed in this book is that, in a sense, much of the critical literature on arms control is not relevant to the thesis of this book. Arms control may or may not be a flawed tool of diplomacy and strategy. However, the key point is that it has always been seen to be a part of the diplomatic and strategic language of polities engaged in political–strategic relations with adversaries. If it has been such a central part of the diplomatic and strategic landscape, it is a pattern of behaviour that needs greater understanding.

Yet such an argument is not always universally accepted. The criticisms of arms control have grown with the end of the cold war, as already seen. In many ways, Colin S. Gray's *House of Cards: Why Arms Control Must Fail* represents a culmination of the critique of arms control.[7] As such, it is an extremely important volume, doubly so as it was published as part of the prestigious *Cornell Studies in Security Affairs* series. Gray's argument in *House of Cards* is of great significance for this volume, for Gray presents arms control as a fundamentally flawed twentieth-century policy tool, aimed at preventing war (when it has often made war more likely), and based on fairly simple propositions. No book on arms control can begin its analysis without thoroughly assessing *House of Cards*, for Gray attempts not only to condemn the practice of arms control, but also to invalidate its study in that his condemnation could be seen as the last word on the subject. Thus, rather than examine a school of thought on this subject, a lengthy consideration of *House of Cards* follows. However, the purpose of this critique of Gray is not only to fundamentally disagree with his propositions, but it is also to use this extreme critique of arms control to illustrate three key problems with the literature on arms control in general. Too often, arms control is seen in too restricted a historical perspective; in too narrow a sense in terms of its purposes; and in too shallow a fashion in terms of its complexity.

The condemnation of arms control

Colin Gray's *House of Cards: Why Arms Control Must Fail* is perhaps the most wide-ranging condemnation of arms control ever produced. For Gray, 'History, logic, and common sense all point to the futility of arms control.'[8] Although the author tries to moderate his argument in places, it is clear throughout the text that arms control is to be completely condemned.[9] Arms control has an appeal which is 'the appeal of a chocolate diet to chocoholics. Like chocolate, arms control is superficially attractive but is really bad for us'.[10] It is also 'a mild virus that has infected the body politic and has proved to be resistant to antimicrobial drugs.'[11] Further, we learn that 'Arms control theory and policy advocacy ... postulates a value – political, strategic, economic – for its ideas that powerful theory, historical evidence, and common sense condemn as unfounded';[12] that 'any grand design for international security which relies critically upon support from an arms control process is doomed to fail';[13] that 'The historical record is so rich that anybody who would claim that the future of arms control will be noticeably different from its past should be weighed down with the requirement of a very large burden of proof';[14] and that 'the time is long overdue for arms control quackery to be exposed'.[15]

The central problem with arms control is that it is riddled with five paradoxes, although in *House of Cards* it is clear that one of these paradoxes is of overwhelming importance. Gray's central arms control paradox is that 'if arms control is needed in a strategic relationship because the states in question might go to war, it will be impractical for that very reason of need, whereas, if arms control should prove to be available, it will be irrelevant'.[16] Thus:

> Arms control regimes worthy of the name are achievable only between states who do not need them ... The motive to cooperate is overridden by the motive to compete. The arms control paradox argues that the reasons why states may require the moderating influence of an arms control regime are the very reasons why such a regime will be unattainable.[17]

Gray's theory of the irrelevance of arms control revolves around four key arguments. First, a view of international relations in which the stakes are relatively clear cut, with an easy identification of states committed to order, and those committed to revisionism. Second, a view of the nature of states in which assessments of political culture are central in affecting strategy and, by extension, their arms control policy. Third a view of the history of arms control which is limited to the twentieth century. Fourth, a view of arms control that confuses diplomatic activity, theory and definition. Each of these arguments will be taken in turn.

The first assumption in House of Cards is that international relations can best be approximated by a fairly crude, although obviously value-laden, Realist perspective. Most explicitly, Gray claims that 'High policy is not made by an all but autonomous public mood; at least it was not in 1914, 1939, or the early 1980s. Things were different in the direct democracy of ancient Athens and the First French Republic, but such exceptions to the rules should not guide theory and practice today.'[18] The calculation of interests is key; and in this calculation, Gray postulates that the opposite of arms control is defence planning. Unilateral improvements in force posture can be undermined by cooperative arms control agreements which, when put to the test, will fail under intense political pressure. Thus, states risk weakening their military forces by entering into arms control, and those weaknesses may be exposed when the arms control regime collapses under political pressure. There is no sense that arms control regimes can develop any robustness, for it is politics that leads states to war, not weapons. The scope for cooperation between antagonistic states is, thus, all but non-existent.[19]

The second assumption is that, in this world, one can identify revisionist states, and those interested in order. In fact, implicit in the analysis is a further assumption, which is that any combination of antagonistic powers can be defined in this manner. Unsurprisingly, we find that in the inter-war period the powers interested in order were Britain and the United States, and the revisionist powers were Germany and Japan. In the post-war period, those working for order were the United States and the Western powers, and the revisionists were the Soviet Union and its allies. In the post-cold war period, the 'good guys' are the Americans, the West and Israel, the revisionists the Russians, Iraq and Israel's Arab foes. This is clearly where the value-laden nature of the analysis bursts forth. One can argue over whether the Soviet Union should be correctly identified as a revisionist or a status quo power. This categorisation also ignores the security dynamics of the non-aligned world. Equally significantly, Gray overlays the importance of political culture onto this analysis. The problem with American culture is that it devotes scant attention to strategy.[20] However, the problem with Russian culture is much worse. We learn of 'The proclivity of Russians to evade and avoid what Washington believes it has settled';[21] that 'Notwithstanding all of the new thinking that has so shaken the former Soviet system, the scope and scale of Moscow's misbehaviour – both legal, if improper, as well as illegal – toward compliance with the terms of the CFE treaty of 1990, are wholly in the Russian tradition of caveat emptor';[22] and that 'a cultural proclivity to cheat is very much the Russian way in statecraft. Cheating for advantage or simply for convenience is probably inalienably, though certainly far from uniquely, Russian ... Moreover, Moscow will cheat in matters small as well as great'.[23] Importantly, Gray claims that 'Few people who recognise the practical force of Russian strategic culture expect the successor states of the Soviet Union to behave very much better in the future.'[24]

What is to be made of Gray's first two assumptions? The world is starkly competitive, with the forces of order arrayed against the revisionists, and the latter are (for political and strategic–cultural reasons) liable to cheat and lie. This raises many questions, not only regarding the fit of this picture with the complexity of international relations involving a whole range of actors, and not just states, and a whole range of issues, not just strategic relations. Assuming that the picture painted of political and strategic culture is correct, how does change occur? How did political culture change from the negative picture of Germany and Japan in the 1930s portrayed by Gray, to the more positive picture of the latter half of the century? Without a theory of political change, the order-revisionist picture of strategic military relations seem to be two-dimensional, unable to explain transformation.

Most centrally, these assumptions lead Gray to criticise and reject what he calls the 'fallacy of political engineering' through arms control.[25] Behaviour cannot be changed by arms control: revisionist states remain revisionist, cheats remain cheats. As Gray states, 'arms control cannot be useful as an intended means to change policy'.[26] If behaviour cannot be changed, then the argument that post-Soviet Russia had to be locked in to a series of agreements by the United States in order to limit the scope of action of a future leadership in Moscow more hostile to the West has to be rejected. If future Russian, or other governments, want to threaten the United States, they will do so regardless of agreements:

> The urge to compete for national advantage does not preclude arms control as a tool of grand strategy. Italy, Japan and Germany in the 1920s and 1930s, and the Soviet Union since 1945 have all illustrated the point that predatory regimes, bent upon the radical revision of their national security circumstances, can find value in, among other things, the cover of respectability provided by a formal arms control framework.[27]

This may be true. However, it is not applicable for most of the time. Between absolute war and absolute peace, states seek to influence one another over the present and the future. The provisions of START II cannot be externally imposed on the signatories and if a future Russian leadership seeks to exceed those limits, they can do so. However, they would have to explain an act that arms control had made illegal. This would not necessarily prevent action; but normative constraints, at the very least, complicate decision making, particularly if they are complemented by sanctions.

Arms control has various purposes that can be served in relations between war and peace. The Lisbon Protocol attached to START would lead to the removal of nuclear forces from the territory of three states. Each might develop nuclear weapons, but the agreement moved any possible nuclear status into the future. START II legitimised American help for the destruction of large numbers of Russian nuclear weapons in circumstances where there was great concern about the security of the storage of such weapons inside Russia. Gray argues that the development of the Iraqi nuclear programme, despite being a signatory of the NPT, is much more significant than any notions of a taboo that the NPT might have helped create regarding non-proliferation.[28] However, without the NPT could the United Nations' Security Council have legitimised the destruction of the Iraqi programme after the war over Kuwait? Without the NPT, what could even be said about the North Korean nuclear programme? Thus, arms control provides a legal as well as a moral framework for action.

The third assumption in *House of Cards* is that any examination of the historical record of arms control in the twentieth century would reveal its failure:

> The historical basis for the argument presented here comprises the better part of a century of frequently renewed arms control negotiations. The enduring character of the states' system and the nature of state behaviour toward security ensure the persistence of the conditions which guarantee that arms control must fail.[29]

To demonstrate this argument, Gray examined two sets of arms control activity: firstly 'the Washington–London naval arms control' regime of the inter-war period; and then that which Gray identifies as 'the mystery tour from SALT to START'. However, there are grave problems with Gray's use of this material, as will be examined by looking at Gray's 'mystery tour'.[30] Gray's argument that SALT and START add up to a mystery tour is based on his assertion that arguments focusing on strategic stability have no merit. Without that, there has been no strategic purpose to SALT and START: they have licensed an increase in strategic arsenals; they have not eliminated 'destabilising' weapons (with the one exception of strategic defences); and they do not provide predictability, for arms control agreements only reflect the state of the world when they are signed.[31] There are two fundamental problems with this analysis.

Firstly, Gray asserts that one of the problems with SALT and START is that they have not led to reductions. Yet despite arguing that arms control is political, Gray ignores the politics. It is extremely difficult to compare the SALT agreements with START I, or with START II. The contexts are different, and the latter two agreements have included significant reductions.[32] Gray retorts that reductions in START II reflect the new circumstances, in which 'if the superpowers are politically at peace, it will not matter where the level of Russian treaty-accountable warheads eventually settles.'[33] However, this does not accord with his earlier condemnation of Russian political culture, and his inability to explain cultural change. More importantly, it confuses end points with process. If Russian–American relations become similar to American–Canadian relations, the number of weapons that the two states have will not be a direct issue for those countries. But how do states move from cold war hostility to political friendship? Surely through a process of agreements over a variety of issues. Further, in a utopian Russ-ian–American world, the number of Russian nuclear weapons may matter if Russia and China are still rivals. Finally, the additional utility of the START agreements has been to disarm the new post-Soviet states, an argu-ment ignored in *House of Cards*.[34]

The second problem with Gray's analysis is his discomfort with restric-tions on strategic defences. However, this argument seems contradictory and ill at ease with the thrust of the book. The United States, of course, has not deployed strategic defences as Gray would want, preferring instead to remain bound by the narrow interpretation of the ABM (Anti-Ballistic Mis-sile) Treaty. Is this the example of successful arms control, even though unwanted? Gray argues in favour of amendment of the ABM Treaty (should this not be abolition?) in favour of defences against proliferators.[35] However, the reader is also told that 'Even in the absence of the ABM treaty the United States would not have deployed BMD (ballistic missile defence) in the 1970s or 1980s.'[36] Again, there is a strange separation of arms control and poli-tics: why would the United States not have deployed ballistic missile defences? Surely because the view that deterrence would be better served by preventing ballistic missile defence (BMD) predominated, and the best way for achieving that end was through arms control.[37] This conventional wisdom came under great attack during the first Reagan administration, during which the ABM Treaty was threatened, but not broken, by the American government.[38] In advocating movement to strategic defences, Gray argues that SALT and START have served the purpose of preventing the deployment of strategic missile defences 'magnificently well'.[39] But how can this be the case, given that arms control is bound to fail? Is it really true, as Gray argues, that limits over missile defences in the 1980s were more a control of national budgets and lack of political will than arms con-trol restraint?[40] Given the bitter debates over SDI within the United States, between the Reagan administration and its West European allies, and in Soviet–American relations, many of which revolved explicitly around the ABM Treaty, one may not be convinced.[41]

The final assumption in *House of Cards* is that the purposes of arms con-trol should be defined in a very narrow way.[42] Gray's critique of arms con-trol is based on his claim that 'Above all else, arms control is about helping to prevent the outbreak of war.'[43] The argument that will be advanced in this book, however, is that the practice of arms control has shown that it has been viewed as a tool designed to achieve many different purposes. It has been used to try to prevent the outbreak of war. But it has also been used to try to create post-war stability in relations between states; to create and strengthen norms of behaviour about the uses and targets of weapons; to legitimise the possession and non-possession of certain forms of weaponry, partly to prevent war, but partly also to create political advantage; and it has also been used by international organisations to impose the interests of 'the international community' upon others. Arms control is thus broader than Gray allows.

Arms control is also defined by Gray in a narrow way in another sense, in that the increasing detail of arms control agreements is seen to be a problem:

> The SALT II Treaty and accompanying documentation betrayed a virulent case of growing legalism, while the START treaty and its protective packaging is of a length and specificity of detail which will gladden the hearts of the legal-minded. Perhaps American consumers have come to expect the provision of excruciating detail on the packages that they buy.[44]

In contrast, the argument in this book is that increasing complexity, which will be referred to as depth, has been deliberately designed in order to strengthen those agreements, to ensure robustness. Thus Gray's view of arms control is, in the context of the argument of this book, both too narrow and too shallow.

Given the limitations placed upon Gray's argument demonstrated by the problems with his four underlying assumptions, it is clear that Gray's arms control paradox is not as stark as he would suggest. The argument was that arms control cannot work when it is needed – when states are on the verge of war – only when it is not needed, when conflict is inconceivable.[45] However, this postulates two extremes which are rarely commensurate with political reality. Governments are more usually concerned with relations with states with which they are neither on the brink of war, nor with whom they are at total peace.

The dimensions of arms control

This lengthy examination of the arguments put forward in *House of Cards* is not designed simply to refute the arguments put forward by Colin Gray. The purpose is to demonstrate the range of issues covered by the term 'arms control', and how easy it is to ignore many of the more important issues. The critique of *House of Cards* presented here is not intended to lead to the conclusion that arms control must be inherently and inevitably a national and international good. This is clearly not the case. Arms control can lead to a worsening of relations politically, and a destabilisation of relations strategically. In political terms, arms control can provide a focus for weakening relations and a source of domestic dissent (such as over the SALT process in the 1970s). In strategic terms, an arms control agreement may not achieve its goals (some examples are examined in the next chapter), may be damaging (some argued this was the case for NATO (North Atlantic Treaty Organization) with regard to the INF Treaty), may lull a state into a false sense of security (as critics argued was the case for the United States over SALT I), while an agreement may simply become irrelevant. But the success or failure, or indeed relevance, of arms control is not the focus of this book which will, rather, seek to develop a typology.

Rather than eulogise arms control, the critique of Gray enables the analysis to move forward in two senses. First, it re-establishes that arms control is a subject worthy of investigation. This book does not suggest that arms control is always successful in the strategic sense defined by Gray. Rather, it represents a pattern of behaviour. As will be examined in the next chapter, for many centuries, polities have used the diplomatic tool of arms control in order to advance various interests. The key element taken here for this book is not to examine how arms control might 'work', but rather to examine the range of different patterns of behaviour which have been subject to arms control. This leads to the second sense in which the examination of *House of Cards* takes the analysis forward. Arms control has not, in historical terms, been an independent factor in international politics as is implied by Gray in his critique of American arms control theory and practice. One is given the impression in *House of Cards* that legions of arms controllers have put their fallacies and careers ahead of the national interests of their countries: for example, 'an arms control process takes on a life of its own, and its supervising officials naturally assume a solicitous concern for the welfare of that process which exceeds strategic considerations of national security'.[46] However, the reality of the phenomena that Gray describes is the politics that he argues should be seen to be central. National interests, and international security, are always subject to political debate, not objective mathematical formulae. Arms control has been about furthering political interests. The key question becomes, therefore, whose interests are furthered and legitimised by different forms of arms control? This does not mean that arms control agreements and negotiations inevitably contribute to a thickening web of arms control welcomed and recognised by all. Rather there are different interests within and between polities which are significant in terms of whether an arms control agreement can be produced at all and, if it is, what it looks like.

Arms control will be defined in a very broad sense in this book. This broader approach to arms control may seem a little uncomfortable initially, in that it combines conventional and unfamiliar notions of arms control. There are at least three elements in this.

First, distinctions will not be made between agreements over arms control and those over disarmament although such a distinction is usually seen to be axiomatic. For Hedley Bull, 'Disarmament and arms control intersect with one another. They are not the same, for there can be disarmament which is not controlled, and control which does not involve a reduction of armaments. On the other hand, they are not exclusive of one another.'[47] Unilateral disarmament lies outside of the definition of arms control provided by Bull, for it is not about the cooperation of antagonistic states.[48] However, internationally agreed measures of disarmament most definitely lie within the definition and, indeed, such agreements have been something of the hallmark of the end of the cold war.

Second, arms control is not presented as an institution that ensures equality for all participants, for in negotiations parties will have different levels of influence, and differing abilities to conclude a satisfactory agreement. Equal outcomes have been sought in many arms control negotiations, but not always, and the historical record illustrates many examples of this (as will be demonstrated in Chapter 1). And as will be seen, in particular in the analysis of arms control at the conclusion of conflicts, sometimes equal outcomes are most certainly not sought.

Third, arms control is not simply about START and CFE and, at a push, the NPT; it will also be defined to include such agreements and issues as the Geneva Convention, and UN disarmament activities in Mozambique.[49] Arms control will be defined to include restrictions on the use and possession of arms. In this sense, the laws of war, which seek to set normative restrictions on the use of violence, must be seen to be arms control. The laws of war set limits on who may be targeted (that is, who can be classed as non-combatants), with what weapons (the outlawing of inhumane weapons), and have sometimes forbidden violence at certain times (such as on the Sabbath) and in certain places. Arms control defined broadly must therefore include norms that have sought to limit the use of arms. But it must also be defined to include restraints on the possession of arms. This obviously includes restrictions on vertical and horizontal proliferation. But it must also include efforts to disarm warring parties and, in this sense, the United Nations' efforts to disarm groups and states in countries such as Mozambique, Cambodia, Somalia and Iraq are arms control.

Arms control will be defined in this book, therefore, to include treaties on disarmament (the INF Treaty, for example); unequal treaties (such as the Treaty of Zama between Rome and Carthage); the laws of war (like the Geneva Conventions); restraints on proliferation (such as the NPT); and United Nations' disarmament efforts. This should not be seen, however, to take the definition of arms control too far away from that developed by analysts such as Schelling, Halperin and Bull. For example, for Thomas Schelling and Morton Halperin the importance of arms control lay 'essentially on the recognition that our military relation with potential enemies is not one of pure conflict and opposition, but involves strong elements of mutual interest in the avoidance of a war that neither side wants'.[50] Certainly, all the activities outlined in the broader approach to arms control outlined above fit with this definition. Indeed, Hedley Bull, in *The Control of the Arms Race*, argued that 'Arms control in its broadest sense comprises all those acts of military policy in which antagonistic states cooperate in the pursuit of common purposes even while they are struggling in the pursuit of conflicting ones.'[51] In the period since the publication of that definition, there has been a temptation to focus on superpower relations, negotiations and agreements in the analysis of arms control. The result has been for arms control to be interpreted in narrow terms, not with the broad approach advocated by Bull. This book seeks to re-broaden the concept.

Arms control will be examined in a very wide sense. There will not, however, be an investigation into the motivations of arms control. For Bull, the primary motivation is to make war less likely and, should it nevertheless still break out, to make it less destructive. A secondary motive is to reduce the economic costs, and a tertiary motive to combat the militarisation of society.[52] This may or may not be persuasive; however, as the investigation into which arms control agreements are successful, and which are not, lies outside the scope of this article, so does a direct examination of motivations. Instead, the book will set out a typology of arms control in the spirit of Bull's definition of the phenomenon.

As will be examined in Chapter 1, arms control has been used throughout history in relations between, for example, Egyptians and Hittites, Romans and Carthaginians, the Christian and Saracen worlds, France and Britain in the eighteenth century, Britain and the United States in the nineteenth century, and the United States and the Soviet Union in the twentieth. Throughout recorded history, arms control has been used to set limitations on the scale of violence in warfare whether through prescribing the space in which hostilities could take place, or through proscribing the use of certain forms of warfare, such as poison and gas. All of these various arms control arrangements, and others like them, had three main characteristics. These related to the participants, the focus of arms control and the implications of arms control agreements. Each of these aspects will be briefly examined.

First, in relation to the participants, arms control agreements were reached between states, or their pre-modern equivalents, based on the assumption that it would be both possible and desirable to develop some form of cooperation in the military field in order to avoid war, manage crises and, should war nevertheless occur, to limit the ensuing damage. However, although most analyses of arms control tend to focus upon treaties, it is important to note that it has not been necessary for an agreement to be formalised in terms of a treaty since tacit agreements (or indeed unilateral reciprocal measures) may also produce a new form of stability after implementation.[53] The key issue is not that there may be negotiations and a treaty, although this is often the case, but rather that there is agreement between states on the nature of a new post-agreement balance of military forces. This book will, therefore, examine not only arms control treaties, but also political agreements and some reciprocal unilateral measures.

Second, in relation to the focus, arms control agreements have been concerned with the control of the use of certain forms of weaponry, the possession of different forms of weaponry, and/or the means of production of weaponry. However, this has allowed for a tremendous variety in arms control agreements not only between quantitative and qualitative arrangements, but also between those prohibiting use and those outlawing possession, between agreements designed to have an impact in a region and those global in scope, between agreements aimed at preventing war and those regulating the conduct of war should it break out, and between those arms control agreements designed to be narrowly in the interests of one state and those with pretensions to benefit the whole of the international society of states. Generalising about such a range of behaviour in international relations only becomes possible with the aid of a wider historical vision than that limited to the cold war period.

Third, in relation to the implications of arms control arrangements, many agreements were based on a hope, whether implicit or explicit, that they would lead to an improvement in political relations between the participants. This was due not only to the expectation that the agreement would represent the minimisation of a security concern between the participants, but also that an agreement might serve as the basis for further confidence-building measures. Yet if they did not, even an expectation of future political cooperation might have been sufficient to weaken reliance on worst-case analysis which might in turn have lessened the powerful pressure of the security dilemma.[54] Thus, arms control has always been about creating and/or supporting norms of behaviour in international politics.

This book takes a broad approach to arms control and seeks to use it to develop a framework of understanding which can be applied to the arms control agreements of the post-cold war period. It will include in its definition of arms control not only traditional arms control agreements between states over the relative size of their military arsenals, but also agreements over the forcible disarmament of groups and states by international bodies (the United Nations' disarmament of Iraq after the Gulf War, for example) and agreements concerning the behaviour of states (the 1949 Geneva Conventions, for example). Thus, a working definition of arms control for this book would be as follows: a search for collaborative arrangements between political entities that seeks to set restraints on the possession and use of certain forms of arms, whether in complete form or in component parts. The definition uses 'political entities' to include sub-state groups, supra-state institutions, and pre-modern states; 'possession' refers to types of weapons, and who may deploy, build, store and operate them, in what numbers, and in what conditions; and 'use' refers to questions related to legitimate targets and geographical areas. Arms control is collaborative, but may include unilateral measures, but only when they are designed primarily to induce reciprocal measures or to enhance international security. It is about setting political limits on military policy.

Chapter One develops the central arguments of the book developed from this definition, arguments which are contained within two theses. The first thesis is that over time, the nature of arms control has *widened* in scope from very limited functions to the broader definition of arms control utilised in this book. The second thesis is that particular arms control agreements can be assessed on the basis of a concept of the *depth* of that agreement.

Widening refers to the different types of arms control activity practised over several thousand years. In early arms control practice, polities reached agreements about the size, strength and disposition of their forces at the end of conflicts in order to formally create a new balance between them, and to create or perpetuate strategic stability at other times. During the Middle Ages, agreements were reached over norms of behaviour limiting the scope, means and timing of violence between polities. During the following centuries, as technology became increasingly sophisticated, growing attention was placed on the problems associated with the proliferation of weaponry. Finally, during the twentieth century, a new form of arms control developed, one that was managed by global international organisations.

Thus, new types of arms control developed as arms control practice widened over time. As a result of this process, conceptually five types of arms control may be said to exist at the beginning of the post-cold war period: (1) arms control at the conclusion of conflicts; (2) arms control to further strategic stability; (3) arms control to create norms of behaviour; (4) arms control to manage the proliferation of weapons; and (5) arms control by international organisation. Chapters Two to Six of this book are divided into these conceptual categories in order to examine over twenty arms control arrangements reached in the post-cold war world.

The second thesis introduced in Chapter One is that arms control can be assessed on the basis of *deepening*. This concept of deepening refers to a process over time whereby the depth of arms control agreements may be said to have increased. By depth, three factors can be identified as significant. The first factor refers to the detail provided in the terms of the agreement. Does the drafting of the agreement cover the scope intended by the states involved? Are definitions clarified? Are mutual understandings spelt out? The second factor relates to provisions for verification. Without adequate provisions for verification within the terms of the agreement the effectiveness of the treaty may be seriously compromised. The final factor refers to regime formation/continuation.[55] Often this is related to the depth of verification, for a detailed verification regime implies at least a medium-term commitment to implementing the agreement. Regime formation/continuation also refers to the degree to which follow-on agreements are expected to be reached within the broad framework of the agreement, and the mechanisms for ensuring progress towards such an end. During Chapters Two to Six, while categorising the arms control agreements of the post-cold war world into the five categories of arms control, each agreement will also be assessed in terms of its depth.

Through the concepts of widening and deepening, this book sets out a framework for understanding and analysing the arms control agreements reached at the beginning of the post-cold war period.

Notes

1   See, for example, Thomas Schelling and Morton Halperin *Strategy and Arms Control* New York: Twentieth Century Fund, 1961; Hedley Bull *The Control of the Arms Race* London: Weidenfeld and Nicolson for the Institute for Strategic Studies, 1961; Louis Henkin (editor) *Arms Control* New York: Ballantine Books, 1960; and Donald G. Brennan (editor) 'Arms Control, Disarmament and National Security' a special issue of *Daedalus* Vol. 89, No. 4, 1960.

2   Examples of these arguments may be found in the following: Malcolm Wallop and Angelo Codevilla *The Arms Control Delusion* San Francisco: Institute for Contemporary Studies, 1987; Joseph Douglass, Jr, *Why the Soviets Violate Arms Control Treaties* Washington DC: Pergamon–Brassey's, 1988; and Robin Ranger 'Learning from the Naval Arms Control Experience' *Washington Quarterly* Vol. 10, Summer, 1987, pp. 47–58.

3   See, for example, Kenneth Adelman 'Arms Control with and without Agreements' *Foreign Affairs* Vol. 63, Winter, 1984–5; Colin Gray 'Arms Control Does not Control Arms' *Orbis* Vol. 37, No. 3, 1993; and Patrick Glynn *Closing Pandora's Box: Arms Races, Arms Control and the History of the Cold War* New York: Basic Books, 1992.

4   For these arguments see, for example, E. P. Thompson *Zero Option* London: The Merlin Press, 1982; Ken Booth 'Unilateralism: A Clausewitzian Reform?' in Nigel Blake and Kay Pole (editors) *Dangers of Deterrence: Philosophers on Nuclear Strategy* London: Routledge and Kegan Paul, 1983; The Alternative Defence Commission *The Politics of Alternative Defence* London: Paladin, 1987; Jonathan Schell *The Abolition* London: Pan, 1984; Regina Cowen Karp (editor) *Security without Nuclear Weapons* Oxford: Oxford University Press for SIPRI, 1992; Stephen King-Hall *Defence in the Nuclear Age* London: Gollancz, 1958; Marek Thee, 'Arms Control: The Retreat from Disarmament, the Record to Date and the Search for Alternatives' *Journal of Peace Research* Vol. 14, No. 2, 1977; Paul M. Cole and William J. Taylor *The Nuclear Freeze Debate: Arms Control Issues for the 1980s* Boulder CO: Westview, 1983; and Edward Kennedy and Mark Hatfield *Freeze* New York: Bantam Books, 1983.

5   See, for example, Christopher Coker *A Farewell to Arms Control: The Irrelevance of CFE* London: Institute for European Defence and Strategic Studies, 1991.

6   See, for example, R. Smith 'The Marginalization of Superpower Arms Control' *Security Studies* Vol. 1, No. 1, 1991, pp. 37–53.

7   Colin Gray *House of Cards: Why Arms Control Must Fail* Ithaca: Cornell University Press for the Cornell Studies in Security Affairs, 1992.

8   *Ibid.*, p. 5.

9   For example, on page 219 he says 'I do not argue that arms control is always of absolutely no, or even negative, value for peace and security.'

10 *Ibid.*, p. 221.

11 *Ibid.*, p. 234.

12 *Ibid.*, p. 225.

13 *Ibid.*, p. 227.

14 *Ibid.*, p. 16.

15 *Ibid.*, p. 73.

16 *Ibid.*, p. 17.

17 *Ibid.*, p. 27.

18 *Ibid.*, p. 194. Further, 'Statesmen compete in arms, foment crises, and wage wars for their vision of security, no matter how pernicious or sensible that vision may seem in retrospect to others.' *Ibid.*, p. 54.

19 Gray's contempt for more liberal perspectives becomes, on rare occasion, extreme. Charles Kupchan and Clifford Kupchan's thought-provoking and challenging article on collective security is condemned in the most extreme terms. According to Gray, the authors 'inadvertently do their best to demonstrate why political scientists should not be entrusted with the serious business of national security ... Not to mince matters, this constitutes a stew of liberal fallacies.' *Ibid.*, pp. 156–7, note 47. The original article is Charles A. Kupchan and Clifford A. Kupchan 'Concerts, Collective Security, and the Future of Europe' *International Security* Vol. 16, Summer, 1991.

20 See Gray *House of Cards*, pp. 228–9.

21 *Ibid.*, p. 137.

22 *Ibid.*, p. 156.

23 *Ibid.*, p. 169.

24 *Ibid.*, pp. 174–5.

25 *Ibid.*, p. 155. Later, he argues that 'arms control process bear witness to the illusion that security can be engineered' *ibid.*, p. 229.

26 *Ibid.*, p. 41.

27 *Ibid.*, p. 55.

28 *Ibid.*, p. 199. Gray argues that 'The apparent fact that Iraq, a signatory to the NPT, covertly could come plausibly within eighteen to twenty-four months of acquiring nuclear weapons, is vastly more impressive datum than is the general opinion that the NPT helped forge a useful taboo. Again, arms control could not handle the really tough challenge.'

29 *Ibid.*, p. 2.

30 For a critique of the first period as analysed by Gray, see S. Croft 'In Defence of Arms Control' *Political Studies* forthcoming 1996. Also see Emily O. Goldman *Sunken Treaties* Pennsylvania: Penn State Press, 1994; C. Hall *Britain,*

America and Arms Control, 1921–37 New York: St Martin's Press, 1987; and E. Goldstein 'The Evolution of British Diplomatic Strategy for the Washington Conference', and Sadoa Asada 'From Washington to London: The Imperial Japanese Navy and the Politics of Naval Limitation, 1921–30' *Diplomacy and Statecraft* Vol. 4, No. 3, 1993.

31   Gray, *House of Cards*, pp. 128–33.
32   On SALT see, for example, Raymond Garthoff *Detente and Confrontation* Washington DC: Brookings Institute, 1985; Dan Caldwell *The Dynamics of Domestic Politics and Arms Control: The SALT II Ratification Debate* Columbia South Carolina: University of Carolina Press, 1991; A. Platt *The US Senate and Strategic Arms Policy 1969–77* Boulder CO: Westview, 1978; John Newhouse *Cold Dawn: The Story of SALT* New York: Holt, Rinehart and Winston 1973; and Gerard Smith *Doubletalk: The Story of SALT I* Lanham: University Press of America, 1985. On START, see Ivo H. Daalder and Terry Terriff *Rethinking the Unthinkable: New Directions for Nuclear Arms Control* a special issue of *Arms Control: Contemporary Security Policy* Vol. 14, No. 1, 1993, and the sections on START in Chapters 2 and 3 of this book.
33   Gray *House of Cards*, p. 123.
34   On the centrality of this concern in the process, see Steven Miller 'Western Diplomacy and the Soviet Nuclear Legacy' *Survival* Vol. 34, No. 3, 1992.
35   Gray *House of Cards*, p. 52.
36   *Ibid*, p. 154.
37   Such a view came under fierce attack from groups such as the Committee on the Present Danger. See Charles Tyroler III *Alerting America* Washington DC: Pergamon-Brassey's, 1984. Also see notes 2 and 3 of this chapter. For analysis, see Mike Bowker and Phil Williams *Superpower Detente: A Reappraisal* London: Sage for the RIIA, 1988; David H. Dunn 'The Politics of Threat: Minuteman Vulnerability in the Carter and Reagan Administrations' unpublished Ph.D. thesis, University of London 1995; Fred M. Kaplan *The Wizards of Armageddon* New York: Simon and Schuster, 1983; Robert Scheer *With Enough Shovels: Reagan, Bush and Nuclear War* New York: Vantage, 1983; and Lawrence Freedman *The Evolution of Nuclear Strategy* London: Macmillan for IISS, second edition, 1989, especially Chapter 26.
38   This was over the question of whether the ABM Treaty could be reinterpreted in a 'broad' fashion to allow the development of the Strategic Defense Initiative. For a view in favour of reinterpretation, see the Heritage Foundation 'US–Soviet Arms Accords Are No Bar to Reagan's Strategic Defense Initiative' *Heritage Foundation Backgrounder 421* Washington DC: The Heritage Foundation, April 1985. For a view against, see Raymond Garthoff *Policy Versus the Law: The Reinterpretation of the ABM Treaty* Washington DC: The Brookings Institution, 1987. For a proposed compromise, see Donald G. Gross 'Negotiated Treaty Amendment: The Solution to the ABM–SDI Treaty Conflict' *Harvard International Law Review* Vol. 28, Winter, 1987, pp. 31–68. Also see William Durch *The ABM Treaty and Western Security* Cambridge MA: Ballinger, 1988.
39   Gray *House of Cards*, p. 130.
40   *Ibid.*, p. 13.
41   See, for example, Hans Gunter Brauch *Star Wars and European Defence* London:

Macmillan, 1987; Ivo H. Daalder *The SDI Challenge to Europe* Cambridge MA: Ballinger, 1987; Stuart Croft 'The Impact of Strategic Defences on European American Relations' *Adelphi Paper 238* London: IISS, 1989; Samuel F. Wells and Robert S. Litwak *Strategic Defenses and Soviet–American Relations* Cambridge MA: Ballinger, 1987; and John Holden and Joseph Rotblat *Strategic Defences and the Future of the Arms Race* London: Macmillan for Pugwash, 1987.

42 Gray also sets out to provide a general theory of why arms control is bound to fail, but seeks to achieve this, in part, by focusing upon the arms control policy of the United States. The general and the particular tend to become confused and overlap, to the detriment of the general theoretical propositions.

43 Gray *House of Cards*, p. 2. This claim is repeated throughout the book. See, for example, p. 69: 'More arms control agreements will be signed in the 1990s. But that fact will have no importance for what arms control primarily is supposed to be about – the prevention of war.'

44 *Ibid.*, p. 137.

45 By this, it is meant that, for example, arms control agreements between France and Germany would have been insubstantial in 1939 on the verge of war, and meaningless in 1990 when both states were firmly at peace.

46 Gray *House of Cards*, p. 232. Elsewhere, the Arms Control Association and the Federation of American Scientists are condemned for showing greater loyalty to a theory of arms control than to the reality of Soviet cheating. *Ibid.*, p. 166.

47 Hedley Bull *The Control*, p. vii.

48 One exception to this is when unilateral reductions are designed to be reciprocal. A very important example of this will be examined in Chapter Two which, in part, will analyse the Bush–Gorbachev unilateral nuclear reductions announced at the end of 1991.

49 Strategic Arms Reduction Treaty (START), Conventional Forces in Europe (CFE) Treaty, and Nuclear Non-Proliferation Treaty (NPT).

50 T. Schelling and M. Halperin *Strategy*, p. 1.

51 Hedley Bull *The Control*, p. xiv.

52 *Ibid.*, pp. 3–4.

53 See, for example, Hedley Bull *The Control*, p. xi, and Thomas Schelling and Morton Halperin *Strategy*, p. 77. The issue of reciprocal unilateral measures is examined in Chapter Two of this book.

54 See, for example, Joseph S. Nye 'Arms Control and International Politics' *Daedalus* Vol. 120, No. 1, 1991.

55 On the importance of regimes in this area see, for example H. Mueller 'The Internationalization of Principles, Norms and Rules by Governments: The Case of Security Regimes' in V.Rittberger with P. Mayer (editor) *Regime Theory and International Relations* Oxford: Clarendon, 1993; M. Enfinger and V. Rittberger 'The CSBM Regime In and For Europe: Confidence Building and Peaceful Conflict Management' in Michael Pugh (editor) *European Security – Towards 2000* Manchester: Manchester University Press, 1991; and O. Young 'International Regimes: Toward a New Theory of Institutions' *World Politics* Vol. 39, No. 1, 1986; and Frank Schimmelfennig 'Arms Control Regimes and the Dissolution of the Soviet Union: Realism, Institutionalism and Regime Robustness' *Cooperation and Conflict* Vol. 29, No.2, 1994, pp. 115–48.

1

The evolution of
arms control

Introduction

The Introduction to this book has suggested that one of the problems with the debate over arms control has been that the phenomenon of arms control has not been defined in a sufficiently comprehensive manner. Too often, arms control has not been seen to be significant before, at best, the early part of the twentieth century. In fact, as this chapter will seek to demonstrate, arms control has a long and rich history across many different cultures. Further, since there has been little emphasis on the historical record of arms control, there has been little focus upon one of the most important changes introduced in the twentieth century, and certainly developed in the cold war era: the process of deepening. All of these issues will be illuminated by a more thorough examination of the arms control record.

Arms control has been a significant area of human activity throughout recorded history. However, many different types of enterprise have been emphasised during this historical development, since arms control activities have always reflected the norms and concerns of the international political system of the time. Nevertheless, it is the argument of this chapter that common practices of arms control can be identified, despite the differing nature of international relations over long periods of time.

This chapter will first examine the historical development of arms control from its origins in the ancient world to the practice of the inter-war period. Second, it will examine the contribution of the cold war period both in terms of the nature of the treaties, and in terms of the arms control theory developed during the late 1950s and early 1960s. Finally, drawing on the first two sections, the chapter advances a typology for the understanding of arms control that suggests that five distinct types of arms control can be identified.

The historical development of arms control

Arms control is often seen to be a modern invention, a creation of the cold war. However, the practice of arms control is many thousands of years old. Arms control agreements can be identified not only in the inter-war period of the twentieth century, but also in the eighteenth and nineteenth centuries, in the Middle Ages, and even in the ancient world. Arms control in one form or another has in fact been practised throughout history. In the centuries before Christ, examples would include the Rome–Carthage Treaty; in medieval Europe, agreements included Canon 29 of the Second Lateran Council of 1139 (which outlawed the use of crossbows against Christians and Catholics), and Canon 71 of the Fourth Lateran Council of 1215 (which banned the transfer of weapons to the Saracens); in the period before the First World War, examples would include the Anglo-French Naval Limitation Pact of 1787, the Franco-Prussian Treaty of 1808 (by which the Prussian army was limited in size), and the 1902 Argentine-Chilean Protocol limiting naval forces; in the inter-war period, one would consider the 1919 Agreement to Restrain Trade in Arms and Munitions of War with China, the 1925 Geneva Protocol regarding prohibition on the use of gas, and the League of Nations One Year Armament Truce of 1931; and finally, there were many arms control agreements in the cold war period, such as the SALT agreements.

An examination of the history of arms control is useful, therefore, not only in terms of correcting an emphasis on the post-1960 history of arms control, but also in defining different emphases in the practice of arms control. For the purposes of this analysis of the historical development of arms control, five distinct periods can be identified: the ancient world; the medieval world; the period between the Peace of Westphalia and the end of the First World War; the inter-war period; and the cold war period. Each of these phases will be examined in turn in order to illustrate the dynamic nature of the development of arms control.

Arms control in the ancient world

Two factors distinguish much of the arms control activity of the ancient world from later arms control practice. First, warfare was endemic, whether in the Middle East, pre-Han China, ancient Greece or the Roman world.[1] Second, warfare, sometimes highly stylised, often very violent, was essentially fought with relatively unsophisticated concussion or cutting weaponry. These two factors had important implications for arms control. With warfare so common, and so important to the cultures of many of the peoples of the ancient world, incentives to prevent conflict in general, as opposed to limiting violence in specific circumstances (when it was clear that no victor would easily emerge) were low. Some exceptions to this have been noted; for example, amongst Iron Age peoples, the League of the Iroquois in pre-colonial North America prevented warfare between the constituent nations for over three hundred years.[2] Further, it was difficult to control weaponry given its relative simplicity, (although some limited attempts were made: note the Philistines' efforts at preventing the Israelites from acquiring iron-based weapons in around 1100 BC).[3] Thus, both the political culture and the practical problems were not conducive to arms control solutions. However, arms control still occurred, notably at the end of wars or when significant technological advance occurred (for example, the development of the Greek trireme naval vessel).

Arms control in the ancient world largely took one of two forms: the establishment of buffer regions; and the disarmament of the defeated. Examples of the former include the agreement between the Egyptian Rameses II and the Hittite Hattusilis III following the Battle of Qadesh around 1280 BC, or the agreement between Rome and the Parthians to manage the buffer state of Armenia between them.[4] Examples of arms control which led to the disarmament of the defeated would include the imposition of the *foedus inaequuum*, or unequal treaty, by the Romans on Carthage in 201 BC, and on Macedon in 196 BC. Under the *foedus inaequuum*, the Romans insisted that the defeated states accept widespread measures of disarmament. Both Carthage and Macedon had their navies largely eliminated, and Carthage had to destroy its war elephants. Both states had to pay reparations, and were forbidden to undertake any military action in regions adjacent to their home cities.[5] A further example occurred at the end of the Peloponnesian War in 404 BC, when Sparta imposed terms on Athens which included the destruction of Athens' walled defences, and the destruction of all but twelve of the Athenian warships.[6]

Arms control in medieval Europe

Arms control had developed little by the Middle Ages. While the limited arms control moves of the ancient world tended to focus on relations between empires, arms control in the medieval world was placed in an altogether different context. While war between states was a significant issue, of perhaps greater concern to the medieval world was the degree of violence within states. This violence was both extra-legal (with the operation of bandits on the edges of society wreaking damage on both towns and countryside), and legal (with the acceptance of the feud and the joust, which in the early medieval period frequently led to widespread violence in the region). The international and extra-legal forms of violence often came together during periods of warfare. Major wars tended to be short, with armies fighting only during the late spring to early autumn period; however, mercenaries and some knights would continue wreaking destruction outside these times for their own gain. Thus private and public violence were frequently hard to distinguish. Yet violence was not limited to actions within

Christian Europe. There were many incursions and invasions from outside – whether from Muslim, Viking or Mongol sources – which in part led local rulers to centralise their powers behind new and more powerful fortifications. As Michael Howard put it, 'War is really too benign a term to describe the condition of the European continent.'[7]

This centralisation of power was in itself to contribute to change in the nature of relations within the medieval world. The major political debate of the period focused upon the secularisation of power, and consequently the somewhat troubled relationship between Church and state, although both Church and state recognised the need to impose limits on the scope of violence.[8]

Would moves to limit violence, both public and private, and within as well as between polities, best be organised by bishops, or by local political leaders? In the former category were the Peace of God in the Synod of Charroux in 989, the Truce of God in the Diocese of Elne in 1027 and the Truce for the Bishopric of Terouanne in 1063. The penalty for breaking the set restrictions on behaviour was to be declared anathema and face excommunication. In the latter category fell the Peace of the Land for Elsass from 1085 to 1103, and the Peace of the Land established by Henry IV in 1103. The penalty for breaches was to be capital punishment or, for lesser offences, the removal of the eyes or the hand of the offender.

The medieval response to this confusion was to attempt to limit violence through a series of agreements. Through what were termed the Peace of God and the Truce of God, and the Peace of the Prince and Peace of the Land, agreements were reached which were designed to control violence.[9] Restrictions were set on the justification for resorting to violence, and limits were set on the scope of the violence in terms of both time and legitimate targets. For example, the Peace of God proclaimed in the Synod of Charroux in 989 decreed:

> 1. Anathema against those who break into churches. If anyone breaks into or robs a church, he shall be anathema unless he makes satisfaction.
> 2. Anathema against those who rob the poor. If anyone robs a peasant or any other poor person of a sheep, ox, ass, cow, goat, or pig, he shall be anathema unless he makes satisfaction.[10]

The Truce of God proclaimed in the Diocese of Elne in 1027 included a requirement not to fight on the Sabbath:

> throughout the whole of the said country and bishopric no one should attack his enemy from the ninth hour on Saturday until the first hour on Monday, so that everyone may perform his religious duties on Sunday.[11]

Part of the Peace of the Land established by Henry IV in 1103 included the requirement 'to keep the peace with churches, clergy, monks, merchants, women, and Jews'.[12] Of course, this is not to argue that such declarations were successful in protecting large numbers of people from the violence of the times. Indeed, these exemptions 'did not apply if they were suspected of giving "aid and countenance" to the war, which they usually were'.[13] But these were initial attempts to set normative constraints upon violence and, in the broad sense, were therefore arms control measures.

In these general attempts to codify and enforce the Just War, the control of weapons themselves had a limited role. The clearest example of direct control took place at the Second Lateran Council of 1139 which prohibited the use of the crossbow under the following decree: 'We forbid under penalty of anathema that that deadly and God-detested art of slingers and archers be in the future exercised against Christians and Catholics.'[14] Three factors are important to note about this Canon, which emphasises the context of arms control during the medieval period.[15] First, the legitimising authority for the prohibition of the crossbow was the Church, and the penalty for breaching the prohibition was an ecclesiastical one. The relationship between secular and religious authority was still confused, as illustrated by the differences between the Peace of God and the Peace of the Prince.[16] Second, the prohibition on the use of the crossbow was not a general one. It was acceptable to use the weapon against non-Christians whether they be invading the Christian world, or being confronted in the Holy Land. Also, the weapon was acceptable for use against heretics within the Christian world. Third, the pressure for the ban on crossbows came from the nobles. The crossbow was the most significant military innovation of the twelfth century. Crossbows were used by relatively unskilled lower class soldiers, yet were able to pierce the armour of the knights and, if laced with poison, were almost certain to produce a fatality. Thus the crossbow was a weapon with potentially socially revolutionary implications. Arms control in this period was thus clearly a product of the confused political relations of the medieval world, and yet had a relatively clear focus: to assist in the regulation and limitation of certain types of violence by creating norms of behaviour.

Arms control from 1648 to 1914

In the period from the Peace of Westphalia in 1648 to the outbreak of the First World War, arms control began to develop much more clearly into its modern form. Many of the activities in the medieval period had laid the foundations for the modern state system, conveniently although not always accurately dated to the Peace of Westphalia.[17] Some early examples showed a degree of continuation with the medieval concern to limit the scope of violence, thereby creating norms of behaviour. For example, in Article XXIII of the Treaty between the United States and Prussia, signed in 1785, both states committed themselves to follow some of the precepts of the Peace of God and the Truce of God, and the Peace of the Prince and Peace of the Land, although no penalties, either ecclesiastical or secular, were stipulated. Part of the Article read:

> If war should arise between the two contracting parties ... all women and children, scholars of every faculty, cultivators of the earth, artisans, manufacturers and fishermen unarmed and inhabiting unfortified towns, villages or places, and in general all others whose occupations are for the common subsistence and benefit of mankind, shall be allowed to continue their respective employments and shall not be molested in their persons, nor shall their houses or goods be burnt, or otherwise destroyed.[18]

In a similar agreement in a Treaty of Commerce between the Netherlands and the United States in 1782, it was agreed that:

> For the better promoting of commerce, on both sides it is agreed that if a war should break out ... there shall always be granted to the subjects on each side, the term of nine months after the date of the rupture, or the proclamation of war, to the end that they may retire, with their effects, and transport them where they please.[19]

These concerns with limitations on the scope of war developed further. Perhaps most obviously, in the latter part of the nineteenth century and the early part of the twentieth many conventions were negotiated and signed concerned with creating and perpetuating rules and laws of war. These ranged from the creation of codes of conduct to the abolition of certain forms of weapons. In the former category, The Hague Conventions (1899 and 1907) set out a series of restrictions on the right to wage war; for example, prohibiting the use of poisoned weapons, the killing or wounding of prisoners, and the unnecessary destruction or seizure of the property of the enemy.[20] In the latter category, the Declaration of St Petersburg in 1868 renounced the use of 'any projectile of less weight than four hundred grammes, which is explosive, or is charged with fulminating or inflammable substances' since such use would 'uselessly aggravate the suffering of disabled men.'[21] This was further developed in the Declaration Concerning Expanding Bullets of 1899, which outlawed 'the use of bullets which expand or flatten easily in the human body, such as bullets with a hard envelope which does not entirely cover the core or is pierced with incisions'.[22] However, in a further echo of the medieval debate in which norms were designed only to exist only amongst like-minded states, the Declaration of St Petersburg forbade the use of certain projectiles 'among civilised nations', while the Declaration Concerning Expanding Bullets would not be 'binding from the time when, in a war between the contracting Powers, one of the belligerents is joined by a non-contracting Power'.[23]

Elements of the ancient world approach to arms control also reasserted themselves in this period. It has already been argued that arms control in the ancient world largely took one of two forms: the establishment of buffers or neutralised areas; and the disarmament of the defeated, sometimes through the *foedus inaequuum*, or unequal treaty.

There were a number of examples of agreements on neutralisation. In the Treaty of Utrecht in 1713, under Article IX the French agreed to British demands:

> that all the Fortifications of the City of Dunkirk be Razed, that the Harbour be filled up, and that the Sluices or Moles which serve to cleanse the Harbour be Levelled, and that at the said King's own Expence, within the space of Five Months after the Conditions of Peace are Concluded and Signed.[24]

Similarly, under Article XXVII of the British–Spanish–Dutch Treaty of 1715, 'The fortifications and all the works of the citadel at Liege, and also those of the chateau of Huy, including all forts and works, shall be razed and demolished, in such a way that they can never be rebuilt or restored.'[25] In the nineteenth century, treaties were signed neutralising countries (Belgium 1831, Luxembourg 1867) and regions (the Black Sea, in 1856).[26] One of the most interesting of these arms control agreements was the Rush–Bagot Agreement of 1817. Under Rush–Bagot the United States and the United Kingdom (subsequently Canada) agreed to the naval demilitarization of the North American Great Lakes. Under this agreement, each side was allowed to deploy a maximum of one ship on Lake Ontario, two ships on the Upper Lakes, and one on Lake Champlain; none of the ships could exceed one hundred tons and one eighteen pound cannon.[27] This agreement did not take the form of a treaty; rather it took the form of an exchange of notes. Nevertheless, this arms control agreement assisted in the general improvement of Anglo-American relations in the period after the war of 1812, which had witnessed a massive build up of naval force to an extent where the British had deployed a ship in the lakes more powerful than the *Victory* which had been so successful at Trafalgar in 1805, while the Americans were in the process of building the two largest warships in the world. Disarmament had begun before Rush–Bagot was agreed; the agreement was nevertheless a stabilising factor in relations between the two states for the rest of the century.[28]

In a further echo of the arms control practices of the ancient world, unequal treaties were also arranged. In 1807, the Prussians and Russians were defeated by Napoleon at Friedland and, following the deal between France and Russia in the Treaty of Tilsit, Prussia was forced to accept a treaty with France that limited the total size of the Prussian army to 42,000 troops, with exact sub-limits of infantry regiments, cavalry regiments, artillery miners and sappers, and the King's Guard, for a period of ten years from 1 January 1809.[29] In addition, under Article V, Prussia would be com-

pelled to send 16,000 troops to fight with the French should a Franco-Aus-
trian war break out.[30] A further example was the series of restrictions
imposed on the Egyptians by their imperial overlords, the Ottoman Turks.
In 1841, a limit of 18,000 was imposed on the Egyptian army, although
this could rise if troops were needed by the Sultan of Turkey in wartime,
and the Egyptians were prohibited from building ironclad warships.
Increases in the size of the Egyptian army were allowed in 1866 and 1873,
but in 1879 the original limitations were reimposed.[31]

Arms control in the inter-war period

The inter-war period in many ways brought many of the disparate arms
control approaches of the past together. There had been arms control connected with attempts to end conflicts, to create stability between states, and
connected with attempts to develop rules of war. The inter-war period was
to witness arms control of all these different types, but in addition was to
strengthen a focus upon the problem of proliferation which had not previously been a major issue, and was to introduce one new form – international control.

Firstly, there were arms control agreements connected with the ending of
conflicts. As already seen before the dawning of the inter-war period, arms
control had been used on several occasions as a part of a post-war settlement. The clearest examples of this form of arms control in the inter-war
period were, of course, in the terms of the post-First World War peace settlements. The Treaty of Versailles of 1919 limited Germany in Part V to an
army of 100,000 (Article 160), a navy of six battleships (Article 181), and
prohibited the development of a German air force (Article 198).[32] The Treaty
of St Germain-en-Laye of 1919 limited the Austrian army to a maximum of
30,000 troops. The Treaty of Neuilly of 1919 prohibited the Bulgarian army
from exceeding a limit of 33,000 troops. Finally, the Treaty of Trianon of
1920 limited the Hungarians to an army of 35,000. Each of these treaties
set detailed terms for not only the size of the armed forces, but also their
structure (for example, Germany was allowed a maximum of seven infantry
divisions and three cavalry by Article 160 of the Treaty of Versailles). For
some, the treaties at the end of the First World War were forms of the *foedus
inaequum*; for others, they were similar to the more limited forms of arms
control designed to create a new post-war stability as, for example, had been
the Treaty of Utrecht.

Second, there had been arms control agreements designed to create or
strengthen strategic stability between two or more states that did not result
from the immediate aftermath of a war. In the inter-war period there were
also many agreements negotiated and signed that were designed to stabilise
relations between particular states. For example, in 1930 Turkey and

Greece reached an agreement on a Naval Protocol by which both states undertook:

> to effect no order, acquisition or construction of war units or armaments, without having notified the other Party six months previously, so that both Governments may thus be enabled if necessary to prevent any competition in the sphere of naval armaments by means of a friendly exchange of views and explanations on either side in a spirit of perfect sincerity.[33]

Similarly, the following year Turkey and the Soviet Union exchanged a protocol under which both states agreed not:

> to lay down any naval fighting unit whatsoever for the purpose of strengthening its fleet in the Black Sea or in neighbouring seas, or to place orders for any such unit in foreign shipyards, or to take any other measure the effect of which would be to increase the present strength of its war fleet in the above-mentioned seas without having notified the second Contracting Party six months previously.[34]

More substantial naval agreements were negotiated and signed between the major naval powers. The Washington Naval Treaty of 1922 between the United States, Great Britain, France, Italy and Japan created a ratio of naval force between the five powers. Great care was taken over the definition of types of ships, their dimensions and the sizes of their armaments, and in a series of attached tables a schedule for the replacement of named ships was set out.[35] The London Naval Treaty of 1930, under Article 1, stipulated that the 'High Contracting Parties agree not to exercise their rights to lay down the keels of capital ship replacement tonnage during the years 1931-6 inclusive as provided in Chapter II, Part 3 of the Treaty for the Limitation of Naval Armament signed between them at Washington.'[36] In 1935, the British and Germans exchanged notes setting the ratio of naval tonnage between their two countries at 100:35 (excluding submarines, which were subject to a different ratio).[37] During 1935 to 1936 the British, Americans, Japanese, French and Italians met to negotiate an extension to their 1930 Treaty. The resulting London Naval Treaty of 1936 differed markedly from the previous naval treaties, however, in that the quantitative approach was abandoned, and instead the treaty set out a series of qualitative restrictions such as, under Article 4, limits to the standard displacement of a capital ship (35,000 tons), and to the maximum gun calibre of a capital ship (14 inches).[38] Over the next two years, Great Britain sought to extend the treaty regime by signing agreements similar to the London Naval Treaty with Germany (1937, and a protocol was added in 1938), the Soviet Union (1937), Poland (1938), and the Scandinavian countries (1938).[39]

Third, as in previous periods, there were many efforts to develop the rules of war and create a general world order in the inter-war period. In common with the practice of the past, these efforts focused upon limiting types of weapons, identifying illegitimate targets and the setting of restraints on the acceptable space for warfare. In the first category, perhaps the most famous agreement was the Geneva Protocol of 1925. Under the Protocol, states agreed that:

> the use in war of asphyxiating, poisonous or other gases, and of all analogous liquids, materials or devices, has been justly condemned by the general opinion of the civilised world ... the High Contracting Parties, so far as they are not already Parties to Treaties prohibiting such use, accept this prohibition, agree to extend this prohibition to the use of bacteriological methods of warfare and agree to be bound as between themselves according to the terms of this declaration.[40]

The clearest example of further setting limits upon acceptable violence in warfare was the Red Cross Convention of 1929, which set terms for the treatment of the wounded, and the Convention of the Treatment of Prisoners of War, also of 1929.[41] In terms of restraints on the space for warfare, the Treaty of Lausanne of 1923 demilitarised the Straits of the Dardanelles, the Sea of Marmora and the Bosphorus, even though the Montreux Convention of 1936 allowed a certain amount of fortification by Turkey.[42] A more esoteric example was the so-called Roerich Pact of 1935, by which states in the Americas agreed to the protection of artistic and scientific institutions and historic monuments in time of conflict.[43]

Much of the above activity was in many ways a continuation of the arms control efforts of previous periods. The issues changed, but the forms of arms control had much in common with the past. Of course, this is not to argue that there were not also significant developments. The level of detail certainly increased, notably in agreements such as the Treaty of Versailles and the Washington Naval Treaty. Further, a growing concern with verification began to become apparent. This deepening of the arms control process was also matched in the inter-war period with a widening as new types of arms control – proliferation and international control – came to the fore.

The fourth area of inter-war arms control was a growing concern with proliferation. To a limited degree, this concern was not new. The Third Lateran Council of 1179 in part focused on the proliferation problem of medieval Christian Europe:

> Greed so filled their souls that although they were Christians they nevertheless provided to the Saracens arms, iron and wood for their ships, and helped them become superior in evil from the provision of arms and necessities to fight the Christians ... These we condemn to be cut off from the Communion of the Church and subject to excommunication for their iniquity and condemned to the loss of their goods, to be confiscated by the Catholic princes of cities. If they are captured they are to be enslaved by their captors.[44]

Such efforts at the control of the proliferation of weapons and technologies were inevitably circumscribed in the Middle Ages due in part to the limited sophistication of weapons technology. In the immediate aftermath of the Great War, in a very different context in which the technological development of weaponry had led to the vast destruction of the 1914-18 war, states attempted to create a legal framework for the limitation of the spread of weapons. An initial agreement, focused on a particular conflict, was reached in May 1919 whereby:

> The Governments of Great Britain, Spain, Portugal, the United States, Russia, Brazil, France and Japan have agreed effectively to restrain their subjects and citizens from exporting to or importing into China, arms and munitions of war and material destined exclusively for their manufacture until the establishment of a government whose authority is recognized throughout the whole country.[45]

Four months later, twenty-three states signed the Convention for the Control of the Trade in Arms and Ammunition, providing a more general level of proliferation restraints, motivated in part by the desire to prevent the escalation of limited wars, in part by the hope that such an action might facilitate the more comfortable control of colonies. Under Article 1, the Convention prohibited the export of:

> artillery of all kinds, apparatus for the discharge of all kinds of projectiles explosive or gas-diffusing, flame-throwers, bombs, grenades, machine guns and rifled small-bore breech-loading weapons of all kinds, as well as the exportation of the ammunition for use with such arms. The prohibition of exportation shall apply to all such arms and ammunition, whether complete or in parts.[46]

Further, under Article 2, the importation of 'firearms and ammunition, whether complete or in parts' was prohibited in the regions set out in Article 6:

> The whole of the continent of Africa with the exception of Algeria, Libya and the Union of South Africa ... all islands situated within a hundred nautical miles of the [African] coast ... Transcaucasia, Persia, Gwadar, the Arabian Peninsula and such continental parts of Asia as were included in the Turkish Empire on August 4, 1914 ... the Red Sea, the Gulf of Aden, the Persian Gulf and the Sea of Oman.[47]

In addition, sections of the Convention dealt with forms of supervision of the Convention both on land and sea. This Convention was developed further in 1925 into the Convention for the Supervision of the International Trade in Arms and Ammunition and in Implements of War.[48] A further attempt was made to control the proliferation of weapons in 1929, with a more detailed Draft Convention with Regard to the Supervision of the Private Manufacture and Publicity of the Manufacture of Arms and Ammunition and of Implements of War under the auspices of the League of Nations.[49]

The fifth and final area of inter-war arms control was a completely new

innovation, arms control through international agency. This was first instituted in the Covenant of the League of Nations. Under Article 8:

> 2. The Council, taking account of the geographical situation and circum-
> stances of each State, shall formulate plans for such [arms] reduction for the
> consideration and action of the several Governments.
> 3. Such plans shall be subject to reconsideration at least every ten years.
> 4. After these plans have been adopted by the several Governments, the limits
> of armaments therein fixed shall not be exceeded without the concurrence of
> the Council.[50]

Several attempts were made to take these provisions further. Perhaps the
clearest example of subsequent efforts can be read into the text of the
Preparatory Commission's draft on arms limitations written in 1930 and
presented to the General Disarmament Conference of 1932. Detailed forms
of limitations were set out, but the key section illustrating the importance
of international control was Part VI. Under Article 40, it was proposed that:

> There shall be set up at the seat of the League of Nations a Permanent Disar-
> mament Commission with the duty of following the execution of the present
> Convention ... Members of the Commission shall not represent their Govern-
> ments.[51]

The success of such efforts at international control during the inter-war
period was, of course, very limited. However, they were to be a forerunner
of more extensive efforts later in the century.

The widening and deepening of arms control

This brief examination of the practice of arms control in the past has
included agreements and treaties from many different contexts and circumstances. What is plain is that the form of arms control practised is always
a product of the international political culture and context of the time. Yet
this historical overview illustrates that, up to the beginning of the Second
World War, the process and scope of arms control had both widened and
deepened.

The widening of arms control relates to the areas in which arms control
has been deemed to be politically appropriate. In the ancient world, in a
context of endemic warfare and simple weapons, arms control had two purposes: it was used at the end of conflicts to impose a new balance (for example, the Rome–Carthage Agreement of 201 BC); and it was used by political
leaders to create or perpetuate stability between their political entities (such
as the Egyptian–Hittite Agreement of 1280 BC). During the Middle Ages, in
the context of the confusion between public and private violence, and the
changing relationship between church and state, arms control was used to
only one purpose: to develop a more orderly state of affairs in the world,

defined at the time as the Christian world (for example, the Truce of God proclaimed in the Diocese of Elne in 1027). During the period between the Peace of Westphalia and the Treaty of Versailles, in a context of the emergence of nation-states, the development of the technology of warfare, and the further development of concerns to devise rules for the use of violence, arms control had three purposes: it was used at the end of conflicts to create a new balance (as in the Treaty of Utrecht); it was used to develop or perpetuate stability between states (the Rush–Bagot Agreement); and it was used to develop norms of behaviour in international relations (as in the Hague Conventions).

Thus in the period up to 1919, arms control had developed in three distinct areas, and arms control of all these three types was pursued in the inter-war period: at the end of conflicts to create a new balance (as in the Treaty of Versailles); to devise or perpetuate stability between states (the 1930 Greco-Turkish Naval Protocol); and it was used to develop norms of behaviour in international relations (as in the Geneva Protocol). In addition, arms control developed in two further areas: the control of the proliferation of weapons (such as the 1919 Convention for the Control of the Trade in Arms and Ammunition); and international control (clearly in the Covenant of the League of Nations). However, in these latter two areas there was much less deepening of the process of arms control compared to the other three types.

The deepening of arms control refers to the nature of the agreements themselves in three areas. First, over time there was a trend away from agreements set in broad terms to much more detailed agreements (compare, for example, the arms control provisions of the Treaty of Utrecht with the Treaty of Versailles). Second, issues of verification became increasingly important. Whereas there was no method of verification on the limitation of the Prussian army in the Treaty of Paris in 1808, and the Prussians were able to break the spirit of the Treaty, the Treaty of Versailles set up Inter-Allied Commissions of Control under Section IV with wide ranging powers; for example, under Article 209, it was the Naval Inter-Allied Commission of Control's 'duty to proceed to the building yards and to supervise the breaking-up of the ships which are under construction there, to take delivery of all surface ships or submarines, salvage ships, docksand the tubular docks, and to supervise the destruction and breaking-up provided for'.[52] Third, agreements increasingly became seen in terms of a regime that could contribute to stability over time, rather than an agreement that merely dealt with an immediate problem. The arms control process began to be seen as a means of managing political difficulty; for example, the Rush–Bagot Agreement (especially in the middle and latter part of the nineteenth century), or the naval arms control agreements of the 1920s and 1930s. By the standards of the debate over arms control during the cold war, such a deepening was very shallow and uneven in different treaties (especially with regard to verification); however, there had been a series of significant developments up to the outbreak of the Second World War.

There was, therefore, a process of the widening and deepening of arms control in the period up to the dawning of the nuclear age. Did the practice of arms control during the cold war further this development? And how did the development of a theory of arms control in the late 1950s and 1960s affect the way in which arms control was perceived?

The influence of the nuclear age

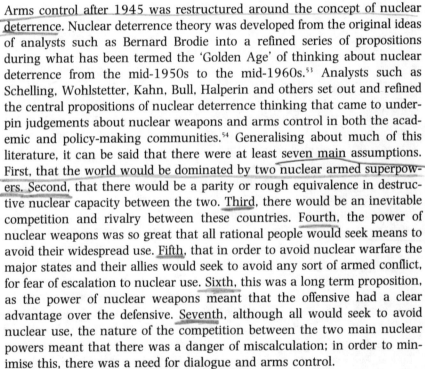

Arms control after 1945 was restructured around the concept of nuclear deterrence. Nuclear deterrence theory was developed from the original ideas of analysts such as Bernard Brodie into a refined series of propositions during what has been termed the 'Golden Age' of thinking about nuclear deterrence from the mid-1950s to the mid-1960s.[53] Analysts such as Schelling, Wohlstetter, Kahn, Bull, Halperin and others set out and refined the central propositions of nuclear deterrence thinking that came to underpin judgements about nuclear weapons and arms control in both the academic and policy-making communities.[54] Generalising about much of this literature, it can be said that there were at least seven main assumptions. First, that the world would be dominated by two nuclear armed superpowers. Second, that there would be a parity or rough equivalence in destructive nuclear capacity between the two. Third, there would be an inevitable competition and rivalry between these countries. Fourth, the power of nuclear weapons was so great that all rational people would seek means to avoid their widespread use. Fifth, that in order to avoid nuclear warfare the major states and their allies would seek to avoid any sort of armed conflict, for fear of escalation to nuclear use. Sixth, this was a long term proposition, as the power of nuclear weapons meant that the offensive had a clear advantage over the defensive. Seventh, although all would seek to avoid nuclear use, the nature of the competition between the two main nuclear powers meant that there was a danger of miscalculation; in order to minimise this, there was a need for dialogue and arms control.

It was these assumptions that created the context for much of the nuclear debate during the cold war period. This thinking was important as it became clear that under these assumptions the practical implication was that nuclear deterrence had to be constantly worked at by policy-makers in order to maintain stability within the competitive relationship between the superpowers. Political will to maintain a deterrent relationship had to be communicated and made credible, based on an evolving capability. On the other hand, political reassurance also had to be worked at, to ensure that natural worst-case analyses on all sides would not lead to the outbreak of war in times of crisis or arms race instability; this was the central role for arms control. For James E. King:

> if it is to be the function of arms control to safeguard the stability based upon mutual deterrence, proposals to *abolish* the 'terror' in the 'balance of terror' are clearly out of order. It may be appropriate, nevertheless, to seek early agreement to *limit* the number ... on each side, and thereby to diminish the implicit threat of terror.[55]

In this new intellectual and political framework it became possible for analysts to argue that 'The history of arms control is quite short.'[56] Of course what is meant here is that the history of the form of arms control practised and theorised about in the nuclear age was quite short. This 'arms control in the nuclear age' was seen by its originators to be something quite new.[57] The core of the theory was that in a nuclear world with two ideologically opposed blocs competing politically and strategically, the outbreak of nuclear war was a possible, but was never a desirable, outcome. Thus the leaders of both blocs had a mutual interest in limiting the possibility of conflict occurring. As Herman Kahn noted, 'Neither the United States nor the Soviet Union wants a war that would annihilate us both – neither side wants the cost of the arms competition to become more onerous; neither side wants to permit lax operational practices for nuclear forces.'[58] These common interests provided a basis for arms control in the nuclear age which therefore rested 'essentially on the recognition that our military relation with potential enemies is not one of pure conflict and opposition, but involves strong elements of mutual interest in the avoidance of a war that neither side wants'.[59] Arms control thus had to ensure strategic stability, and to prevent it from being undermined by technological developments which in turn could lead to incentives being developed which might encourage a surprise attack. Under crisis conditions such an attack would be designed to destroy the opponent's strategic nuclear arsenal in a situation in which the advantages of striking first clearly outweighed those of being second in terms of achieving strategic goals, and in particular in terms of damage limitation. The key task for the originators of arms control in the nuclear age was, therefore, the reduction of the vulnerability of retaliatory forces to ensure that any second strike capability remained invulnerable, thus ensuring the stability of nuclear deterrence.

Five periods of arms control may be identified in the cold war era: the focus on nuclear disarmament to the late 1950s; 'pure' arms control to 1972; political arms control to 1979; the collapse of arms control to 1985; and the new arms control of the late 1980s. Each of these periods will be examined in turn in terms of the influence of the new concepts of arms control.

In the first period, from the origins of the cold war to the end of the 1950s, the political debate was framed by notions of general and complete disarmament mainly, although not exclusively, of nuclear weapons. For example, the Baruch Plan of 1946 proposed 'the creation of an International Atomic Development Authority, to which should be entrusted all phases of the development and use of atomic energy' and further that:

1.   Manufacture of atomic bombs shall stop;
2.   Existing bombs shall be disposed of pursuant to the terms of the treaty; and
3.   The Authority shall be in possession of full information as to the know-how for the production of atomic energy.[60]

Thirteen years later, ambitions – or the desire for good publicity – had grown greater, with a proposal by the Soviet Union to the General Assembly of the United Nations that:

over a period of four years, all States should carry out complete disarmament ... land armies, naval fleets and air forces will cease to exist ... All atomic and hydrogen bombs at the disposal of States will be destroyed, and all further production of such bombs will cease.[61]

It was the dissatisfaction with what was thought to be the unrealistic nature of such proposals that led to the work of the late 1950s and early 1960s to develop an approach to arms control that was deemed appropriate for the nuclear age. As James E. King put it:

total disarmament is a tragic illusion, if not a deliberate fraud. No conceivable inspection system could prevent the 'internal security' forces envisaged by every such proposal from being a threat to neighbouring countries, nor commercial aircraft from being converted for military purposes.[62]

However, as Robert Bowie put it, 'Within these limits ... there appears room for substantial arms control if the parties wish to pursue it.'[63] Arms controllers, therefore, sought reductions in a strategic context in which it was clear that:

very small forces are more vulnerable to a clandestine attacking force that lead many who concern themselves with arms control to think of a goal well short of the complete elimination of strategic weapons. It is not simply that a reduction to modest levels is a less ambitious goal. It is that the situation may become safer in the event of war, and more stable with respect to the likelihood of war, if forces are substantially reduced, but that *beyond a certain point* further reductions may increase both the fears and the temptations that aggravate the likelihood of war.[64]

It was these considerations that provided the context for the development of arms control theory, an approach which revolved around two major assumptions: that nuclear states had an overriding and mutual desire to avoid warfare, since nuclear war would completely devastate their own states; and that arms control would have to be used to reduce the incentives to launch a first strike, thus lessening crisis and arms race instability, and hence strengthening strategic stability.[65] This was the basis for the second period, which might be termed 'pure' arms control, by which is meant that there was an attempt to create a close relationship between arms control theory and practice. The major goal of the nuclear arms control thinkers of this period was to achieve strategic stability based on MAD (mutually assured destruction), in which instabilities through either the arms race or crises would be minimised. In bringing about this situation, arms control had a role in both commission and omission.

In terms of commission, the Anti-Ballistic Missile Treaty of 1972 ensured that mutual assured destruction had become and would remain the central strategic reality. As agreed in Article I, 'Each Party undertakes not to deploy ABM systems for a defense of the territory of its country and not to provide a base for such a defense'.[66] With national defence prohibited by arms control, the nuclear superpowers would always be vulnerable to nuclear destruction thus, in the logic of nuclear deterrence, giving the strongest possible incentives to each state to avoid any form of conflict between them. Further, through the Interim Agreement on Limitation of Strategic Offensive Arms of 1972, both sides acknowledged that an acceptable level of nuclear parity had developed between them. Under Article I, 'The Parties undertake not to start construction of additional fixed land-based intercontinental ballistic missile launchers after July 1, 1972.'[67] Under Article III, 'The Parties undertake to limit submarine-launched ballistic missile launchers and modern ballistic missile submarines to the numbers operational and under construction on the date of the signature of this Interim Agreement.'[68] The arms balance in terms of missile launchers (although not warhead numbers) was to be stabilised at existing levels of parity.[69]

In terms of omission, arms control had not restrained developments in three areas. First, it had not regulated the increase in the size of the Soviet nuclear arsenal during the 1960s as it approached parity with the United States. A 'natural' parity was allowed to emerge which was then codified through arms control, rather than arms control being used to shape that emerging parity. Second, it had not been used to control the emergence of certain new technologies (such as the SLBM (submarine-launched ballistic missile) and the MIRV (multiple independently-targetable re-entry vehicle), which were deemed to be stabilising. Third, arms control in this period produced an Interim Agreement on OffensiveArms between the United States and Soviet Union at levels of weapons which ensured that there would be a level of nuclear overkill in which a second strike capability should always seem survivable. As Hedley Bull argued in *The Control of the Arms Race* it was necessary in arms control efforts to recognise 'those kinds and quantities of forces and weapons that promote the stability of the balance of power, and those which do not; to tolerate or even to promote the former, and to restrict the latter'.[70]

This approach to arms control was highly successful in that by the mid-1970s, many of the fears which initially animated the new arms controllers had largely been allayed. However, this form of arms control, in which theory and practice were to be closely linked, was to be heavily compromised from the mid-1970s onwards in two ways. First, arms control expanded its scope from the central strategic question – ensuring the survivability of a second strike capability – into a range of other forms of arms control. There were negotiations over biological weapons, conventional weapons and over the level of the arms trade. In other words, the original focus of the new arms control of the nuclear age was blunted as a process of widening took place. Second, political issues – which had originally been ruled out of the new nuclear arms control – grew enormously in importance. For much of the 1970s it seemed that the terms 'arms control' and 'detente' had become synonymous. Further, as political debate raged around the value of detente, so arms control was taken from its realm of expert discussion and placed into the public political debate. In the United States, there was great argument over whether there was any value to this new form of arms control, with the political right wing, in the form of the Committee on the Present Danger, arguing for less emphasis on bilateral and multilateral measures, and for a greater focus on unilateral efforts.[71] In contrast, in many European countries the debate became polarised between those who supported arms control efforts on a multilateral basis, and those who sought disarmament, arguing that arms control merely legitimised the arms race.[72]

The new arms control of the nuclear age thus fell into disrepute by the late 1970s and early 1980s. There were essentially two reasons for this. First, it had probably never been feasible to limit the discussion over arms control to the technical, expert level, and the introduction of partisan politics into the debate, along with the widening of the arms control agenda, in retrospect appear almost inescapable. This widening was perhaps inevitable, not only because of the success of arms control (at least as widely perceived at the time) in improving strategic and political relations, but also given that the security concerns of the 1960s related not only to the stability of the central nuclear relationship between the superpowers, but also to the fear of nuclear proliferation. The success of the negotiation and signing of the Non-Proliferation of Nuclear Weapons Treaty in 1968 represented a success for the process of arms control, but a challenge for the theoretical base of the arms control of the nuclear era, since arms control theory could at best only partly explain and shape the drive for non-proliferation.

Second, as already seen, much of the immediate arms control agenda of the early 1960s had, by the mid-1970s, been achieved. The strategic focus of increasing strategic stability seemed less urgent in a period in which strategic parity had been achieved and ratified, and at a time in which mutual assured destruction had clearly become the reality of nuclear deterrence.[73] In such circumstances, the essence of the drive to create an arms control theory in the early 1960s had been transformed. As Phil Williams noted, 'Schelling and Halperin (along with Hedley Bull) had provided much of the philosophy which was to inform arms control efforts during the 1960s. During the 1970s, however, this philosophy appeared increasingly less relevant to the arms control experience.'[74] This separation of the theory and practice of arms control had been a subject that had worried the theorists in the early 1960s. As Schelling and Halperin had warned:

> One of the difficulties with a substantial agreement on arms limitation might be the difficulty of reaching a common expectation of just how much of a 'truce' in diplomacy, propaganda, and even military activity is involved ... The least favourable prognosis is probably for an agreement that one party expects to symbolise the burying of the hatchet, a new era of good feeling, and a resolution to live up to new standards of international friendship, while the other takes for granted that 'realistic' diplomacy will prevail, subject only to the concrete matters agreed on. In this case acute disappointment and recrimination might result, and the greatest of misunderstandings.[75]

If Schelling and Halperin had mentioned the possibility of such division, disappointment and misunderstanding occurring within states as well as between them, they would have given an almost perfect prediction of the problems facing arms control in the late 1970s. Perhaps nowhere was the loss of the theoretical focus of arms control more evident than in the SALT II negotiations and treaty. SALT I had ratified and confirmed strategic parity and the reality of mutual assured destruction. In contrast, SALT II produced an agreement with no such fundamental results, and a general increase in the levels of nuclear warheads.

In the fourth period of arms control in the cold war era, the early 1980s, the new arms control introduced by the theorists of the 1960s had lost its central focus, been broadened to issues beyond its theoretical base, and become politicised in a manner most unwelcome to its originators. The debate over arms control in this period recognised the collapse of many of its initial assumptions.[76] The fate of SALT II and the difficulty of identifying a strategic logic for arms control, along with the worsening of cold war relationships, led to a period from 1983 to 1985 in which for the first time since 1969, there were no nuclear arms control negotiations between the superpowers.

However, arms control re-emerged as a major international issue in the mid- and late-1980s, from the elevation of Mikhail Gorbachev to General Secretary of the Soviet Communist Party. In this final period of arms control in the nuclear age during the cold war, a different purpose emerged.

Whereas arms control had been initially conceived of by the nuclear arms control theorists in terms of enhancing bilateral stability, it had been broadened by the mid-1970s to include certain elements of world order and proliferation control. Increasingly after 1985, Gorbachev and the reformist element in the Soviet Union sought to broaden arms control further by seeking to use the process in order to end the cold war conflict. This theme will be developed later in this book when looking at the transition to the post-cold war world.

Arms control, therefore, moved through five periods during the cold war. Initially there was little arms control, largely the rhetoric of disarmament.[77] In the second period from the early 1960s, a new theory emerged which focused arms control efforts on the need to create a particular form of weapons stability between the nuclear superpowers. The success of this ambition led to a third period in which arms control was broadened to include attempts at proliferation control (most notably with the Nuclear Non-Proliferation Treaty), and to create new norms of behaviour (the Environmental Modification Treaty of 1977, for example).[78] In the fourth period, arms control fell into disrepute during the early 1980s, as the theoretical underpinning to arms control collapsed. Finally, from the mid-1980s, arms control increasingly came to be concerned with regulating the end of conflict as the cold war came to an end.

Thus, the pattern of development in arms control identified in the first section of this chapter continued after the hiatus of the first two decades of the cold war, and after having been forgotten at a time when a new theory of arms control was developed. The pattern of the past – the widening of the areas in which arms control was used – was again repeated. However, there was one particularly significant contribution made by arms control in the cold war period, and that was to accelerate the process of deepening, in three ways.

First, the trend towards increasing the level of detail of agreements continued, although admittedly unevenly. The Interim Agreement on Offensive Arms, the ABM Treaty and SALT II all used a series of attached statements and understandings to the treaty by both signatories in order to clarify as far as possible the exact meaning of the relevant articles.[79] However, such attempts to further increase the amount of detail and precision in treaties did not prevent argument over issues of interpretation, as was seen, for example, in the middle of the 1980s in relation to the debate over the ABM Treaty.[80]

Second, issues of verification further increased in importance, although the technical possibilities for more detailed verification tended to be constrained by the politics of the cold war. Whereas the Partial Test Ban Treaty of 1963 made no provisions for verification in the terms of the treaty, the Interim Agreement on Offensive Arms, the ABM Treaty and the SALT II

Treaty all provided for verification by national technical means in Article V, Article XII and Article XV respectively. Some of the difficulty of judging the required level of verification had been foreshadowed by the debate amongst the arms control theorists in the early 1960s. For some, verification was of only limited importance; Schelling and Halperin, for example, suggested that 'even if violation cannot with great confidence be completely deterred, it may be sufficient to deter the most profitable violations, or to make violation so costly that little can be gained by it'.[81] In contrast, Fred Iklè feared that democratic governments might be tempted to ignore repeated violations for fear of suffering domestic political damage, especially were the violations only to be apparent through clandestine sources, and were the government to be politically committed to the arms control agreement.[82]

Third, many agreements increasingly came to be seen as part of a regime: for example, the non-proliferation regime, the ABM Treaty regime, the biological weapons regime, and even the SALT regime. Particularly by the end of the 1980s, policy-makers and analysts came to see arms control not only in terms of aiding the prevention of a movement towards war, but also in terms of being able 'to lay the foundation for a movement in relations toward those characteristic of a pluralistic security community'.[83]

Thus the historical pattern of the development of arms control reasserted itself during the cold war, even if much of the arms control practice that pre-dated the nuclear age was largely ignored in the creation of arms control theory in the early 1960s. The process of widening was demonstrated in microcosm during the cold war period, while the process of deepening continued further. The remainder of this chapter will seek to explore the concept of widening in order to develop a typology of arms control.

A typology of arms control

The debate over arms control theory in the cold war period was initially very narrow by historical comparisons. Although bilateral arms control designed to create strategic stability is an important function of arms control, it represents only one of five different approaches that have been identified from the history of arms control: arms control used to end conflicts; arms control focused on strategic stability; arms control to create norms of behaviour; proliferation control; and arms control by international organisation. Each of these forms of arms control is important to the understanding of the concept. In order to demonstrate this argument and the validity of these categories, historical examples of each form of arms control will be examined in turn.

Arms control at the conclusion of conflicts

This category refers specifically to arms control agreements that have been reached at the end of wars or major conflicts. The focus in these cases has not been the strengthening of strategic stability and the aversion of impending conflict; rather, the attempt has been made to create a new series of post-war relationships. These have been treaties in which the terms have been overwhelmingly dependent upon the nature of the military and political outcome.

Four possibilities exist. First, where one state has been overwhelmingly defeated, an initial response may be to totally disarm that state, as in the cases of Germany and Japan at the end of the Second World War. Second, where a participant may be largely – although not completely – defeated, such as Carthage by the Romans, arms control terms may be very unequal: the *foedus inaequum*, designed to create strategic and political inferiority. A third possibility is that where there has been a clear military success, the victors may wish to dictate terms to the defeated states that would impose a semi-permanent strategic stability through the superiority of the forces of the victors in order to create the conditions for peace, rather than conditions to perpetuate the political inferiority of the defeated states. Examples of such arms control would be the post-First World War peace treaties, or the peace treaty between the victorious allies and Italy and other defeated states in 1947. Finally, where one group of forces is merely in the ascendancy, but has not achieved an overwhelming victory, the terms of the treaty have been rather more balanced, although still in favour of the dominant parties, as is clear in the terms of the Peace of Westphalia. Each of these alternatives will be examined in turn.

The first possibility is that an overwhelmingly defeated state may be completely disarmed by its vanquishers. At Potsdam in 1945, the powers that were to occupy defeated Germany – Great Britain, the United States, France and the Soviet Union – reached a Protocol in which they agreed that:

> The purposes of the occupation of Germany by which the Control Council shall be guided are:
>
> (i) The complete disarmament and demilitarisation of Germany and the elimination or control of all German industry that could be used for military production. To these ends:
> (a) All German land, naval and air forces, the SS, SA, SD, and Gestapo, with all their organisations, staffs, and institutions, including the General Staff ... shall be completely and finally abolished in such manner as permanently to prevent the revival of German militarism and Nazism.[84]

A slightly different form of the same approach may be seen in the disarmament of Japan after the Second World War. Limitations on Japan did not take the form of a treaty: rather, Japanese disarmament took the form of a constitutional commitment. That this was imposed by outside forces, above all the United States and the personal influence of General MacArthur, is clear in the context of the American occupation and role in the political restructuring of Japan following its military defeat. Article 9 of the Japanese constitution declares:

> Aspiring sincerely to an international peace based on justice and order, the Japanese people forever renounce war as a sovereign right of the nation and the threat or use of forces as means of settling international disputes.
>
> In order to accomplish the aim of the preceding paragraph, land, sea, and air forces, as well as other war potential, will never be maintained. The right of belligerency of the state will not be recognised.[85]

Of course in both cases, the prohibition on the development of military forces did not last, and the permanency implied in the phrases 'completely and finally abolished' and 'never be maintained' soon took on a rather fleeting character.

In contrast to the attempt to establish permanent disarmament, another form of establishing a new series of relationships at the end of conflict has been to impose severe military, and political, limitations upon the defeated state. Whereas the former may seek to impose permanent disarmament, the latter seeks to create permanent political inferiority. At the end of the Second Punic War, the terms of the Treaty of Zama in 202 BC were overwhelmingly in favour of Rome. Whereas the Romans had only to 'cease their raiding attacks', the Carthaginians had to observe strict limitations:

> all warships to be surrendered, with the exception of ten triremes, and all the trained elephants in their possession were to be handed over and no more to be trained. They were not to make war on anyone inside or outside Africa without permission from Rome; they were to make restitution to Masinissa [the Numidian prince] and draw up a treaty with him; they must supply grain and pay to the allied troops until their own envoys had returned to Rome. They were to pay 10,000 talents of silver spread by equal instalments over fifty years, and to hand over 100 hostages.[86]

Such use of arms control was designed to cement political relations whereby the defeated, through the limitations on their arms, would be kept in semi-permanent weakness in relation to the victor. It was not the strategic balance that was the key to the treaty for the Romans, but rather the effect of maintaining political dominance over Carthage. In this case, a Carthaginian attempt to change the power balance some fifty years later through rearming and waging war on the Numidians led to the complete destruction of Carthage at the hands of Rome.

The third possibility is that where there has been a clear military success, the victors may wish to dictate terms to the defeated that would impose upon them a semi-permanent position whereby the defeated state would not be able to upset strategic stability. This did not imply a position of political inferiority; rather, a guarantee to the victors that they would not be placed in a position of strategic inferiority and therefore, since the victors interpreted their behaviour and desires as non-threatening, peace would be kept. The clearest examples of such agreements were those arrived at in the aftermath of both the First and Second World Wars. The Treaty of Versailles, for example, identified Germany as a destabilising power and therefore set a series of restrictions upon the German armed forces 'In order to render possible the initiation of a general limitation of the armaments of all nations.'[87] In a similar way, in the case of the restrictions placed on Italy, Bulgaria, Finland, Hungary and Romania in the peace treaties of 1947, limitations were placed on the size and quality of the army, navy and air force in the interests of preventing these states from being able to engage in militarily destabilising behaviour.

The final possibility is that at the conclusion of a war, there is no overwhelming victor, and that any arms control agreements reached would thus tend to be more balanced than the above. A good example of this would be the seven-year negotiations that eventually led to the Peace of Westphalia in 1648. The nature of the negotiations changed with the fortunes of war throughout the period. At the end of the conflict, the balance of advantage lay with France and its allies against the Holy Roman Emperor, and consequently the treaty terms reflected this. Taken as a whole, the treaty appeared to offer the prospect for a general peace between France, Sweden and their German allies on the one hand and the Holy Roman Empire on the other. There was a general disarmament section, Article CXVIII, in which it stated 'that the troops and armies of all those who are making war in the Empire, shall be disbanded and discharged; only each party shall send to and keep up as many men in his own dominion, as he shall judge necessary for his security'.[88] Under Article III:

> that a reciprocal amity between the Emperor, and the Most Christian King [of France], the Electors, princes, and states of the Empire, may be maintained so much the more firm and sincere ... the one shall never assist the present or future enemies of the other, under any title or pretense whatsoever, either with arms, money, soldiers, or any sort of ammunition; nor no-one, who is a member of this pacification, shall suffer any enemy's troops to retire through or sojourn in his country.[89]

Yet although these articles were designed to create a more pacific central Europe at the end of the Thirty Years War, they were also to be used specifically in the interests of the French, for not only had the French been at war with the Emperor, but also the Spanish who were close allies of the Emperor. Through Article IV, the French forced the Emperor to make a separate peace, thus making the Circle of Burgundy (the Spanish Netherlands) vulnerable to France. Article IV stipulated that:

the Circle of Burgundy shall be and continue a member of the Empire, after the disputes between France and Spain (comprehended in this treaty), shall be terminated. That nevertheless, neither the Emperor nor any of the states of the Empire shall meddle with the wars which are now on foot between them. That if for the future any dispute arises between these two kingdoms, the above said reciprocal obligation of not aiding each others' enemies, shall always continue firm between the Empire and the kingdom of France.[90]

Other elements of the treaty were to be more balanced. The French ally, the Elector of the Palatinate, was restored to power, but the Elector of Bavaria, one of the Emperor's closest allies, was recognised in a more powerful position. The French won the right to 'keep a garrison in the castle of Philippsburg' and thereby control of part of Alsace, but their further ambitions were to be constrained since they were to be 'limited to such a number of soldiers, as may not be capable to give any umbrage, or just suspicion to the neighbourhood'.[91] Further, sovereign control of the region was not to be ceded, since 'the King shall pretend to nothing more than the protection and safe passage of his garrison into the castle ... but the property of the place, all jurisdiction, all its profits, revenues, purchases, rights, *regales*, servitude, people, subjects, vassals ... shall appertain' to the Chapter of Speyer in the Empire.[92]

Arms control at the end of conflicts, therefore, has covered a large sphere of political and military activity. In addition, some elements of treaties such as those at Westphalia, Utrecht and Versailles have also sought to develop new norms of international behaviour.

Arms control to strengthen strategic stability

The second type of arms control focuses upon the attempt to create a greater measure of strategic stability between two or more states. There are many examples of this form of arms control, but in the classic form generally such measures focus upon one form of weaponry or upon one particular military concern. Often these agreements have taken place between two or more states equally concerned about the threat from the other. The use of arms control to strengthen strategic stability between two or more states has a long history, and may be traced back at least as far as the Egyptian–Hittite Agreement of 1280 BC. On certain occasions, such agreements have been brought about by the desire to strengthen crisis stability, sometimes in the context of a perception that war may be imminent; thus arms control has been used as a war prevention measure. The Anglo-French Naval Limitation Pact of 1787 is one example. On other occasions arms control has been used to strengthen arms race stability, and thereby also to avoid a costly arms race at some stage in the future; here the Argentine–Chile Naval Limitation Convention of 1902 is examined as an example.

The Anglo-French Naval Limitation Pact of 1787 was clearly designed to strengthen strategic stability between the two countries in the context of a high probability of war breaking out between Great Britain and France. After the outbreak of civil war in Holland both the British and French sought to avoid being drawn in on opposite sides. In a Reciprocal Declaration both sides decided that:

> in the current position of affairs, to agree that no one on either side will prepare any naval armaments beyond the peacetime establishment; and that neither will make any attempt to place in the water a greater number of ships-of-the-line than the six whose armaments have already been reciprocally communicated; and that in a situation where one of the two sovereigns should find it necessary to make some different arrangement, it would not take place until after preliminary notification.[93]

Within three weeks of this agreement, however, direct conflict between Britain and France appeared even more likely over Holland; yet, as a result of negotiations, a further strengthening of an arms control regime took place with the signing of a joint declaration at Versailles on 27 October, in which:

> the undersigned, in the name of their respective sovereigns, agree, that the armaments, and in general all warlike preparations, shall be discontinued on each side; and that the navies of the two nations shall be again placed upon the footing of the peace establishment, as it stood on the 1st of January of the present year.[94]

Through the use of arms control, both the British and French were able to convince themselves that war over Holland, an objective that neither desired, could be avoided by obtaining sufficient confidence that the adversary would be unable to mobilise an adequate force to intervene fully in the Dutch civil war.

In contrast to the tense relations of 1787, the Argentine–Chilean Naval Limitation Convention of 1902 took place in a general context in which war was not seen to be imminent. Strongly encouraged by the British, both Argentina and Chile decided to enter into an arms control agreement which would prevent the two countries from entering into a direct naval arms race.[95] Article 1 of the Convention required that:

> the Governments of Chile and of the Argentine Republic desist from acquiring the vessels of war now building for them, and from henceforth making new acquisitions. Both Governments agree, moreover, to reduce their respective fleets, with which object they will continue to exert themselves until they arrive at an understanding which shall establish a just balance between the said fleets. This reduction to take place within one year, counting from the date of the exchange of ratification of the present Convention.[96]

Under Article 2, 'The two Governments bind themselves not to increase their naval armaments during a period of five years, without previous notice; the one intending to increase them shall give the other eighteen months notice.'[97]

Such classic forms of arms control to strengthen strategic stability should not exclude other forms of agreement in this category. At least two other examples need to be given to illustrate the variety of different arms control measures designed to strengthen strategic stability: bilateral measures over neutralisation to strengthen crisis stability; and multilateral efforts to avoid arms race instability.

The first of these forms concerns the limitation on weapons within a particular area in order to strengthen crisis stability. The Aaland Islands Convention of 1921 between Finland and the Soviet Union set measures for the neutralisation of the area. Article 3 stipulated that 'No military or naval establishment or base of operations, no military aeronautical establishment or base of operations, and no other installations utilized for war purposes shall be maintained or created in the zone.'[98] In such cases, areas over which conflict might occur were identified and neutralised in order to reduce the likelihood of conflict occurring between the parties.

The second type concerns multilateral efforts to strengthen arms race stability. The Central American Arms Limitation Treaty of 1923, amongst other arms control measures, set firm limits on the total size of the Army and National Guard of Guatemala (5200), El Salvador (4200), Honduras (2500), Nicaragua (2500) and Costa Rica (2000) for a period of five years (Article 1); a maximum of ten 'war aircraft' and no 'war vessels' excluding armed coast guard boats (Article 4); and forbade the export of arms to other Central American countries (Article 3). The treaty's limits could be exceeded in cases of civil war or impending attack by another state (Articles 1 and 4), but states had no right to withdraw from the treaty for five years, and after that period states had to give twelve months notification of withdrawal. States had to provide 'a report on the measures adopted by said Government for the execution of this Convention' every six months.[99] Clearly designed to strengthen arms race stability and to control the costs of an arms race in the region, the agreement applied the concept of strategic stability to a multilateral environment.

There have therefore been a number of agreements reached which were designed to strengthen strategic stability between one or more nations by reducing the dangers of crisis and arms race instability in the context of strategic relationships in which war may always be possible. In contrast, arms control at the end of conflicts seeks to create a new set of strategic relationships. Whereas arms control to create strategic stability is likely to be balanced between the participants, arms control at the conclusion of conflicts is much more likely to be uneven in the treatment of the parties.

Arms control to create norms of behaviour

There have been a number of agreements and treaties that have sought to create norms in international relations, particularly as they affect the use of arms. Arms control that has sought to create or develop such norms may be divided into three categories. First, there have been efforts to contain the destructive effect of warfare by prohibiting the use of certain weapons. Examples of this include the Declaration of St Petersburg in 1868, and the 1925 Geneva Protocol. Second, there have been attempts to create rules on the identification and treatment of non-combatants, such as the Peace of God, proclaimed by Guy of Anjou in 990, or the 1923 Rules of Air War. Third, some agreements have sought to identify geographic areas in which conflict is illegitimate, as with the 1881 Straits of Magellan Treaty and the Antarctic Treaty of 1959. Each of these categories will be examined in turn.

Numerous attempts have been made over the course of human history to constrain the use of certain forms of weapons which have been deemed to be unacceptable because of the level and nature of destruction which their use would bring. Certain basic forms of weapons have repeatedly been the focus of arms control efforts. For example, a prohibition on the use of poison is attributed by Leon Friedman to the Seventh Book of the Hindu *Book of Manu* in the fourth century BC.[100] The Treaty of Strassbury in 1675 prohibited the use of poison and poisoned weapons in warfare in France and Germany.[101] Such prohibitions later included gas along with poisons, and were included in agreements such as the Declaration of Brussels of 1874, the Hague Convention of 1899, and the Washington Treaty on Use of Submarines and Gases in Wartime of 1922.[102] The Geneva Protocol on Poisonous Gases of 1925 added to this list a prohibition on 'bacteriological methods of warfare'.[103] There are many other examples. Canon 29 of the Second Lateran Council of 1139 outlawed the use of crossbows against Catholics, as has already been mentioned. In the more contemporary period, as technology has increased the level of possible destructiveness, and as humanitarian concerns have grown, arms control has focused on other forms of weapons. Prohibitions have been issued against other weapons, such as exploding bullets in the Declaration of St Petersburg in 1868. In each of these and other examples, it was deemed possible to identify weapons that could be defined as uncivilised, barbarous tools of violence which it was the duty of political leaders to attempt to eliminate. Especially in the earlier agreements, a key notion was that of 'civilisation'. The prohibition on the use of the crossbow did not include heretics and Saracens. The ban on the use of expanding bullets was suspended 'with regard to non-contracting powers, or powers that shall not have acceded to it ... [and] ... from the moment when, in a war between contracting and acceding parties, a non-contracting party, or a non-acceding party, shall join one of the belligerents'.[104] Rules of conduct, which included expectations of the social order, required restrictions on certain forms of weapons where those rules were recognised and the suspension of the rules where they were not.

An examination of arms control agreements thus also indicates the nature of the world in which decision-makers believed that they were operating. This is most evident with respect to the two most extreme arms control initiatives of this type, for both the Kellogg–Briand Pact and the Saavedra Lamas Treaty sought to identify all weapons as uncivilised, and thereby to make all war illegal and unacceptable. An early forerunner of these efforts took place at the Fourth Lateran Council of 1215 during which the Pope proclaimed that 'for four years peace be observed in the whole Christian world.'[105] Nine states signed the Kellogg–Briand Pact of 1928, under which they 'solemnly declare in the names of their respective peoples that they condemn recourse to war for the solution of international controversies, and renounce it as an instrument of national policy in their relations with one another'.[106] The more extensive Saavedra Lamas Treaty of 1933 between states in the Americas declared under Article I that 'the settlement of disputes or controversies of any kind that may arise among them [the signatories] shall be effected only by the pacific means of international law'.[107] The treaty also attempted to create a conciliation service.

Across many centuries there has been a remarkable continuity in the efforts to control the most destructive forms of weapons. And continuing this trend in the cold war period, the United Nations declared that:

(a) The use of nuclear and thermo-nuclear weapons is contrary to the spirit, letter and aims of the United Nations and, as such, a direct violation of the Charter of the United Nations;
(b) The use of nuclear and thermo-nuclear weapons would exceed even the scope of war and cause indiscriminate suffering and destruction to mankind and civilization and, as such, is contrary to the rules of international law and to the laws of humanity;
(c) The use of nuclear and thermo-nuclear weapons is a war directed not against an enemy or enemies alone but also against mankind in general, since the peoples of the world not involved in such a war will be subjected to all the evils generated by the use of such weapons;
(d) Any State using nuclear and thermo-nuclear weapons is to be considered as violating the Charter of the United Nations, as acting contrary to the laws of humanity and as committing a crime against mankind and civilization.[108]

Regardless of the level of success of these agreements, and treaties such as Kellogg–Briand were clearly failures, repeatedly states have sought to control the destructive effect of warfare by prohibiting the use of certain weapons. Some agreements have been rather more successful: for example, the prohibitions on the use of exploding bullets and on the use of poison.

The second area of interest has been connected with the attempts to identify and protect non-combatants. As early as 990, the Bishop of Puy, Guy
of Anjou, declared the Peace of God in which rules for the control of violence were set out including prohibitions on the seizure of peasants and
merchants.[109] More precisely, the Peace of the Land of Elsass from 1085 to
1103 decreed that 'All clergy and women, merchants, hunters, pilgrims,
and farmers while they work in the fields and on their way to and from their
labour, shall have peace.'[110] In the seventeenth century, it became common
practice to ransom prisoners of war, which led to some improvements in
their treatment. In an agreement of 1673 between France and the States
General of the United Provinces (the Netherlands), prices were agreed that
ranged from 50,000 *livres* for a General to 25 *livres* for an auditor.[111] Later
norms developed which stipulated that the sick and wounded should be well
treated in wartime (for example, the Geneva Convention of 22 August
1864) and that prisoners of war should be treated as non-combatants. Two
of the most extensive treatments of this subject were in the Hague Conventions of 1899 and 1907, in Chapter II of the Annexe to the Convention. In
those documents, signed by twenty-four states in 1899 and forty-one in
1907, nations agreed on a series of limitations on the violence in war relating to issues such as sieges, flags of truce, armistices, and on the behaviour
of an occupying army.[112] In the inter-war period, many of these norms were
taken further in agreements such as the Red Cross Convention of 1929 on
the Amelioration of the Condition of the Wounded and Sick of Armies in the
Field, and the Convention on Treatment of Prisoners of War of 1929.[113] The
Hague Rules of Air Warfare of 1923 even went so far as to attempt to regulate the use of military aircraft at a time when surgical precision was a
technical impossibility, in order to try to define civilians as non-combatants
in air war. Article XXIV stipulated that:

1. Aerial bombardment is legitimate only when directed at a military objective, that is to say, an object of which the destruction or injury would constitute a distinct military advantage to the belligerent.
2. Such bombardment is legitimate only when directed exclusively at the following objectives: military forces; military works; military establishments or
depots; factories constituting important and well known centres engaged in the
manufacture of arms, ammunition, or distinctively military supplies; lines of
communication or transportation used for military purpose.
3. The bombardment of cities, towns, villages, dwellings, or buildings not in
the immediate neighbourhood of the operations of land forces is prohibited ...
4. In the immediate neighbourhood of the operations of land forces, the bombardment of cities, towns, villages, dwellings, or buildings is legitimate provided
that there exists a reasonable presumption that the military concentration is
sufficiently important to justify such bombardment, having regard to the
danger thus caused to the civilian population.[114]

49

Such attempts to control the use of weapons against particular targets have frequently been ignored in warfare, and this discordance between what has been prescribed and the action actually taken has been one area that from time to time has led the whole process of arms control into disrepute.

The final area where arms control has been used in the attempt to create norms has been related to preventing warfare occurring in particular areas. In the Middle Ages, efforts were made to eliminate violence from churches and church land, as is clear in the Peace of God proclaimed by Guy of Anjou in 990: 'From this hour forth no one shall seize ecclesiastical lands, whether those of a bishop, chapter or monastery.'[115] Later arms control efforts sought to focus on particular geographic regions, not so much in order to stabilise relations between states, but in order to avoid national competition in the region. One such example was the Clayton–Bulwer Treaty of 1850 regarding the Panama Canal, by which both Great Britain and the United States agreed 'that neither the one nor the other will ever obtain or maintain for itself any exclusive control over the ship-canal; agreeing that neither will ever erect or maintain any fortifications commanding the same.'[116] In 1881, Argentina and Chile agreed under the Straits of Magellan Treaty to the neutralisation of the region to allow free navigation.[117] A final example would be the Antarctic Treaty of 1959 which declared, under Article I, that:

> Antarctica shall be used for peaceful purposes only. There shall be prohibited, *inter alia*, any measures of a military nature, such as the establishment of military bases and fortifications, the carrying out of military manoeuvres, as well as the testing of any type of weapons.[118]

Attempts to create or develop norms affecting the use of arms may therefore be divided into those efforts to contain the destructive effect of warfare by prohibiting the use of certain weapons, the attempts to create rules on the identification and treatment of non-combatants, and the agreements that have sought to identify geographical areas in which conflict is deemed to be illegitimate. These activities have been a part of the history of war and peace for at least a thousand years, certainly in Europe. The next area of arms control, the management of the proliferation of arms, has been a much less significant issue until more recent times.

Managing the proliferation of weapons

Political leaders have always been concerned with the proliferation of weapons into the hands of their potential enemies, and have sought agreements to contain such threats. However, in the twentieth century, there have also been agreements designed to control proliferation not simply because there may be a direct threat to a participating state, but rather because weapons in general, or particular forms of weapons specifically, have been seen to be generally destabilising in international relations either to a region or country, or to the world as a whole. Thus three types of proliferation control may be identified: first, defensive, such as the agreement between Great Britain and Spain in 1814 to limit the arms trade in Spain's American colonies; second, arms control designed to control proliferation in order to try to enhance global stability, with the Non-Proliferation Treaty of 1968 being a good example; and third, arms control to try to limit violence and the danger of war and escalation in a particular country or region, such as the 1950 Tripartite Arms Declaration to limit instability in the Near East. Each of these different forms of proliferation control will be examined in turn.

In terms of defensive management of proliferation, many of the examples pre-date the twentieth century. As already seen, both the Third Lateran Council of 1179 and the Fourth Lateran Council of 1215 sought to prevent military supplies, and especially naval materials and skills, from being sold to the Saracens. During the Middle Ages, it was fairly common practice to insert clauses into commercial treaties which would limit the arms trade to the enemies of the governments of the signatories. For example, the *Confirmatio Tractatus Flandriae* of 1370 between the English King, Edward III, and the Count of Flanders included the stipulation that:

> it is agreed that none of the subjects of the Count of Flanders will bring, or will have brought, by sea, any arms, artillery or supplies for the aid and comfort of the enemies of the King of England. Excepted from this are the arms, artillery and suppliers necessary for the guard and defence of their own bodies of masters, merchants, sailors and shipboard servants on board the boats and vessels of the Count.[119]

In the 1814 agreement between Great Britain and Spain, in the context of the rebellion of the colonies in the Americas against Spanish rule:

> His Britannic Majesty being anxious that the troubles and disturbances which unfortunately prevail in the Dominions of His Catholic Majesty in America should entirely cease, and the Subjects of those Provinces should return to their obedience to their lawful Sovereign, engages to take the most effectual measures for preventing his Subjects from furnishing Arms, Ammunition, or any other warlike article to the revolted in America.[120]

A third example may be drawn from the Convention as to the Pacific Ocean and Northwest Coast of America in 1824, in which the Russians and Americans agreed to occupy part of the northwestern coast of the North American continent, and sought to ensure that they would be relatively safe from destructive attack by the indigenous peoples. Article V set limits upon the type of trade that the Americans and Russians could engage in with the indigenous peoples, and stipulated that:

> fire-arms, other arms, powder, and munitions of war of every kind, are always

to be excepted from this same commerce permitted; the two powers engage, reciprocally, neither to sell, nor suffer them to be sold, to the natives by their respective citizens and subjects, nor by any person who may be under their authority.[121]

A final example of efforts to limit the area in which certain weapons could be used would be the Brussels Convention of 1890, which stated that:

> The experience of all nations that have intercourse with Africa having shown the pernicious and preponderating part played by fire-arms in operations connected with the slave-trade as well as internal wars between the native tribes ... the powers decide, so far as the present state of their frontiers permits, that the importation of fire-arms, and especially of rifles and improved weapons, as well as of powder, ball and cartridges, is ... prohibited in the territories comprised between the 20th parallel of North latitude and the 22nd parallel of South latitude, and extending westward to the Atlantic Ocean and eastward to the Indian Ocean.[122]

Such measures were designed to assist in the management of colonial Africa by further controlling the slave trade.

Thus, the control of the proliferation of weapons prior to the twentieth century focused on the defence of the particular state against rebels, indigenous peoples and other actual or potential enemies. The contribution of the inter-war period, however, was to see the introduction of the idea into arms control that the regulation of weapons in general might lead to global peace. Although many of the roots of this argument lay in the interpretations of the causes of the First World War, others pre-dated 1914. An example of the official thinking behind the arms control and peace efforts of the pre-1914 period can be seen in the letter issued by the Russian Foreign Minister on behalf of the Tsar inviting participants to attend what became the First Hague Conference. The Tsar called for a meeting to agree:

> the most effective means of assuring to all peoples the blessings of real and lasting peace, and above all of limiting the progressive development of existing armaments ... the accumulation of war material renders the armed peace of today a crushing burden more and more difficult for the nations to bear. It consequently seems evident that if this situation be prolonged, it will inevitably lead to that very disaster which it is desired to avoid, and the horrors of which make every humane mind shudder by anticipation.[123]

In the immediate aftermath of the First World War, the Tsar's overt agenda was taken up with renewed enthusiasm. In 1919 the Convention for the Control of the Trade in Arms and Ammunition was signed, stating that 'the long war now ended, in which most nations have successively become involved, has led to the accumulation in various parts of the world of considerable quantities of arms and munitions of war, the dispersal of which would constitute a danger to peace and public order'.[124] Yet this enthusiasm quickly waned. In 1925, a follow-up Convention for the Supervision of the International Trade in Arms and Ammunition and in Implements of War was signed; however, it was never ratified. Further illustrating the decline of the globalist vision, the Convention with Regard to the Supervision of the Private Manufacture and Publicity of the Manufacture of Arms and Ammunition and of Implements of War drawn up in 1929 was submitted to the League of Nations' World Disarmament Conference of 1932, but was not even signed.

If the globalist approach declined markedly in the late 1920s, it was to re-emerge strongly in the cold war period in the context of the control of nuclear weapons. During the 1950s, the context for arms control was set by the public pronouncements of the need to obtain general and complete disarmament; of course it was the reaction to this that led to the development of arms control theory in the late 1950s and early 1960s. But those theories relegated the subject of proliferation control to secondary importance. The practice of globalist proliferation control, however, was moving ahead. The Statute of the International Atomic Energy Authority of 1956 was the first such measure. Article II defined the objectives of the IAEA as follows:

> The Agency shall seek to accelerate and enlarge the contribution of atomic energy to peace, health and prosperity throughout the world. It shall ensure, so far as it is able, that assistance provided by it or at its request or under its supervision or control is not used in such a way as to further any military purpose.[125]

This globalist drive for nuclear non-proliferation reached its height, of course, with the signing of the Treaty on the Non-Proliferation of Nuclear Weapons in 1968. In the preamble, the globalist intentions were made clear: the Treaty was important given

> the devastation that would be visited upon all mankind by a nuclear war and the consequent need to make every effort to avert the danger of such a war and to take measures to safeguard the security of peoples,
> ... the proliferation of nuclear weapons would seriously enhance the danger of nuclear war.[126]

Globalism in the 1980s was extended even further with the agreement on the Guidelines for Sensitive Missile-Relevant Transfer, the Missile Technology Control Regime. As stipulated in the first line of the agreement, 'The purpose of these Guidelines is to limit the risks of nuclear proliferation by controlling transfers that could make a contribution to nuclear weapons delivery systems other than manned aircraft.'[127]

Globalist arms control in the cold war era was thus more successful than globalism in the inter-war period. The failure of inter-war endeavours, along with the disillusion over the rhetoric of general and complete disarmament in the 1950s, may in part explain why many efforts were made to create partial agreements in the cold war period, attempts to limit the proliferation of weapons to third countries or regions that might lead to a lessening of violence in that area, or might limit the likelihood of war breaking out. Only one significant partial proliferation control agreement was reached in the inter-war period, the Restraining Sales of Armaments in China agreement of 1919. In the cold war period, several such agreements were reached. One of the earliest was the very limited Tripartite Arms Declaration of 1950. This Declaration built upon United States' and United Nations' arms embargoes on the combatants in the Arab–Israeli war of 1948. In the Tripartite Arms Declaration of 1950, Great Britain, the United States and France recognised:

> that the Arab states and Israel all need to maintain a certain level of armed forces for the purposes of assuring their internal security and their legitimate self defence and to permit them to play their part in the defence of the area as a whole. All applications for arms or war material for these countries will be considered in the light of these principles ... The three Governments take this opportunity of declaring their deep interest in and their desire to promote the establishment and maintenance of peace and stability in the area.[128]

More substantial than this were the two nuclear weapons free zones treaties. Under the Treaty of Tlatelolco of 1967:

> The Contracting Parties hereby undertake to use exclusively for peaceful purposes the nuclear material and facilities which are under their jurisdiction, and to prohibit and prevent in their respective territories:
>
> (a) The testing, use, manufacture, production or acquisition ... of any nuclear weapons ...
> (b) The receipt, storage, installation, deployment and any form of possession of any nuclear weapons.[129]

Also, the South Pacific Nuclear-Free-Zone Treaty under which each Party undertook 'not to manufacture or otherwise acquire, posses or have control over any nuclear device'.[130]

Thus there was a major difference in the forms of proliferation control in the twentieth century in comparison to those which had gone before. Strictly defensive limitations were much less in evidence, and efforts to create partial and global proliferation controls developed and grew. Partly the globalist efforts were connected to one of the most significant developments of the twentieth century: the rise of the international organisation. The final form of arms control to be examined is that directly related to control by international organisation.

Arms control by international organisation

The history of arms control by international organisation is, of course, completely dominated by the activities of the League of Nations and the United Nations. Both organisations sought a role in arms control and disarmament.[131] The League, under Article 8 of the Covenant, gave the Council a role in setting the level of armaments with individual states, and after agreement had been reached those limits could 'not be exceeded without the concurrence of the Council'.[132] In contrast, very little was mentioned in the Charter of the United Nations with regard to arms control; it certainly was not given the prominence as an issue that it had received in the League's Covenant. The major reference in the Charter was in Article 26, which stated:

> In order to promote the establishment and maintenance of international peace and security with the least diversion for armaments of the world's human and economic resources, the Security Council shall be responsible for formulating, with the assistance of the Military Staff Committee referred to in Article 47, plans to be submitted to the Members of the United Nations for the establishment of a system for the regulation of armaments.[133]

The actual activities of arms control in both organisations were in essentially different areas. Under the League, most efforts concerned global controls. As Resolution XIV of the League of Nations General Assembly noted in 1922, 'No scheme for the reduction in armaments, within the meaning of Article 8 of the Covenant, can be fully successful unless it is general.'[134] Under the United Nations, although attempts to secure global controls have been an important part of its work, arms control efforts have widened into two other areas: there have been efforts to control individual countries; and security guarantees have also been given in order to elicit agreement on arms control. This section will examine all three of these activities of international organisations in relation to arms control.

In terms of global controls on weapons, it is clear that most of the work of the international organisations has taken the form of providing a forum for discussion rather than generating a great deal of activity. The League of Nations was the host for a large number of draft treaties and arms control proposals, particularly in the period of the General Disarmament Conference in the early 1930s. The Soviet Union made detailed proposals for general and complete disarmament in 1927 and 1928; the Preparatory Commission for the Conference made a further detailed draft in 1930; the United States made a series of proposals in 1932; the French also in 1932; the British in 1933; the United States again in 1933: this list is by no means exhaustive.[135] Similarly, the United Nations played host in the 1950s to a further series of proposals for global disarmament, examples of which included: the Soviet plan of 1952; the Western countries' proposals, 1952; the Soviet Union again in 1955; the United States in 1956; India, 1956; the Soviet Union and Western countries exchanged plans in 1957; and so forth – again the list is not exhaustive.[136] In all this diplomatic effort, only one clear (and very limited) achievement can be identified. In 1931 the Twelfth Assembly of the League of Nations adopted a One-Year Armament Truce, which was formally adopted by forty-five states. The truce declared that 'a renewal of the competition in armaments would necessarily lead to an international and social catastrophe;' and therefore:

> The Assembly,
> Requests the Governments invited to the Disarmament Conference to prepare for this event by means of an armaments truce, and, accordingly,
> Requests the Council to urge the Governments ... to refrain from any measure involving an increase in their armaments.[137]

Such modest achievements in the light of so much diplomatic effort certainly implied to the arms control theorists of the early 1960s that alternative routes to arms control needed to be devised.

However, it would be wrong to ignore other areas in which international organisations have been involved in arms control. The United Nations has on several occasions imposed arms restraints on an individual member, South Africa. In 1963, Security Resolution 181 initiated the United Nations involvement in imposing arms restraints upon South Africa:

> *Noting with concern* the recent arms build-up by the Government of South Africa, some of which arms are being used in furtherance of that Government's racial policies ...
> *Being convinced* that the situation in South Africa is seriously disturbing international peace and security ...
> *Solemnly calls upon all* States to cease forthwith the sale and shipment of arms, ammunition of all types and military vehicles to South Africa.[138]

Four months later, with the South African refusal to accept the above Resolution, the Security Council unanimously passed a Resolution appealing 'to all States to comply with the provisions of Security Council resolution 181 (1963) of 7 August 1963'.[139] However, it was not until after Resolution 392 (1976) condemning killings by the police and army in South Africa that the Security Council moved from voluntary to mandatory compliance. In Resolution 418 of November 1977, the Security Council declared the following:

> *Recognising* that the military build-up by South Africa and its persistent acts of aggression against the neighbouring States seriously disturb the security of those States;
> *Further recognising* that the existing arms embargo must be strengthened and universally applied, without any reservations or qualifications whatsoever, in order to prevent a further aggravation of the grave situation in South Africa ...
> *Decides* that all States shall cease forthwith any provision to South Africa of arms and related matériel of all types, including the sale or transfer of weapons and ammunition, military vehicles and equipment, paramilitary

police equipment; and spare parts for the aforementioned, and shall cease as well the provision of all types of equipment and supplies and grants of licensing arrangements for the manufacture and development of nuclear weapons.[140]

Finally, Resolution 558 of 1984 reaffirmed Resolution 418, and requested 'all States to refrain from importing arms, ammunition of all types and military vehicles produced in South Africa'.[141] Of course, Resolution 558 indicated that one of the effects of Resolution 418 had been to further increase the effectiveness of South Africa's own military industrial base; nevertheless, the United Nations had, through the force of international law, significantly isolated the military forces of South Africa, and thereby affected the structure of those forces.[142]

The third area, the giving of security guarantees to elicit arms control, has only occurred on one, very significant, occasion. In 1968, the Treaty on Nuclear Non-Proliferation was submitted to the General Assembly for consideration. Although there was general support, some nations were concerned at what they saw as a treaty that would impose nuclear disarmament on some, but not all states. In order to attempt to alleviate these concerns, and therefore to clear the way for the treaty to be as widely supported as possible, Security Council Resolution 225 was passed. It stated that:

> *Taking into consideration* the concern of certain of these States that, in conjunction with their adherence to the Treaty on the Non-Proliferation of Nuclear Weapons, appropriate measures be undertaken to safeguard their security ...
>
> 1. *Recognises* that aggression with nuclear weapons or the threat of such aggression against a non-nuclear-weapon State would create a situation in which the Security Council, and above all its nuclear-weapon States permanent members, would have to act immediately in accordance with their obligations under the United Nations Charter;
>
> 2. *Welcomes* the intention expressed by certain States that they will provide or support immediate assistance, in accordance with the Charter, to any non-nuclear-weapon State Party to the Treaty ... that is a victim of an act or an object of a threat of aggression in which nuclear weapons are used.

Such a guarantee by the nuclear haves of the security of the nuclear have-nots against threats or aggression by the possessors of nuclear weapons made a significant contribution to the wide – although by no means unanimous – acceptance of the Treaty. They were confirmed by unilateral statements by the Soviet Union, the United States and the United Kingdom in May and June 1978.[143]

Arms control through international organisation has thus been a mixed experience. The majority of the activity in this sphere has been in terms of discussion rather than agreement, and yet some limited and specific measures have been enacted. Although clearly the area in which the least arms control has been agreed, arms control by international organisation has nevertheless still had a role to play.

Conclusion

The main purpose of this chapter has been to examine the *widening* of arms control from its limited beginnings in the ancient world to its complex practice in the inter-war and cold war periods. This notion of widening will be applied in the rest of this book to the arms control agreements that have been reached in the post-cold war world in order to demonstrate the importance of the widening concept to the understanding of arms control. However, before beginning that investigation, there is an important second theme that has emerged in the course of this chapter that merits some further analysis, and that is the notion of *deepening*.

Deepening, it will be recalled, refers to three factors related to the nature of agreements reached: the increasing amount of detail placed in agreements; the growing stress on verification; and the evolution of regimes around arms control agreements. The development of each of these elements will be briefly noted in this section.

First, many arms control agreements in the twentieth century have been far more detailed than those which had been reached before. Partly this was due to experience and increasing diplomatic sophistication. If an agreement is not carefully drawn up, it may be broken in spirit if not in letter. After the Franco-Prussian Treaty of 1808 in which the Prussian army was limited to 42,000 troops, Scharnhorst began a strategy by which recruits were given intensive training, and then sent on extended leave, during which time they received extra tuition in their towns and villages. In this way, the Prussian army never formally exceeded the limit of 42,000, yet was also developed into the army of Blücher that was so effective at Waterloo. In the period before the nuclear age one of the clearest examples of deepening in terms of greater precision was the Washington Naval Treaty of 1922. Running to twenty-three articles, the treaty was one of the first to set out technical details regarding limitations. Signed by Great Britain, the United States, France, Italy and Japan, the treaty set out acceptable sizes for ships and their weapons, and also a ratio for the total size of the relative navies in which the United States and the British Empire were to be allowed the largest navies with a maximum tonnage of 525,000, Japan 315,000 tons and both France and Italy 175,000 tons.[144] This detailed treaty set out which ships the High Contracting Parties were able to retain, and a schedule for the laying down of new ships and their completion against the scrapping of old ships. In Chapter 2, the treaty set out definitions, rules on which ships each state could retain, and also rules for the destruction of excess ships, along with a schedule for the replacement of ships, thus setting out a clear plan for the transformation of the navies of all five parties to a situation in which by 1942 all capital ships of the parties would have been built post-Jutland.[145] In the cold war period, the SALT I and SALT II treaties took this process further through issuing common understandings and agreed statements with the treaty in order to clarify the nature of the process.

Second, the growing importance of verification has also been a feature of the arms control of the twentieth century, and in particular an attribute of the cold war period for both technical and ideological reasons. During the cold war period the development of satellite imaging has provided for a level of information that was previously inconceivable, while the nature of the East–West political rivalry was such that, with very little trust on either side, national or independent information with regard to compliance was naturally deemed to be of great importance. Five forms of verification can be identified in arms control agreements. First, the implicit understanding that information will be gathered by national technical means. Neither the Partial Test Ban Treaty nor the Biological Weapons Convention mention any verification procedures, and thereby rely not only on national restraint, but also on national intelligence gathering facilities. Second, national technical means may be explicitly mentioned in the terms of the agreement. This is the case with the Interim Agreement on Limitation of Strategic Offensive Arms, the ABM Treaty and SALT II, and in each treaty there is a prohibition on interference with such means (Article V, XII and XV respectively) which states that 'Each party undertakes not to interfere with the national technical means of verification of the other Party.'[146] Third, states may be explicitly required to provide information under the terms of the treaty. Under both the Antarctic Treaty and the Outer Space Treaty (Articles III and XI respectively) parties were committed to informing others of their activities in the regions concerned. Fourthly, measures of on-site inspection may be allowed by the signatories. An example of such provision is included in the Peaceful Nuclear Explosions Treaty of 1976.[147] Finally, states may be required to allow international bodies to inspect national facilities and activities in order to obtain information. This is most clearly the case with the Treaty on the Non-Proliferation of Nuclear Weapons, where states must accept International Atomic Energy Agency safeguards under Article III.

Third, the process by which arms control agreements tended to be seen as part of a regime to be protected and developed as a cornerstone of a political relationship pre-dated the twentieth century. Early examples include the Rush–Bagot Agreement, and also to a certain extent the Treaty of Utrecht. In the twentieth century, however, these efforts developed further. In the inter-war period, the naval arms control agreements of the five major naval states were seen, until the late 1930s, to form an arms control regime around which policy could be built between the powers, and into which other naval states – such as Germany and the Soviet Union – could be incorporated. Further, the post-First World War peace treaties and arms limitations were also seen to be part of a regime that would allow a general disarming of states under the League of Nations. In the cold war period, one of the purposes of the arms control theory of the early 1960s was to advocate the development of a regime for the strengthening of strategic stability through a series of arms control agreements, which in practice began with the 1972 SALT I agreements. Finally, the Non-Proliferation Treaty of 1968 was seen as only one element in a non-proliferation of nuclear weapons regime which includes the Partial Test Ban Treaty and the IAEA (International Atomic Energy Agency), amongst other elements.

This chapter has argued that an analysis of the history of arms control demonstrates that there are five areas in which arms control has been practised as arms control procedures have widened. This typology will now be applied to those agreements that have been reached in the post-cold war world in order to demonstrate the validity and significance of the widening concept. Chapter 2 will examine those agreements that have been reached in order to end the cold war conflict; Chapter 3 will analyse the agreements that have been reached in order to strengthen strategic stability; Chapter 4 assesses agreements designed to strengthen norms of behaviour in relation to weapons and the use of arms; Chapter 5 examines proliferation concerns; and Chapter 6 analyses the role of the United Nations in the international control of weapons.

Notes

1 Trevor Dupuy and Gay Hammerman in *A Documentary History of Arms Control and Disarmament* New York and London: R. R. Bowker and Co., 1973, quote Edward Parker's account (*Ancient China Simplified* London: Chapman and Hall, 1908) of a peace conference held in 546 BC attempting to end seventy-two years of war (pp. 2–4). The Peloponnesian wars lasted for some thirty-nine years. Thus not only were wars frequent, but they sometimes lasted for generations.

2 See Neta C. Crawford 'Cooperation Among Iroquois Nations' *International Organization* Vol. 48, No. 3, 1994, pp. 345–85.

3 Evidence for this may be found in the Bible: I Samuel 13: 19–22, reproduced Richard D. Burns (editor) *Encyclopedia of Arms Control and Disarmament* New York: Charles Scribner, 1992, p. 1409.

4 The Egyptian–Hittite Agreement was poorly drawn up in that the area of the buffer region was not adequately defined. See Stanley M. Burstein 'Arms Control in Antiquity' in Richard D. Burns (editor) *Encyclopedia*, p. 552.

5 *Ibid.*, p. 559.

6 *Ibid.*, p. 556.

7 Michael Howard *War in European History* Oxford: Oxford University Press, 1976, p. 1. Also see R. A. Preston, S. F. Wise and H. O. Werner *Men in Arms: A History of Warfare and its Interrelationship with Western Society* New

York/London: Holt, Rinehart & Winston.

8   See Udo Heyn 'Medieval Arms Control Movements and the Western Quest for Peace' in Richard D. Burns (editor) *Encyclopedia*, pp. 563–79.

9   Excerpts from these proclamations can be found in Richard D. Burns *Encyclopedia*, pp. 1489–96.

10   Reproduced in *ibid.*, p. 1489.

11   Reproduced in *ibid.*, p. 1491.

12   *Ibid.*, p. 1495.

13   Michael Howard *War*, p. 5.

14   Canon 29 of the Second Lateran Council of 1139, reproduced in Richard D. Burns *Encyclopedia*, p. 1367.

15   There is some debate on the nature of the interpretation of Canon 29. Dupuy and Hammerman, for example, suggest the possibility that the Latin *ballistrariorum* and the English 'slingers' referred to in Canon 29 should be interpreted in that the 'prohibition against the crossbow also applies to other bow-and-arrow weapons' (p.11). Indeed, a reliable source for the widely held assumption that *ballistrariorum* means crossbow alone is very illusive. However, this study has interpreted *ballistrariorum*, in accordance with the common usage, to mean crossbow.

16   However, secular leaders were often associated with the Peace and Truce of God, and spiritual leaders with the Peace of the Land and the Peace of the Prince, so the distinction should not be overly emphasised.

17   The sense in which this was a symbolic beginning of the state system is made clear in David Armstrong *Revolution and World Order* Oxford: Clarendon, 1993, pp. 32–4.

18   Reproduced in Leon Friedman (editor) *The Law of War: A Documentary History* New York: Random House, 1972, p. 150.

19   Cited in *ibid.*, p. 149.

20   See *ibid.*, pp. 204–50 for details of the 1899 Conference, and pp. 270–394 for the 1907 Conference.

21   Reproduced in Richard D. Burns (editor) *Encyclopedia*, p. 1500.

22   *Ibid.*, p. 1501.

23   Reproduced in *ibid.*, p. 1500.

24   Excerpted in *ibid.*, p. 1322.

25   Reproduced in *ibid.*, p. 1323.

26   The Neutralisation of Belgium, the Neutralisation of Luxembourg and the Black Sea Convention are excerpted in *ibid.*, pp. 1326–9.

27   The exchange of letters is reproduced in *ibid.*, pp. 1325–6.

28   On the Rush–Bagot Agreement see Ron Purver 'The Rush–Bagot Agreement: Demilitarising the Great Lakes, 1817 to the Present' in Richard D. Burns (editor) *Encyclopedia*, p. 592.

29   Reproduced in Trevor Dupuy and Gay Hammerman *A Documentary History*, pp. 36–7.

30   Due to the scale of Prussia's defeat, and the reorganisation of the country after the loss of much territory, this figure was reduced to 12,000 for the year 1809 only. *Ibid.*

31   Reproduced in Richard D. Burns *Encyclopedia*, pp. 1141–2.

32 See Trevor Dupuy and Gay Hammerman *A Documentary History*, p. 86.
33 See Richard D. Burns, *Encyclopedia*, p. 1193.
34 Cited in *ibid.*, pp. 1193–4.
35 The treaty is reproduced in *ibid.*, pp. 1166–75.
36 *Ibid.*, p. 1176; the whole treaty is reproduced on pp. 1176–83.
37 See *ibid.*, pp. 1183–4.
38 Excerpted in *ibid.*, pp. 1185–91.
39 See Trevor Dupuy and Gay Hammerman *A Documentary History*, pp. 273–82.
40 See Leon Friedman *The Law of War*, p. 454.
41 Reproduced in *ibid.*, pp. 476 and 493.
42 See Richard D. Burns *Encyclopedia*, pp. 1531–4.
43 Excerpted in *ibid.*, p. 1508.
44 Cited in *ibid.*, p. 1410.
45 Reproduced in *ibid.*, p. 1413.
46 Reproduced in Trevor Dupuy and Gay Hammerman *A Documentary History*, pp. 96–7.
47 Excerpted in *ibid.*, p. 98.
48 Richard D. Burns *Encyclopedia*, pp. 1419–28.
49 The text can be found in *ibid.*, pp. 1428–32.
50 Reproduced in *ibid.*, p. 1154.
51 Italics added. For the whole treaty, see *ibid.*, pp. 1155–62.
52 Trevor Dupuy and Gay Hammerman *A Documentary History*, p. 95.
53 Much of nuclear deterrence thinking is dated back to the publication of Bernard Brodie's *The Absolute Weapon: Atomic Power and World Order* New York, Harcourt Brace, 1946.
54 For examples of the 'Golden Age' thinking see Thomas Schelling *Arms and Influence* New Haven: Yale University Press, 1966; Thomas Schelling and Morton Halperin *Strategy and Arms Control* New York: Twentieth Century Fund, 1961; Hedley Bull *The Control of the Arms Race* London: Weidenfeld and Nicolson for the Institute for Strategic Studies, 1961; Albert Wohlstetter 'The Delicate Balance of Terror' *Foreign Affairs* Vol. 37, 1959; Morton Halperin *Limited War in the Nuclear Age* New York: John Wiley, 1963; John Herz *International Politics in the Nuclear Age* New York: Columbia University Press, 1959; Robert Osgood *Limited War: The Challenge to American Strategy* Chicago: University of Chicago Press, 1957.
55 James E. King 'Arms Control and United States Security' in Louis Henkin *Arms Control* New York: Ballantine Books, 1961, p. 126. This is one of the best early chapters on arms control approaches in the 'Golden Age'.
56 Barry Buzan *An Introduction to Strategic Studies* London: Macmillan for the International Institute for Strategic Studies, 1987, p. 253.
57 See Hedley Bull *The Control of the Arms Race*; and Donald G. Brennan (editor) 'Arms Control, Disarmament and National Security' *Daedalus* Vol. 89, No. 4, 1960.
58 Herman Kahn *On Escalation: Metaphors and Scenarios* London: Pall Mall Press 1965, p. 192.
59 Thomas Schelling and Morton Halperin *Strategy and Arms Control*, p. 1.
60 'The Baruch Plan: Statement by United States Representative to the United

Nations Atomic Energy Commission, 14 June 1946', reprinted in Trevor Dupuy and Gay Hammerman *A Documentary History*, p. 304.

61   'Address by Soviet Premier Khrushchev to the General Assembly, 18 September 1959', extracted in *ibid.*, p. 447.

62   James E. King 'Arms Control and United States Security' in Louis Henkin *Arms Control*, p. 140.

63   Robert R. Bowie 'Arms Control and United States Foreign Policy' in *ibid.*, p. 93.

64   Thomas Schelling and Morton Halperin *Strategy and Arms Control*, p. 57 (italics in the original).

65   See Hedley Bull *The Control of the Arms Race*, Chapter 3.

66   Excerpted in Trevor Dupuy and Gay Hammerman *A Documentary History*, p. 604.

67   Cited in *ibid.*, p. 608.

68   *Ibid.* An attached Protocol set out the agreed numerical levels.

69   For more on this, see note 32 in the Introduction.

70   Hedley Bull *The Control of the Arms Race*, p. 61.

71   See C. Tyroler II (editor) *Alerting America: The Papers of the Committee on the Present Danger* Washington DC: Pergamon-Brassey's, 1984. For more on this, see note 37 in the Introduction.

72   See, for example, Marek Thee 'Arms Control: The Retreat from Disarmament, the Record to Date and the Search for Alternatives' *Journal of Peace Research* Vol. 14, No. 2, 1977, and note 4 in the Introduction.

73   Of course, those on the right would not have agreed with this, suggesting instead that the product of SALT was to increase the threat to the United States' second strike force due to the power of the Soviet's heavy missile force.

74   Phil Williams 'Thomas Schelling' in John Baylis and John Garnett (editors) *Makers of Nuclear Strategy* London: Pinter Publishers, 1991, p. 130.

75   Thomas Schelling and Morton Halperin *Strategy and Arms Control*, p. 133.

76   See, for example, Thomas Schelling 'What Went Wrong with Arms Control?' *Foreign Affairs* Vol. 64, No. 2, 1985–6; and Barry Blechman 'Do Negotiated Arms Limitations Have a Future?' *Foreign Affairs* Vol. 59, No. 1, 1980.

77   There were some important exceptions, such as the Austrian State Treaty which neutralised Austria, and the creation of a demilitarised zone between the Koreas after the Korean War. There were also limits set on Japan and Germany at the end of the Second World War, which will be examined later.

78   Under Article I, 'Each State Party to this Convention undertakes not to engage in military or any other hostile use of environmental modification techniques having widespread, long lasting or severe effects as the means of destruction, damage or injury to any other State Party.' Richard D. Burns *Encyclopedia*, p. 1585.

79   In a real sense this represented disagreement, for real agreement would have led to the introduction of this material into the treaty itself. Were it in the treaty, it would be legally binding; outside, it was not. However, it was important in that this was a significant means of dealing with the problem of disagreement by attaching understandings to the agreement itself.

80   See note 38 in the Introduction.

81   Thomas Schelling and Morton Halperin, *Strategy and Arms Control*, pp. 100–1.

82   Fred C. Iklè 'After Detection – What?' *Foreign Affairs* Vol. 39, January 1961.

83   Ivo H. Daalder 'The Role of Arms Control in the New Europe' *Arms Control* Vol. 12, No. 1, 1991, p. 24.
84   Cited in Richard D. Burns *Encyclopedia*, p. 1195.
85   Reproduced in Trevor Dupuy and Gay Hammerman *A Documentary History*, 'The Constitution of Japan, November 3, 1946', pp. 312–13.
86   Excerpted in Richard D. Burns *Encyclopedia*, p. 1137.
87   Part V of the Treaty 'Military, Naval and Air Clauses' in Trevor Dupuy and Gay Hammerman *A Documentary History*, p. 82.
88   Cited in Geoffrey Symcox *War, Diplomacy, and Imperialism, 1618–1763: Selected Documents* London: Macmillan, 1974, p. 59.
89   Reproduced in *ibid.*, p. 42.
90   *Ibid.*
91   Article LXXVIII, *ibid.*, p. 52.
92   Article LXXIX, *ibid.*
93   Reproduced in Richard D. Burns *Encyclopedia*, p. 1139.
94   Cited in *ibid.*, p. 1140.
95   See Andrew D. Farrand 'Chile and Argentina: Entente and Naval Limitation, 1902' in Richard D. Burns *Encyclopedia*, pp. 595–603.
96   The text is reproduced in *ibid.*, p. 1142.
97   *Ibid.*
98   Cited in *ibid.*, p. 1336.
99   *Ibid.*, p. 1192.
100   Cited in Leon Friedman *The Law of War*, p. 3.
101   Excerpted in Richard D. Burns *Encyclopedia*, p. 1368.
102   For the text of the agreements, see: Leon Friedman *The Law of War*, on the Declaration of Brussels, p. 196; and Richard D. Burns *Encyclopedia*, on the Washington Treaty, p. 1369.
103   Cited in Richard D. Burns *Encyclopedia*, pp. 1390–1.
104   Reproduced in Leon Friedman *The Law of War*, p. 193.
105   However, this effort was largely designed in order to focus energies on the Fifth Crusade. See *ibid.*, p. 9.
106   'Kellogg–Briand Pact for the Renunciation of War, August 27, 1928' reproduced in Trevor Dupuy and Gay Hammerman *A Documentary History*, p. 156.
107   The treaty was drawn up by Argentina, and entered into force in 1935. The text is reproduced in Richard D. Burns *Encyclopedia*, pp. 1399–1401.
108   United Nations General Assembly Resolution 1653, 24 November 1961. Leon Friedman *The Law of War*, pp. 697–8.
109   Although 'the bishops or the archdeacon may use such means as are necessary to compel them [monks and those who accompanied them] to pay the taxes which they owe them'. See Richard D. Burns *Encyclopedia*, pp. 1489–90.
110   Cited in *ibid.*, p. 1495.
111   'Cartel for the Exchange of Prisoners Made by the Duke of Luxembourg Acting on Behalf of Louis XIV, and Count Horn Acting for the States General of the United Provinces, 26 May 1673' reproduced in Geoffrey Symcox *War, Diplomacy*, pp. 51–6.
112   The text of both Conventions are published in Leon Friedman *The Law of War*, 'Laws and Customs of War on Land (Hague II) July 29, 1899, pp. 221–35;

and 'Laws and Customs of War on Land (Hague IV) October 8, 1907', pp. 308–23.

113   See the texts reproduced in Richard D. Burns *Encyclopedia*, pp. 1505 and 1506.
114   See Leon Friedman *The Law of War*, pp. 437–49.
115   Quoted in Richard D. Burns *Encyclopedia*, p. 1490.
116   Article I, excerpted in Richard D. Burns *Encyclopedia*, p. 1331.
117   Under Article V. See *ibid.*, p. 1332.
118   United States Arms Control and Disarmament Agency *Arms Control and Disarmament Agreements* London: Transaction Books, 1984, p. 22.
119   The text is reproduced in Richard D. Burns *Encyclopedia*, p. 1311.
120   *Ibid.*
121   Cited in *ibid.*, p. 1412.
122   This is drawn from Article VIII: see *ibid.*, p. 1329.
123   The letter was dated 24 August 1898 (12 August in the Julian calendar then in use in Russia) and is reproduced in Trevor Dupuy and Gay Hammerman *A Documentary History*, pp. 48–50.
124   See the text in Richard D. Burns *Encyclopedia*, p. 1414.
125   *Ibid.*, pp. 1445–54.
126   Reproduced in *ibid.*, pp. 1437–40.
127   Cited in *ibid.*, pp. 1474–80.
128   *Ibid.*, p. 1432.
129   Reproduced in *ibid.*, p. 1348. The treaty covered the whole of Latin America, but did not come fully into effect for several decades.
130   The treaty was signed in 1985; this quote is from Article 3. See *ibid.*, pp. 1359–64.
131   For a contemporary account of the League's work, see Salvador de Madariaga *Disarmament* New York: Coward-McCann, 1929. De Madariaga was Chief of the League's Disarmament Section for five years in the 1920s.
132   Cited in Richard D. Burns *Encyclopedia*, p. 1154.
133   Reproduced in Trevor Dupuy and Gay Hammerman *A Documentary History*, pp. 288–90.
134   Excerpted in *ibid.*, p. 122.
135   These documents are reproduced in *ibid.*, pp. 138–259.
136   Extracts of these proposals are reproduced in *ibid.*, pp. 353–426.
137   See *ibid.*, pp. 187–8.
138   Adopted by 9 votes to 0, Britain and France abstaining, 7 August 1963. This resolution implied voluntary compliance. Reproduced in Richard D. Burns *Encyclopedia*, p. 1433.
139   Adopted 4 December 1963, Resolution 182: *ibid.*, p. 1434.
140   *Ibid.*, p. 1135.
141   Excerpted in *ibid.*, p. 1436.
142   For more information, see *The United Nations and Apartheid, 1948–1994* New York: UN Department of Public Information, 1995.
143   Each state renounced the use of nuclear weapons against non–nuclear states: for the texts of the statements, see Jozef Goldblat *Agreements for Arms Control* London: Taylor and Francis for SIPRI, 1982, pp. 252–3. China and France were not members of the Nuclear Non–Proliferation regime at this time.

144   On this, see for example Emily O.Goldman *Sunken Treaties* Pennsylvania: Penn State Press, 1994.

145   For the text, see Richard D. Burns *Encyclopedia*, pp. 1166–75.

146   This is the same phrase used in all three Treaties.

147   See SIPRI *Arms Control: A Survey and Appraisal of Multilateral Agreements* London: Taylor and Francis, 1978, p. 29.

2

Arms control at the conclusion of major conflicts

Introduction

In the course of the first chapter it was argued that arms control at the end of conflicts takes one of four forms. First, it was suggested that where one state was overwhelmingly defeated, an initial response may be to totally disarm that state. A second possibility was that where a participant may be defeated heavily, although not completely over-run, arms control might take very unequal forms. This was the *foedus inaequuum*, designed to create strategic and political inferiority. Third, where there has been a clear military success, the victors may wish to dictate terms that would create a semi-permanent strategic stability through the superiority of the forces of the victors. The purpose here was to create the conditions for peace. The fourth and final possibility was that where one group of forces is merely in the ascendancy, but has not achieved an overwhelming victory, the terms of the treaty have been rather more balanced, although still in favour of the dominant parties. The purpose of this chapter is to examine these concepts in relation to the arms control agreements reached at the end of the cold war. In addition, it will seek to examine the degree of deepening in those arms control agreements.

However, before initiating such a discussion, one significant issue needs to be addressed. In considering this concept in historical terms, it was related to those arms control issues and agreements reached at the end of major *wars*. There was discussion of the Treaty of Zama at the conclusion of the Second Punic War; the Peace of Westphalia at the end of the Thirty Years War; the Treaty of Versailles and the other post-First World War agreements; and the post-Second World War arrangements over Germany, Japan, Italy and other defeated states. This section seeks to consider the end of the cold war in a similar light, even though the ending of the cold war did not bring about a conclusion to an outright military conflict. Such a perspective may be justified if one considers the two central features of international relations at the conclusion of major conflicts, such as those just outlined. On each occasion, an existing pattern of international relations was overthrown. And on each occasion, attempts were made by states – using arms control amongst other instruments – to create a new series of relationships. Both points will be briefly considered.

First, the end of the cold war was similar to the peace arrangements outlined above in that it witnessed the overthrow of an existing pattern of relations between the major powers. As the end of the Second Punic War brought about the collapse of bipolarity in favour of unipolarity in the Mediterranean, so one might argue that the end of the cold war brought about the collapse of global bipolarity and the emergence of the United States as the 'unipolar' power.[1] As the Peace of Westphalia witnessed the end of the dominance of the Holy Roman Empire and the confirmation of the emergence of the state system, so the end of the cold war has brought about the end of communism as a global force and the re-emergence of a more complicated state system. As both the post-First and post-Second World War settlements sought to lower the significance of the arms race in international relations, with a reduced dependence on great power politics and a greater reliance on international norms and authority, so the post-cold war settlement initially brought about a large degree of disarmament in both conventional and nuclear weapons and a growth in recourse to and reliance on the United Nations.

Second, as at the end of the conflicts mentioned above, the end of the cold war has been a time in which states have sought to create a new framework for relations between themselves. Whereas the CSCE Paris summit of November 1990 cannot be compared with the negotiations and agreements reached in Münster and Osnabrück in the middle of the seventeenth century, nor those in Vienna in 1814-15, nor indeed those in Paris and elsewhere in 1918-20, the series of meetings between states and the growth of new norms and understandings in the late 1980s and early 1990s was as significant in creating a new pattern of international relations as the series of meetings between states and the growth of new norms and understandings was in earlier periods.

Some may wish to argue that the qualitative difference in the nature of the cold war and its aftermath compared to previous conflicts and their conclusions may be explained largely, if not entirely, by the existence of nuclear weapons and nuclear deterrence. This was a conception born in the first months of the nuclear age, when Bernard Brodie wrote 'Thus far the chief purpose of our military establishment has been to win wars. From now on its chief purpose must be to avert them. It can have almost no other useful purpose.'[2] Indeed, it was the purpose not only of deterrence theorists but also of deterrence practitioners to ensure that nuclear weapons did provide a qualitative difference to previous ages. As a British government *Statement on the Defence Estimates* argued:

it is easy to forget that in the first half of this century the world was twice plunged into immensely destructive global conventional war, precipitated on both occasions by a state numerically weaker than the combination of states that faced it. In the last century Europe was torn asunder by several major wars. By contrast, in the 40 years since the end of the Second World War – 40 years of nuclear deterrence – there has been no war in Western Europe, either conventional or nuclear, in spite of deep ideological hostility between East and West. This is a striking achievement.[3]

The purpose of nuclear deterrence was thus to eliminate the probability of any form of warfare breaking out between the major powers. However, this has been by no means a universally shared perspective, with many criticising the power of deterrence as an explanation for a lack of major conflict between the predominant powers during the cold war.[4] Nevertheless, there is a consensus that at the very least thinking about nuclear deterrence created a climate in which international relations appeared to be qualitatively different in the cold war period compared to earlier times. Given the powerful influence of nuclear weapons on the cold war conflict, therefore, it perhaps is not surprising that the cold war ended in a less violent way than earlier conflicts examined in this book.

If it is legitimate to consider the end of the cold war to be comparable to the periods at the conclusion of conflicts such as those in early part of the second century BC, the middle of the seventeenth century, and in the early and middle parts of the twentieth century, which of the four forms of arms control possibilities – total disarmament, the *foedus inaequum*, the creation of a semi-permanent peace through mandated strategic superiority, and the more balanced agreement (which is still in favour of the dominant parties) – is the most appropriate fit? It will be argued throughout this chapter that the fourth of these categories is the most appropriate classification for the arms control agreements that have drawn the cold war period to an end. None of the arms control activity at the end of the cold war was designed to totally disarm the former communist bloc, nor to impose a *foedus inaequum*, nor indeed create a position of strategic and political superiority for the United States and the Western countries. Arms control activity has been shaped by the ascendancy, although not overwhelming victory, of the United States and the Western powers as communism collapsed in Eastern Europe, and then the Soviet Union itself disintegrated. Consequently, the terms of arms control have been balanced, although still in favour of the dominant parties. This argument will be demonstrated by first examining the nuclear reductions of the period, both unilateral cuts and the terms of the Strategic Arms Reduction Treaty of 1991, and second by examining the conventional arms reductions of the post-cold war period, and in particular by focusing on the Conventional Forces in Europe Treaty of 1990. The depth of these agreements will also be examined.

Reductions in nuclear weapons: the START Treaty

One of the central defining characteristics of the cold war confrontation was the nuclear debate between the superpowers. Naturally, therefore, one of the central elements of the negotiations at the end of the cold war was the attempt to reduce the nuclear arsenals on both sides. This section will examine three issues. First, it will assess the START Treaty in terms of its major provisions, and will examine the implications of START. Second, it will analyse the depth of the treaty. Third, the section will assess the nature of the unilateral reductions in nuclear forces announced after the signing of START yet before the collapse of the Soviet Union, and examine the implications for the deepening of nuclear arms control.

Provisions of the START Treaty

The circumstances surrounding the opening of the START negotiations in 1982 and their conclusion with the signing of the treaty on 31 July 1991 could not have been more different. The negotiations began in a context in which relations between the superpowers were very tense over arms control compliance and the arms race, European politics and political relations in many parts of the developing world; the value of the practice of arms control was deeply questioned by many in the United States; significant reductions were seen to be politically desirable although not really practical; and where one of the central issues was the relationship between offensive forces and strategic defences. In contrast, the START Treaty was signed at a time of global cooperation between the superpowers; around a new consensus that arms control had an important role to play in strengthening American security interests; when reductions were seen to be both politically and strategically desirable; and where the question of the relationship with strategic defences was once again relegated in importance. In short, the START negotiations were begun in a context of superpower confrontation at a high point in the cold war; they were terminated with great speed at the conclusion of that cold war. Even in 1989, the authoritative *Military Balance* had argued that:

> Given existing negotiating problems, the prospect for new US positions that could modify the previously agreed START framework, the impact of force modernisation programmes, and the higher priority now being given to conventional force reductions in Europe, it is quite conceivable that it may take several more years of negotiations to complete a START Treaty.[5]

Twelve months later, the *Military Balance* reported that these 'four remaining major issues in START ... have now been resolved'.[6]

START brought about significant reductions in the strategic nuclear arsenals of the United States and Soviet Union. Article II of the treaty set out the specific limitations:

(A) 1600, for deployed ICBMs [submarine-launched ballistic missile] and their associated launches, deployed SLBMs [inter-continental ballistic missile] and their associated launchers, and deployed heavy bombers, including 154 for deployed heavy ICBMs and their associated launchers;
(B) 6000, for warheads attributed to deployed ICBMs, deployed SLBMs, and deployed heavy bombers, including

(i) 4900, for warheads attributed to deployed ICBMs and deployed SLBMs;
(ii) 1100, for warheads attributed to deployed ICBMs on mobile launchers of ICBMs;
(iii) 1540, for warheads attributed to deployed heavy ICBMs.[7]

A heavy ICBM was defined as 'an ICBM of a type, any one of which has a launch weight greater than 106,000 kilograms or a throw-weight greater than 4350 kilograms'.[8] Although the explicit purpose of the negotiations was to bring about 50 per cent reductions in the level of nuclear warheads, the nature of the counting rules were to lead to reductions totalling approximately one-third of the nuclear arsenals, reducing the combined American–Soviet strategic nuclear arsenals from some 24,000 to around 16,000 warheads.

Although in effect the nuclear cutbacks implied in the START Treaty would simply have led the superpowers to reduce the size of their arsenals to the levels of 1982 – that was, when the START negotiations began – this measure of nuclear disarmament was nevertheless highly significant. Under START, some eight thousand nuclear weapons were to be cut. Also, this was the first arms control treaty that would lead to real cuts in strategic nuclear weapons. The Interim Agreement on Offensive Arms in SALT I led to no decrease in the size of the nuclear arsenals; indeed, during the SALT I period both the United States and the Soviet Union massively increased the destructive capability of their nuclear arsenals within the terms of the treaty. SALT II did provide for some cuts, although not in the American arsenal, and only by 250 ballistic missiles and bombers in the slightly larger Soviet arsenal. However, despite the significance of the cuts mandated by START, and the attempt to create parity in the terms of the START Treaty, these reductions and the terms of the treaty would have had an uneven impact upon the arsenals of the Soviet Union and the United States for two important reasons. The first reason related to the real levels of warheads that each nation would have been allowed to possess after the implementation; the second referred to issues that were not included in the terms of the treaty, although limits had previously been sought by the Soviet Union.

First, the nature of the counting rules favoured the United States rather than the Soviet Union. These counting rules favoured bombers rather than ballistic missiles. The argument in favour of this was quite apparent: bombers were seen clearly to be second strike weapons, whereas ballistic missiles – with their speed and accuracy – could be first strike weapons. Thus favouring bombers over ballistic missiles would aid strategic stability. Specific warheads numbers to be counted against each ICBM or SLBM were stipulated in the 'Memorandum of Understanding on the Establishment of the Data Base Relating to this Treaty', and numbers on new systems were to be counted as 'the maximum number of reentry vehicles with which an ICBM or SLBM of that type has been flight tested'.[9] In contrast, under Article III.4(G), 'Each heavy bomber equipped for nuclear armaments other than long-range nuclear ALCMs [air-launched cruise missile] shall be attributed with one warhead', even though such bombers could carry up to 24 nuclear bombs and missiles.[10] A bomber with up to 24 such weapons would therefore only count as one against the limit of 6000 warheads.

Such counting rules favoured the United States rather than the Soviet Union in two related ways. First, the United States possessed a larger bomber fleet than did the Soviet Union. The total non-ALCM loading on American bombers in 1990 was estimated at 2748, for Soviet bombers at only 380.[11] This implied a relatively small reduction in and restructuring of the American bomber force, while the Soviet Union would have had to further expanded its investment in its bomber force to build up to the START levels. Second, the limitations on ballistic missiles would have placed far more strain on the Soviet arsenal than the American. Reductions in warhead numbers would have approached some 50 per cent, and cuts in ballistic missile launchers could possibly have exceeded that figure. In contrast, the United States would have been able to accommodate some 30 per cent reductions essentially by retiring the older Minuteman II and Poseidon C–3 systems. Whereas the Americans would have been affected only by the 4900 ballistic missile warhead limit, the Soviets would have been affected by the total ballistic missile warhead limit, the 1540 limit on heavy missile warheads, and the 1100 limit on mobile missile warheads, thus complicating the reduction and restructuring calculations. Taken together, START implied that the United States would have relatively little restructuring to carry out, while the Soviet Union would have to invest much more heavily, and in addition after implementation the United States might have been in possession of rather more strategic nuclear weapons than the Soviet Union.

The second way in which the terms of the treaty favoured the United States rather than the Soviet Union related to concessions made by the Soviet Union in essentially accepting the American agenda when the treaty was drawn up. This related especially to restrictions over strategic defences, to limitations on submarine-launched cruise missiles (SLCMs), and to a focus on the Soviet SS–18. For much of the 1980s, the Soviet Union had sought to link any prospective START Treaty to a commitment to strengthen the ABM Treaty regime which, it was felt by Moscow, was threatened by President Reagan's Strategic Defence Initiative. In particular, the Soviet Union sought to obtain an agreement on a non-withdrawal period from the ABM Treaty as part of an agreement on offensive forces contained within the START Treaty. However, with the desire to finalise a treaty, this linkage was dropped by Moscow during 1990. The Soviet Union had also sought to obtain specific constraints on SLCMs within the limits of the treaty, a field in which it was felt that the United States had an advantage. Restrictions on SLCMs were agreed, but did not form part of the treaty. Rather, in an attached understanding it was agreed that each side would make annual statements regarding deployment plans for long-range SLCMs (defined as those over 600 kilometres), with a maximum of 880 per nation. Being outside the treaty, these restrictions were not subject to verification procedures as had originally been sought by the Soviet Union. Finally, the provisions of START could have been fulfilled by both nations largely through retiring older systems, and in general no particularly strategically useful system had to be sacrificed. The one exception to this generalisation was the specific reductions mandated in the treaty to the Soviet SS–18, from some 308 missiles to 154, and therefore from 3080 warheads to 1540.

START, although formally an equal and balanced treaty, therefore worked to the advantage of the United States through a variety of means in significant, although not overwhelmingly decisive, ways. As will be seen in the next section, it was also a very deep agreement.

START and the deepening of arms control

The process of deepening in arms control, it was argued in the first chapter, related to three areas: the level of detail involved; the nature of the verification provisions; and the creation of regimes. In all these areas it was clear that START was a very deep agreement. Each of these criteria will be examined in turn.

In terms of detail, START was one of the most complex agreements seen in arms control up to 1991. The treaty, attached protocols, agreed statements, unilateral statements and declarations ran for some 250 pages. Articles II, III and IV provided definitions of weapons types and systems, and limitations and aggregates of weapons and facilities. Article V set limits on testing and deployments. Article VII set out obligations on the conversion and elimination of strategic weapons, subsequently expanded upon in the Conversion or Elimination Protocol. Article VIII set out the requirements of a data base and data exchange. Some reductions were relatively straight forward: for example, under Article II 1(B)(iii) '1540, for warheads attributed to deployed heavy ICBMs'.[12] Other elements were more complicated. For example, on heavy bombers, the ALCM rule stated that:

(E)   For the United States of America, each heavy bomber equipped for long-range nuclear ALCMs, up to a total of 150 such heavy bombers, shall be attributed with ten warheads. Each heavy bomber equipped for long-range nuclear ALCMs in excess of 150 such heavy bombers shall be attributed with a number of warheads equal to the number of long-range nuclear ALCMs for which it is actually equipped ...

(F)   For the Union of Soviet Socialist Republics, each heavy bomber equipped for long-range nuclear ALCMs, up to a total of 180 such heavy bombers, shall be attributed with eight warheads ... in excess of 180 such heavy bombers shall be attributed with a number of warheads equal to the number of long-range nuclear ALCMs for which it is actually equipped.[13]

There was also to be a general limitation on the aggregate throw weight of deployed ICBMs and SLBMs such 'that seven years after entry into force of this treaty and thereafter such aggregate throw-weight does not exceed 3600 metric tons'.[14] Thus, there were to be limits on the numbers of launchers, limits on the numbers of warheads and sub-limits on warheads, and a prohibition on the total throw-weight of each arsenal under START counting rules.

The reductions to the set levels were to be brought about over seven years after ratification in three phases, as shown in Table 2.1.

Table 2.1   *Schedule of START phased reductions*

	By 36 months Phase 1	By 60 months Phase 2	By 84 months Phase 3
Launchers on ICBMs, SLBMs, and Bombers	2100	1900	1600
Warheads on ICBMs, SLBMs and Bombers	9150	7950	6000
Warheads on ICBMs and SLBMs	8050	6750	4900

Source: Compiled from the limitations set out under Article II. Quoted in Richard D. Burns (editor) *Encyclopedia of Arms Control and Disarmament* New York: Charles Scribner, 1993, p. 1288.

On verification, the START Treaty allowed each state the right not only to conduct verification through national technical means (Article IX), but also an ability to conduct very intrusive on-site inspections. Article IX prohibited interfering with national technical means, and also forbade concealment measures designed to impede the collection of data. It also stipulated that 'To aid verification, each ICBM for mobile launchers of ICBMs shall have a unique identifier.'[15] Article X set out the regulations governing

flight tests of ICBMs and SLBMs so that the other state might be able to confirm the parameters of the test.

The heart of the verification provisions of the treaty, however, were in
Article XI, which set out the central elements of the verification provisions.
These related to inspections, exhibitions, and to rights for continuous mon-
itoring. Much more detail on these rights and obligations was set out in the
Inspection Protocol, and also in the Conversion or Elimination Protocol.

In terms of inspection rights, eight different forms were set out. First,
there were to be baseline data inspections to confirm the accuracy of the
data. Second, data update inspections would confirm the accuracy of data
on the numbers and types of items specified. Third, new facility inspections
would confirm the accuracy of data on the numbers and types of items specified. Fourth, suspect site inspections would confirm that covert assembly of
ICBMs for mobile launchers of ICBMs or covert assembly of first stages of
ICBMs was not occurring. Fifth, re-entry vehicle inspections of deployed
ICBMs and SLBMs would confirm that such ballistic missiles did not contain
more re-entry vehicles than the number attributed to them. Sixth, there
would be post-exercise dispersal inspections of deployed mobile launchers of
ICBMs. Seventh, there was provision for conversion or elimination inspections. Finally, formerly declared facility inspections would confirm that facilities were not to be used for reconstitution.[16]

Exhibitions, rights and duties related to three areas. First, 'technical characteristic exhibitions ... during such exhibitions by the other Party to conduct inspections of an ICBM and an SLBM ... to permit the inspecting party
to confirm that technical characteristics correspond to the data specified'.
Second, 'distinguishability exercises for heavy bombers, former heavy
bombers, and long-range nuclear ALCMs'. Finally, 'baseline exhibitions, and
shall have the right during such exhibitions by the other Party to conduct
inspections, of all heavy bombers equipped for non-nuclear armaments, all
training heavy bombers, and all former heavy bombers specified in the initial exchange of data'[17]

The Final part of Article XI specified that 'Each Party shall have the right
to conduct continuous monitoring activities at production facilities for
ICBMs for mobile launchers of ICBMs to confirm the number of ICBMs for
mobile launchers of ICBMs produced.'[18]

In addition to these requirements, Article XII set out responsibilities with
regard to providing information. Both states had to display road-mobile and
rail-mobile ICBM launchers, and heavy bombers and former heavy bombers
in the open should the other state ask for such provision, up to seven times
a year, and twice a year the state asking for such cooperative measures
could also stipulate the site. The display had to begin within 12 hours of
the request being made. Further details were set out in the Notification Protocol.

The START Treaty was, therefore, carefully designed to create a very detailed verification arrangement. Indeed, this verification system was part of the effort to make the START Treaty a part of an American–Soviet regime for the controlled reduction of the massive levels of nuclear forces possessed by each state at the end of the cold war. This attempt at regime creation is most evident in Article XVII (2), which stated:

> This treaty shall remain in force for 15 years unless superseded earlier by a subsequent agreement on the reduction and limitation of strategic offensive arms. No later than one year before the expiration of the 15-year period, the Parties shall meet to consider whether this treaty will be extended. If the Parties so decide, this treaty will be extended for a period of five years unless it is superseded ... This treaty shall be extended for successive five-year periods, if the Parties so decide, in accordance with the procedures governing the initial extension, and it shall remain in force for each agreed five-year period of extension unless it is superseded.[19]

In addition, under Article XV, both states set up a Joint Compliance and Inspection Commission within which problem issues could be resolved, and the START regime in general managed.

The creation of such a regime was an important element providing an anchor around which both the United States and Soviet Union were able to make further moves, this time of a unilateral nature, towards greater nuclear disarmament during the final six months of the existence of the Soviet Union. It is to these unilateral gestures that the analysis now turns.

Unilateral reductions in nuclear forces

In the period immediately after the signing of the START Treaty, the Soviet Union moved more dramatically into terminal decline. With the failure of the August coup of 1991 in the Soviet Union, the cold war appeared to be receding even more hastily into history. In such circumstances, it seemed feasible and desirable to move forward and to build upon the START regime with further disarmament. There were two, linked, moves at this time: from President Bush on behalf of the United States and, less than a fortnight later, from Soviet President Gorbachev.

Bush's initiative was made in a speech on 27 September 1991 in which he announced a series of unilateral concessions and offers.[20] There were four elements to the new American position: the desire to bring about a hastening of the START process; moves to institute a further reversal of the arms race at the strategic level through the cancellation of weapons systems; efforts to widen the disarmament focus to the tactical nuclear level; and attempts to create a framework for further negotiations on the implementation of arms control and on furthering arms control issues.

In the first of these elements, President Bush announced that those American ICBMs scheduled to be deactivated under the provisions of the START Treaty would be demobilised with immediate effect. Further, all American strategic bombers were to be taken off alert status. With regard to the second of these elements, the mobile programme of the MX and Midgetman ICBMs were cancelled, as was the SRAM II (short range attack missile) programme. Third, significant reductions at the tactical level were announced. All naval tactical nuclear weapons – including nuclear armed SLCMs – were to be withdrawn and either destroyed or put into storage. All nuclear artillery shells and warheads for tactical ballistic missiles were to be destroyed. In this way over 4000 tactical nuclear warheads were to be destroyed or placed into storage. Finally, Bush proposed negotiations with the Soviet Union over de-MIRVing the Soviet and American strategic nuclear arsenals (that is, to allow only single warheads on missiles), and cooperation with the Soviet Union over ensuring central control over nuclear weapons on Soviet territory (Bush had also announced that all American strategic weapons would be placed under one command structure), along with an offer to begin detailed collaboration over techniques relating to the safe transport and destruction of nuclear warheads.

Significantly, these unilateral moves were designed to bring about reciprocal gestures from the Soviet Union. As Bush said in his speech, 'We expect our bold initiative to be met with equally bold steps on the Soviet side.'[21] By making such an announcement in offering major American cuts, the United States had sought to structure the nuclear weapons reduction process further around its own agenda. The United States wanted to ensure the safe continuation of the START Treaty which was viewed as making a significant contribution to American security and to strategic stability. Thus, the Bush announcement sought to keep START on the agenda, and to hasten its implementation. The United States also wanted to encourage the Soviet Union not to develop further strategic mobility, which could have been seen as the most problematic area for the verification of START and the most feasible area for a surreptitious breakout from the treaty. Thus, Bush offered the elimination of future mobility for elements of the United States' forces in the form of the MX and Midgetman programmes, encouraging the Soviet Union to focus on an area in which it had developed sophisticated capabilities. Elimination of ground- and sea-based tactical nuclear weapons was proposed in the hope that the Soviet Union might respond, thus removing nuclear forces from possibly falling into the hands of non-state actors or putative governments of new states on the territory of the crumbling Soviet Union. In proposing new talks over deMIRVing, a measure that could be seen as stabilising in its own right, the United States sought to further elements on the START agenda which had focused on eliminating entirely the Soviet hard-target kill capability in the shape of the SS–18, and to therefore eliminate the American fear of a disarming first strike attack to which elements of the American land based force may still have seemed vulnerable in a post-START world without significant further investment. Finally, in proposing American assistance with the management of the Soviet nuclear arsenal, Bush illustrated the emerging Western concern with the possible proliferation of Soviet nuclear weapons outside central control.

Gorbachev's response mirrored the American agenda closely on all four points.[22] First, Gorbachev accepted a hastening of the START agenda. All Soviet strategic bombers were to be taken off alert status, as were all rail-mobile ICBMs, 503 other ICBMs, and three submarines with a total of 48 SLBMs. In addition, Gorbachev went beyond the Bush announcement by declaring that the Soviet Union would cut its strategic arsenal to 5000 warheads rather than 6000 under the START regime. Second, the Soviet announcement stated that development of new launchers for rail-mobile ICBMs, a new small mobile ICBM, and a short range attack missile would all be cancelled. Third, Gorbachev promulgated deep cuts in the Soviet tactical nuclear weapon arsenal. All ground-launched tactical nuclear warheads would be destroyed, (which would account for an estimated 10,000 weapons), and all naval tactical nuclear weapons would also be withdrawn.[23] Finally, Gorbachev demonstrated a willingness to discuss command and control issues with the Americans (he also announced that all Soviet strategic nuclear forces would be placed under a single command), but in addition issued a series of ideas that went well beyond the Bush statement: a one year Soviet moratorium on testing nuclear weapons was announced; Gorbachev suggested further negotiations to reduce START levels by 50 per cent within the START framework; he proposed a ban on the production of fissile material for nuclear weapons; and suggested the possibility of a joint Soviet–American deployment of ballistic missile defences.

In the twilight of the Soviet state's existence, the United States had sought to both hasten the implementation of the START Treaty and to widen the START agenda to include tactical nuclear forces to control the development of new weapons systems. In bringing about this widening, however, there was a price to pay in terms of deepening. Reciprocal unilateralism was a useful arms control technique to short-cut the diplomatic process of arms control negotiations which could prove lengthy, in order to bring about agreements on the significant elements of the force postures on both sides. However, such speed meant that it was not possible to provide detail, nor to develop verification procedures for these unilateral moves: 'in emphasizing speed over negotiations, the administration deliberately decided to forgo verifying agreed undertakings, and to rely instead on an exchange of information about how the commitments were being implemented'.[24] Most significantly, it did not prove possible to move from declarations to implementation of these new arms control ideas and gestures in the period from early October, when the Soviet state looked very ill, to the pronouncement that the illness was terminal when citizens in the Ukraine voted for independence in early December. Soviet–American discussions in this period, although 'undoubtedly constructive engagements ... were unaccompanied by any practical actions'.[25] And with the disintegration of the Soviet Union, the attempt to build and develop a nuclear reduction regime was threatened with collapse.

Reductions in conventional weapons

From the late 1980s, stimulated by a feeling of greater security as the cold war came to an end, many governments in Europe and North America engaged in a process of conventional arms reductions. This activity was motivated in part by the desire to release resources from the defence budget to either be redirected towards other areas of domestic government expenditure, or to reduce total government expenditure, and was legitimised by arms control negotiations in the form of the CFE talks. Indeed, several countries began to suggest making unilateral reductions in their armed forces before the completion of the CFE treaty. In December 1989, the West German Defence Ministry proposed a reduction in the size of the Bundeswehr by 33,000; at the end of January, 1990, the Netherlands' Minister of Defence suggested a reduction in the number of Dutch troops stationed in West Germany by 5500; while also in January 1990, Belgian Defence Minister Guy Coeme asked the Chief of Staff to study the implications of withdrawing all 28,000 Belgian troops from the Federal Republic.[26]

The process of reductions was codified in the Conventional Armed Forces in Europe Treaty signed in 1990, which, along with the allied agreements of 1992 on conventional arms control, constituted a major contribution towards ending the cold war confrontation in Europe through arms control. This section will firstly examine the CFE Treaty and analyse the agreements reached to maintain the relevance of the treaty subsequent to the collapse of the Soviet Union, and will secondly examine the depth of these agreements.[27]

Provisions of the CFE Treaty

The CFE Treaty was clearly a product of the ending of the cold war. The negotiations over Mutual and Balanced Force Reductions (MBFR) occupied much arms control activity in Europe from 1973 to 1989, without ever achieving major success. In contrast, the CFE negotiations opened in March 1989, and a detailed and complex treaty was signed in November 1990. The dilemmas that had prevented real movement in the course of the MBFR talks – what could be the incentives for the Soviet Union and Warsaw Pact to give up a large conventional superiority that played such an important part in Pact military strategy? – were resolved with remarkable alacrity. Argument over the scope of the negotiations (should they cover just tanks, artillery and armoured troop carriers, or be expanded to cover personnel, aircraft and helicopters?) was settled, as was the problem of organising agreed definitions. Under any criteria, the CFE Treaty was one of the most remarkable successes for arms control. However, as Colin McInnes has argued, if 'The signing of the CFE Treaty in Paris on 19 November 1990 represented the final, closing act in the drama of the cold war in Europe ... it appeared in 1990 that the CFE Treaty's time had not only come, but was passing quickly.'[28]

It was the changing political situation in Europe that accelerated the progress of CFE. The process really began with Mikhail Gorbachev's speech to the United Nations in December 1988, in which he announced significant measures of unilateral Soviet disarmament, and subsequently Gorbachev sought to make meaningful concessions in order to obtain a multilateral arms control agreement. However in 1989, Soviet control over Eastern Europe collapsed, removing the *glacis* which had provided a pivotal justification for those concessions as far as many in the Soviet military were concerned. The treaty signed in 1990, although modified slightly to take into account the changed strategic circumstances, brought about a significantly different strategic relationship from that which was envisaged by both sides only eighteen months previously.

The terms of the treaty brought about an equality between both groups of states that hid a clear advantage for the Western group of states. The major implication of the treaty concerned the unprecedented amount of military material that would have to be moved, destroyed or converted. Under the terms of the treaty, 9860 items of Treaty Limited Equipment (TLE) would have to be reduced in the Eastern group of countries, plus another 23408 TLE for the Soviet Union, making a total of 33268. However, the net NATO reduction was only to be 97 TLE. The creation of numerical parity under CFE counting rules was therefore to generate a great deal of work and expense for only one group of states.[29]

The inequality in the treaty went further. Several NATO countries were committed to major reductions, such as the United States (2063 TLE), the Netherlands (775 TLE), Italy (659 TLE) and France (427 TLE). However, this material was not to be destroyed, but transferred. Many NATO countries were able to expand their holdings of TLE: above all Turkey (2015 TLE), along with Greece (918 TLE), Portugal (537 TLE), Germany (400 TLE), and Spain (320 TLE). Not only were many NATO countries allowed to expand their equipment quantitatively, but many would also be encouraged to upgrade their holdings qualitatively through the NATO policy of 'cascading'. This referred to the movement of excess high quality equipment from central Europe to the flanks, where more obsolete equipment would be destroyed. The largest donors were to be the United States and Germany, followed by the Netherlands, and the largest beneficiaries were to be Turkey and Greece, as well as Denmark, Norway, Portugal and Spain.[30]

Thus, although the terms of the CFE Treaty appeared to deal with the interests of NATO countries and those of the Warsaw Pact in an even-handed fashion, in fact the treaty brought about significant advantages for the Western countries in three ways. First, numerical parity was created between Eastern and Western states; however, by the time the treaty was signed, it was clear that the Soviet Union could not rely militarily upon its Warsaw Pact colleagues. The implementation of the CFE Treaty would therefore place the Soviet Union in a position of numerical *inferiority* in conventional forces in Europe. Second, while the Soviet Union and other Eastern forces had to remove and destroy large amounts of material, with all the costs involved, NATO forces had relatively few reductions to make. Third, while reductions were being made in the East, states on the flanks of NATO were increasing not only the quantity but also the quality of their holdings, through the NATO policy of cascading.

Unsurprisingly, an agreement that appeared to be so unequal to the Soviet Union was opposed by many in the Soviet military. Ratification of the treaty was delayed by three problems in 1991. First, the Western nations were dissatisfied with the nature of the data supplied by the Soviet Union at the time of the signing of the treaty, as intelligence estimates suggested that there was a massive under-reporting of the size of the Soviet military machine. Second, NATO countries were unhappy about the movement of large amounts of Soviet equipment east of the Urals (that was, outside the scope of the treaty), which seemed to offer the possibility for major force regeneration. Third, Western countries complained about the resubordination of units from the army to the navy, given that naval forces were excluded from the treaty. Together, these could have been seen as a deliberate attempt by the Soviet military to circumvent the CFE Treaty. Although these problems were resolved, discussion between the States Parties to the treaty and the Soviet Union continued until the middle of 1991, which coincided with the August coup and the subsequent collapse of the Soviet Union. The arguments over data thus delayed the ratification of the treaty until a time when the Soviet Union was in complete collapse, unable to ratify the treaty and thereby impose its terms on the successor states.

The failure of the Soviet Union to complete the ratification process before the collapse of the country, delayed in large part by the disputes over data, movement of TLE east of the Urals and over resubordination, necessitated that all the successor states sign the treaty. This in turn required new subdivisions of equipment in the territory of the former Soviet Union. The resulting negotiations were complex, yet again completed with remarkable speed and clarity, given that the ex-Soviet states had to decide for themselves on the apportionment of the forces of the former Soviet Union. There were inevitable political problems associated with achieving this, and there was also a major geographical problem. The old Soviet military districts were the sub-zonal basis for the treaty. However, these military districts comprised several of the new states, especially on the flanks. The southern subzone included Armenia, Azerbaijan, Moldova, Georgia, parts of Russia and parts of Ukraine, all of which together had to be limited under the terms of the treaty to 1850 tanks, 2775 artillery pieces and 1800 ACVs (armoured combat vehicles), which was only just short of the holdings of Armenia, Azerbaijan, Moldova and Georgia alone. However, despite these apparent problems, on 15 May 1992, the ex-Soviet states were able to announce agreement on the maximum levels of TLE for each country at a meeting in Tashkent, reproduced in Table 2.2.

Table 2.2   *CFE entitlements of the former Soviet Union, by state*

Country	Tanks	ACVs	Artillery	Aircraft	Helicopters
Azerbaijan	220	220	285	100	50
Armenia	220	220	285		50
Belarus	1800	2600	1615	260	80
Georgia	220	220	285	100	50
Kazakhstan	0	0	0	0	0
Moldova	210	210	250	50	50
Russia	6400	11,480	6415	3450	890
Ukraine	4080	5050	4040	1090	330

Notes:
● Total ceilings include active and storage units.
● Kazakhstan may retain no Treaty Limited Equipment in that part of its territory covered by the CFE Treaty.
● Estonia, Latvia and Lithuania are not party to the CFE Treaty.

Source: 'The Tashkent Agreement', reproduced in *Trust and Verify* No. 29, June 1992, p. 2.

Twenty-nine nations became a party to the new version of the treaty, agreed at the Oslo meeting of the North Atlantic Cooperation Council on 5 June 1992.[31] In Helsinki on 10 July 1992 sixteen NATO countries, six former Warsaw Pact countries and seven former Soviet republics signed the Provisional Application of the CFE 1 Treaty, which came into force on Friday 17 July 1992. In all this negotiation and agreement, the CFE Treaty as originally signed and as modified was to be one of the deepest arms control agreements ever reached.

The depth of the treaty, however, would be no guarantee of its survival. Open opposition to CFE in Russia became clear from the end of 1993.[32] In

September, President Yeltsin wrote to the Americans, British, French and Germans outlining the case for a suspension of Article V of the treaty, regarding the flank zone. These arguments revolved around security issues (the many conflicts in Moldova and the Transcaucasus) and socio-economic factors (the existence of greater infrastructure in the south to accommodate forces returning from Central and Eastern Europe).[33] Twelve months later, senior American officials were being informed directly that Russia would not meet the treaty's requirements on the flanks.[34] It was reported that US intelligence estimated that the Russians would be 400 tanks, 2000 APCs and 500 artillery pieces over the flank sub-limits by November 1995, when deadlines had to be met.[35]

Problems with the continuation of CFE demonstrated that success of an arms control agreement depends fundamentally on willing compliance. It is not part of this book to assess the success or failure of arms control agreements; but it is central to assess the depth.

CFE and the deepening of arms control

The CFE Treaty was an excellent example of the level of deepening in certain areas of arms control at the end of the cold war. The process of deepening relates to the level of detail, the nature of the verification provisions, and the creation of regimes.

The CFE Treaty, and its subsequent amendments, was a very deep agreement in all three terms, and it is worth laying out some of the terms of the treaty in order to demonstrate this point. The treaty set out a great deal of detail in three areas: first, the area to be covered by the treaty; second, definitions of the weapons systems to be included; and third, the acceptable equipment holdings in five areas of weaponry. The treaty also outlined detailed verification provisions. Finally, the terms of the treaty were designed to create a regime. Each of these areas will be examined in turn.

In terms of the area to be covered by the treaty, this was defined as the Atlantic to the Urals area (defined in Article IV.1). The zones were broken down into a flank area and three linked central areas, comprising Bulgaria, Greece, Iceland, Norway, Romania, Turkey and four Soviet Military Districts (MDs) – Leningrad, Odessa, North Caucasus, Trans-caucasian – in the Flank region; Belgium, Czechoslovakia, Germany, Hungary, Luxembourg, Netherlands, Poland in Sub-zone IV.4: Belgium, Czechoslovakia, Denmark, France, Germany, Hungary, Italy, Luxembourg, Netherlands, Poland, United Kingdom, and four Soviet MDs (Baltic, Belorussian, Carpathian, Kiev) in Sub-zone IV.3; Belgium, Czechoslovakia, Denmark, France, Germany, Hungary, Italy, Luxembourg, Netherlands, Poland, Portugal, Spain, United Kingdom, and six Soviet MDs (Baltic, Belorussian, Carpathian, Kiev, Moscow, Volga–Urals) in Sub-zone IV.2.

Detailed definitions of the five types of TLE were provided. First tanks, defined under Article II.1(C) as:

> tracked armoured fighting vehicles which weigh at least 16.5 metric tonnes unladen weight and which are armed with a 360-degree traverse gun of at least 75mm calibre. In addition, any wheeled armoured fighting vehicles entering into service which meet all the other criteria stated above shall also be deemed battle tanks.

Second, armoured combat vehicles, which were divided in Article II.1(D) into three categories. Armoured personnel carriers (APCs), 'designed and equipped primarily to transport a combat infantry squad and which, as a rule, is armed with an integral or organic weapon of less than 20mm calibre'. Armoured infantry fighting vehicles (AIFVs):

> designed and equipped primarily to transport a combat infantry squad, which normally provides the capability for troops to deliver fire from inside the vehicle under armoured protection, and which is armed with an integral or organic cannon of at least 20mm calibre and sometimes an antitank missile launcher.

Finally heavy armoured combat vehicles (HACVs), 'with an integral or organic direct fire gun of at least 75mm calibre, weighing at least 60 metric tonnes unladen weight, which does not fall within the definitions of an armoured personnel carrier, or an armoured infantry fighting vehicle or a battle tank'. Third, the Treaty defined artillery under Article II.1(F) as:

> Large calibre artillery systems are guns, howitzers, artillery pieces combining the characteristic of guns and howitzers, mortars, and multiple launch rocket systems with a calibre of 100mm and above. In addition, any future large calibre direct fire system which has a secondary effective indirect fire capability shall be counted against the artillery ceilings.

Fourth, combat aircraft were defined under Article II.1(K) as:

> fixed wing or variable geometry wing aircraft armed and equipped to engage targets by employing guided missiles, unguided rockets, bombs, guns, cannons, or other weapons of destruction, as well as any model or version of such an aircraft which performs other military functions such as reconnaissance or electronic warfare. The term 'combat aircraft' does not include primary training aircraft.

Fifth and finally, helicopters were divided into five different types, each of which was specified.[36] The treaty also set out detailed limits on the number of types of equipment by region as shown in Table 2.3.

Further detail was provided in the attached declarations in Annexe II of the treaty. One of these declarations was a statement that each group of states would not exceed a limit of 430 land based naval aircraft with a single country limit of 400. There was also a unilateral declaration by Germany that the united German armed forces would be limited to 370,000 total, with 345,000 in the air and ground forces.

Table 2.3. *Limitations of military equipment in the CFE Treaty*

		Tanks	ACVs	Artillery	Aircraft	Helicopters
Overall	Total	20,000	30,000[b]	20,000	6800	2000
	active[a]	16,500	27,300	17,000		
Sub-zone IV.2	Total	15,300	24,100	14,000		
	active	11,800	21,400	11,000		
Sub-zone IV.3	Total	10,300	19,260	9100		
	Kiev MD	2250	2500	1500		
Sub-zone IV.4	Total	7500	11,250	5000		
Flank zone V	Active	4700	5900	6000		
	temp[c]	459	723	420		
	1 state	153	241	140		
1 state VI	Total	13,300	20,000	13,700	5150	1500

Notes

[a] Equipment stores in the 'main region' and in two further Soviet Military Districts: Odessa (400 tanks, 500 artillery pieces); Southern Leningrad, defined as south of 60 degree 15 minutes north latitude (600 tanks, 800 ACVs, 400 artillery pieces).
[b] Additional limitations: 18,000 AIFV plus HACV, 1500 HACV
[c] Total temporary additional deployment.

Source: Drawn from *Focus on Vienna* No. 21, December 1990, p. 3.

The CFE Treaty was also very deep in terms of its verification procedures. The reductions to residual limits of the equipment as defined within the various zones were to be complied with within forty months after the treaty entered into force. In order to specify how this was to be achieved, Article VIII.4 set out four phases of the treaty. The first, the Baseline Validation Phase, was to run for the first 120 days, and this was a period in which data could be investigated. The second period, the Reduction Phase, was to last for three years and was to cover the destruction, conversion and recertification of equipment accompanied by detailed inspections.[37] The third period, the Residual Level Validation Phase, was to last a further 120 days, and was designed to allow for the inspection of the data following the reductions. Finally the Residual Phase was to last for an indefinite period in which there would be inspections at declared and undeclared sites to check on whether states were keeping to the provisions of the treaty. Within the terms of the treaty there was a mass of additional detail relating to: methods of destruction of equipment (severing, explosive demolition, deformation, smashing, target drones); an outline of eight methods of equipment reduction (destruction, conversion, static display, use as ground targets, modification, instructional use, reclassification and recategorisation); a list of equipment that could be converted and fourteen accepted uses that could be made of the equipment after conversion; provision for the recategorisation of certain helicopters; and the reclassification of certain named aircraft into unarmed trainer aircraft. Further, there were details of methods of notification and exchange of information, and a great deal of information of verification practices.

Finally, there were also provisions in the terms of the treaty designed to create a conventional arms control regime. Most clearly, this was evident in Article XVIII, which committed the states to follow-on negotiations on levels of personnel, to be completed by the Helsinki 1992 CSCE conference. In the Charter of Paris which had been signed alongside the CFE Treaty, the Heads of Government and State had looked 'forward ... to discussions and consultations among the 34 participating States aimed at establishing by 1992, from the conclusion of the Helsinki Follow-up Meeting, new negotiations on disarmament and confidence- and security-building open to all participating States'.[38] In order to facilitate the operation of the treaty regime, and following the SALT practice, a Joint Consultative Group was set up under Article XVI. The treaty was to be of unlimited duration, although states could withdraw with 150 days notice. Further, the last of the three attached declarations to the Treaty was a declaration by all twenty-two signatories that military manpower would not be increased during negotiations designed to achieve an agreement on troop levels. Throughout the negotiations for the CFE Treaty, there was an expectation that this treaty would merely be the first in a series of agreements designed to reduce the military confrontation in Europe.

Thus, on all three criteria, the terms of the CFE Treaty were very deep. There was a large amount of detail, designed to prevent states from evading restrictions and also designed to reduce the possibilities for misunderstanding. The verification provisions were extensive. Finally, the treaty set the parameters for the creation of a regime in which the CFE Treaty would be the cornerstone, but in which other agreements would subsequently be reached.

The CFE Treaty was, therefore, clearly focused on the criteria related to constructing arms control at the end of major conflicts. It was an agreement that appeared to produce equality, and yet in reality largely benefited the Western states; however, CFE also very significantly furthered the deepening process in arms control.

Conclusion

It is clear from this analysis of the START Treaty and the unilateral reductions in nuclear forces announced in 1991, along with the CFE Treaty, that the major arms control agreements associated with the end of the cold war conformed very closely to one of the four forms which such arms control may take, as identified in Chapter 1 of this book. Unlike many earlier arms control agreements, none of this arms control activity was designed to secure the total disarmament of one party (in this case, the Soviet Union and Warsaw Pact states), nor to impose upon those countries the *foedus inaequuum*, nor to create a semi-permanent peace through the mandated strategic superiority of the dominant powers (in this case, of the United States and its allies). Rather, the United States and its allies were in the ascendancy, but had not achieved an overwhelming victory. The terms of the agreements were thus rather more balanced than one would expect under any of the other three possibilities; nevertheless, those agreements were still in favour of the dominant parties. Under the START Treaty, although numerical parity was mandated, the counting rules meant that the United States would be able to deploy more warheads than the Soviet Union after implementation, while the Soviet Union agreed to accept many items on the American agenda in order to reach agreement. These trends were accelerated in the unilateral statements exchanged in September and October 1991. Under the CFE Treaty, while numerical parity was mandated, by the time of the implementation of CFE it was clear that the treaty would entail a Soviet inferiority in conventional weapons in Europe, require only the Soviet Union and its allies to engage in significant levels of demolition, while allowing states on the flanks of NATO to increase not only the quantity but also the quality of their holdings through the NATO policy of cascading.

If these agreements were to lead to advantages for the United States and the Western countries over the Soviet Union, no criticism is intended by this. As French diplomacy was able to exploit the success of France at the end of the Thirty Years War, and to ensure the predominance of French interests in the Peace of Westphalia, so American and Western diplomats were able to exploit the inherent advantages to their perspectives as the cold war came to a close.

Inevitably, much of the cold war debate over arms control can be seen in the agreements reached at its conclusion. In some senses, the nature of the CFE Treaty and the START Treaty reflected a pinnacle of cold war arms control practice; this is, of course, another way of saying that these agreements were particularly deep ones. Both treaties were extremely detailed documents, with extensive verification provisions, and both documents sought to explicitly create an arms control regime in nuclear and conventional weapons. However, the collapse of the cold war order inevitably threw this approach to arms control into confusion. The attempt to extend the START regime through unilateral measures at the end of 1991 sacrificed both detail and verification to the desire to extend agreement on nuclear disarmament.

However, the whole START regime itself was to be seriously compromised as the cold war order finally collapsed with the dissolution of the Soviet Union at the end of December 1991.

Notes

1 Admittedly a controversial notion. Justifying this label, see Charles Krauthamer 'The Unipolar Moment' *Foreign Affairs* Vol. 70, No. 1, 1991.

2 Bernard Brodie *The Absolute Weapon* New York: Harcourt Brace and Co, 1946, p. 76.

3 *Statement on the Defence Estimates 1987*, London: HMSO, 1987, p. 13.

4 There is a multitude of works in this area: see, for example, Philip Green *Deadly Logic: The Theory of Nuclear Deterrence* Columbus: Ohio State University, 1966; Robert Jervis 'Deterrence and Misperception' *International Security* Vol. 7, No. 3, 1982–3; Patrick Morgan *Deterrence: A Conceptual Analysis* Beverley Hills: Sage 1977; Jack Snyder 'Rationality at the Brink: The Role of Cognitive Processes in Failures of Deterrence' *World Politics* Vol. 30, No. 3, 1978; John Mueller *Retreat from Doomsday* New York: Basic Books, 1989; and John Steinbruner 'Beyond Rational Deterrence: The Struggle for New Conceptions' *World Politics* Vol. 28, No. 2, 1976.

5 *The Military Balance 1989–90* London: Brassey's for the International Institute for Strategic Studies, 1989, p. 213.

6 *The Military Balance 1990–91* London: Brassey's for the International Institute for Strategic Studies, 1990, p. 210.

7 See the Treaty as reproduced in Richard D. Burns (editor) *Encyclopedia of Arms Control and Disarmament* New York: Charles Scribner, 1993, p. 1287.

8 Excerpted in *ibid.*, p. 1306.

9 Article III 4 (A) and (B). *Ibid.*, p. 1288.

10 *Ibid.*, p. 1289.

11 See *The Military Balance 1990–1991*, pp. 212–13. *The Military Balance* concluded that 'Even with those reductions, however, the number of warheads deployed on US bombers could exceed 4,000.' *Ibid.*, p. 210.

12 See Richard D. Burns *Encyclopedia*, p.1287

13 Under Article III, 4. See Richard D. Burns *Encyclopedia*, p. 1288.

14 Under Article II, 3. *Ibid.*, p. 1287.

15 Cited in *ibid.*, p. 1299.

16 See *ibid.*, p. 1300.

17 *Ibid.*, pp. 1300–1301.

18 Reproduced in *ibid.*, p. 1301.

19 *Ibid.*, p. 1305.

20 See 'A new era of reciprocal arms reductions' *Arms Control Today* October 1991. Also see 'US Disarmament Initiative' *Survival* Vol. 33, No. 6, 1991.

21 'A new era of reciprocal arms reductions', *ibid.*, p. 5.

22 See 'President Mikhail Gorbachev, 5 October 1991' in *Arms Control Today* October 1991; and 'Soviet Disarmament Initiatives' *Survival* Vol. 33, No. 6, 1991.

23 On these issues, see 'Comparison of US and Soviet Nuclear Cuts' *Arms Control*

Today November 1991.

24   Ivo H. Daalder and Terry Terriff 'Nuclear Arms Control: Finishing the Cold War Agenda' in a special issue of *Arms Control: Contemporary Security Policy* entitled *Rethinking the Unthinkable: New Directions for Nuclear Arms Control*; Vol. 14, No. 1, 1993, p. 15.

25   Steven Miller 'Western Diplomacy and the Soviet Nuclear Legacy' *Survival* Vol. 34, No. 3, 1992, p. 10.

26   See Jane M. O. Sharp 'Conventional Arms Control in Europe' in *SIPRI Yearbook 1990* Oxford: Oxford University Press for SIPRI, 1990, pp. 477–8.

27   Much of the material on the CFE Treaty is drawn from Stuart Croft (editor) *The Treaty on Conventional Forces in Europe: The Cold War Endgame* Aldershot: Dartmouth, 1994. Also see Sergey Koulik and Richard Kokoski *Conventional Arms Control: Perspectives on Verification* Oxford: Oxford University Press for SIPRI, 1994.

28   Colin McInnes 'The CFE Treaty in Perspective' in Stuart Croft (editor) *The Treaty on Conventional Forces in Europe*, p. 4.

29   See Jonathan Dean and Randall Watson Forsberg 'CFE and Beyond: The Future of Conventional Arms Control' *International Security* Vol. 17 No. 2, 1992, table 1; also *Focus on Vienna* No. 22 February–March 1991, p. 3; and *BASIC Reports* No. 12, 17 December 1990, pp. 2–4. Obviously not all countries would build up to these levels, and there was scope for future changes.

30   By February 1993, Greece had received 916 tanks, 150 ACVs, 72 artillery pieces and 100 mortar systems under the cascading arrangement. Turkey had received 1057 tanks, 600 ACVs, and 71 artillery systems. Dan Plesch, Director of the British American Security Information Council in a letter to the *Financial Times* 17 February 1993. See also Robert Block 'NATO adds fuel to Balkans Arms Race' *The Independent* 21 July 1993.

31   See '29 Sign CFE Treaty' *Jane's Defence Weekly* 13 June 1992, p. 1009.

32   See, on this, Andrew Marshall 'Russia: Kremlin Niggles on Treaty Disturb NATO' *The Independent* 7 October 1993; and David White 'Crisis in Russia: Moscow Hints It May Breach Troop Cuts Treaty' *Financial Times* 7 October 1993.

33   On this, see Jane M. O. Sharp 'CFE Implementation: Is Russia Opting Out?' *Brassey's Defence Yearbook 1994* Centre for Defence Studies, London, Brassey's, 1994. Also see James Woolsey 'Russia is Playing the Great Game with CFE' *Wall Street Journal* 5 May 1995.

34   See James Adams 'Russia Repudiates European Treaty on Force Reductions' *Sunday Times* 23 October 1994. The information had been passed by the Russian deputy foreign minister, Georgi Mamedov, to the US deputy secretary of state, Strobe Talbott. Also see Andrew Marshall 'Russia Wants a Free Hand in Its Old Empire' *The Independent* 29 May 1994.

35   See the report in James Adams 'Too Soft Clinton to Get Tough on Russia' *Sunday Times* 10 April 1994.

36   Under Article II.1(L) combat helicopters were defined as 'a rotary wing aircraft armed and equipped to engage targets or equipped to perform other military functions. The term 'combat helicopter' comprises attack helicopters and combat support helicopters. The term 'combat helicopter' does not include

unarmed transport helicopters'. Under Article II.1(M), attack helicopters were defined as 'a combat helicopter equipped to employ anti-armour, air-to-ground or air-to-air guided weapons and equipped with an integrated fire control and aiming system for these weapons. The term 'attack helicopter' comprises specialised attack helicopters and multi-purpose attack helicopters'. Under Article II.1(N), specialised attack helicopters were specified to be 'an attack helicopter that is designed primarily to employ guided weapons'. Multi-purpose attack helicopters were defined as 'an attack helicopter designed to perform multiple military functions and equipped to employ guided weapons'. Article II,1(O) p. 5. Finally, under Article II.1(P), a combat support helicopter was specified as 'a combat helicopter which does not fulfil the requirements to qualify as an attack helicopter and which may be equipped with a variety of self-defence and area suppression weapons, such as guns, cannon, and unguided rockets bombs or cluster bombs, or which may be equipped to perform other military functions'.

37 From July 1992 to March 1993, some 500 verifications had been carried out. See 'First Joint Multinational Inspection Under the CFE Treaty' NATO Press Release (93) 26, 16 March 1993.

38 Reproduced in *Focus on Vienna* No. 23, May 1991 p. 8.

3

Arms control to strengthen strategic stability

Introduction

In Chapter 1 it was argued that an important form of arms control focused upon the desire to create a greater measure of strategic stability between two or more states. Whereas the terms of arms control agreements at the conclusion of conflicts are likely to be uneven in their impact upon the participants, arms control that is designed to create strategic stability at times other than the end of wars is prone to produce a more balanced arrangement between those states involved. Arms control at the end of major conflicts in part seeks to create a new series of relationships; arms control designed to strengthen strategic stability seeks to improve existing relationships.

It was argued in Chapter One that arms control agreements designed to strengthen strategic stability have two aspects. First, such agreements have been brought about by the desire to strengthen crisis stability; an example of such an agreement might be the Anglo-French Naval Limitation Pact of 1787. The purpose of these agreements is to ensure that in a crisis, neither side would see a military advantage accruing to the state that attacks first, and to try to prevent political crises from developing into military confrontations. Thus, the role for arms control is to take measures designed to reduce the requirement for quick action, and thereby create more time for diplomacy. Second, arms control has been used to strengthen arms race stability, and thereby to avoid a costly arms race at some stage in the future; an example of such an agreement was the Argentine–Chile Naval Limitation Convention of 1902. The objective of such an agreement is to prevent competition in a particular field of activity which would be expensive and potentially threatening should one side be able to develop a breakthrough either in technology or in the number of weapons systems that it was able to deploy.

This chapter will examine four agreements in the post-cold war world in terms of strategic stability. Both the Indian–Pakistani Agreement on the

Prohibition of Attack Against Nuclear Facilities and Installations of 1988 and the Hungary–Romania Open Skies Agreement of 1991 were agreed in order to strengthen crisis stability. The Argentine–Brazilian Joint Declaration on Nuclear Policy of 1990 was an agreement reached in order to strengthen arms race stability. Finally, the START II Treaty of 1993 between Russia and the United States enhanced both crisis and arms race stability. Each agreement will be examined in turn.

Agreements to strengthen crisis stability

There have been many agreements reached designed to enhance stability between states in order to reduce the likelihood of war breaking out at time of crisis. The Egyptians and Hittites accomplished such an agreement in 1280 BC, the British and French agreed a settlement in 1787, Finland and the Soviet Union reached another agreement in 1921, while the Interim Agreement on Offensive Arms between the United States and the Soviet Union as part of the SALT I agreement in 1972 provides a fourth example. Each agreement contained a diplomatic arrangement whereby issues of weapons and territory were settled between states so that the likelihood of one of the states feeling in crisis circumstances incentives to pre-empt would be eliminated. In the post-cold war period, measures of this sort were agreed between India and Pakistan, and between Hungary and Romania.

The Indian–Pakistani Agreement, 1988

On 31 December 1988, leaders of the Indian and Pakistani governments met in Islamabad and signed the Agreement on the Prohibition of Attack Against Nuclear Installations and Facilities. Since the violence of 1947, India and Pakistan have been engaged in a deep rooted rivalry which in both 1965 and 1971 led to further warfare. During the cold war, each side sought superpower support in diplomatic and material terms, both of which was forthcoming. However, as the cold war began to draw to an end, both states were in danger of losing their supporters, especially as the Soviet Union sought a way to retreat from its Afghan quagmire. Yet the lowering of cold war tensions did not imply a reduction of tension on the sub-continent. The dispute over the control of Kashmir continued to be at the heart of Indo-Pakistani rivalry in the 1980s, compounded by Indian accusations that Pakistan provided covert support to Sikh groups struggling for independence in Punjab. Indian and Pakistani forces clashed in 1985 on the Siachen glacier in Kashmir, and from November 1986 to January 1987 both sides massed hundreds of thousands of troops on their shared border as India and Pakistan seemed ready to go to war with each other for a fourth time. Such a conflict seemed to threaten not only bloody devastation through conventional means, but also the hidden menace of nuclear conflict. In the aftermath of its defeat by China in the 1962 border war and the first Chinese nuclear test two years later, India had developed a nuclear programme which led to the detonation of the Indian 'peaceful' nuclear explosion in 1974. Subsequently, Pakistan developed its own nuclear programme which, by the late 1980s, seemed to be approaching fruition. Hence, by that time it was clear that on the sub-continent two states stood in historical antagonism, with a clear area of dispute, with the restraining influence of superpower supporters being lifted, and with probable nuclear arsenals available to the political and military leaders of both states.[1]

Alongside this tense and often acrimonious relationship, limited efforts had been made to ameliorate rivalries. Above all, efforts focused on resolving the Kashmir dispute (although finding a solution has proved elusive) and reducing the nuclear dilemma. Progress on the nuclear relationship was made problematic by the fact that both states had refused to sign the Nuclear Non-Proliferation Treaty and had substantial nuclear programmes. Despite this, in December 1985, India and Pakistan reached an agreement that they would not attack each other's nuclear facilities in the event of war: however, this agreement was not signed for another three years due to military tensions on the subcontinent.

The agreement was short, comprising a general preamble and only three articles. Under Article I (1), 'Each Party shall refrain from undertaking, encouraging or participating in, directly or indirectly, any action aimed at causing the destruction of, or damage to, any nuclear installation or facility in the other country.'[2] In the following paragraph, a limited amount of detail was provided on definitions, as follows:

> The term 'nuclear installation or facility' includes nuclear power and research reactors, fuel fabrication, uranium enrichment, isotopes separation and reprocessing facilities as well as any other installations with fresh or irradiated nuclear fuel and materials in any form and establishments storing significant quantities of radio-active materials.[3]

Under Article II, 'Each Contracting Party shall inform the other on 1st January of each calendar year of the latitude and longitude of its nuclear installations and facilities and whenever there is any change.'[4]

Although this may seem a limited accord, it was significant in that it was the first agreement reached between India and Pakistan since the Simla agreement of 1972, in which the leaders of both states sought to devise a framework for bilateral relations in the aftermath of the 1971 war. Thus, perhaps not surprisingly, the agreement was not very deep on all the three criteria developed earlier: detail, verification and the development of a regime. Little detail was provided in the two main articles (Article III related to ratification, which was completed in December 1990). Although some definitions were given, it was considered sufficient, for example, to define establishments covered by the terms of the Treaty rather imprecisely to include those with 'significant quantities of radio-active materials' without stipulating any thresholds.

As a consequence of the brevity of the document, little was provided in the way of verification. However, Article II did provide a framework for the exchange of information on the location of nuclear sites, although there were no explicit means stipulated for the other state to verify this information itself. Would the incentives to declare a facility to attempt to protect it from any attack outweigh the incentives to keep the location of at least the most important facilities secret, and thereby not declare them? However, the agreement at least meant that were any declared facility ever to be struck by weapons from the other state, it could not be other than deliberate.

Finally, little was achieved in terms of developing a regime in this field. Discussions continued in the years afterwards regarding the creation of a nuclear weapons free zone in the region, and on agreements notifying the other state of military exercises. However, little subsequent progress was made on the nuclear issue. Both states sought to maintain their status of being on the threshold of full nuclear capability, to have a nuclear option but not to be a fully declared nuclear state. The agreement implicitly sanctioned the right of both states to maintain this position, which meant that any further progress would in the medium term be extremely difficult.

Ultimately, the agreement was a very limited step, but nevertheless one which aided the cause of furthering strategic stability. Both states feared that in any future war, nuclear installations would be prime targets; indeed, that in a crisis, advantages might become apparent to the state inflicting damage on its rival's nuclear facility first. Both states wanted to avoid falling victim to the kind of pre-emptive attack that Israel had launched on the Iraqi Osirak reactor in 1982; any such attack could have proved tempting in a crisis, or could have led a crisis into war.[5] In these narrowly defined terms, the Indian–Pakistani Agreement on the Prohibition of Attack Against Nuclear Installations and Facilities was clearly drawn up to strengthen crisis stability.

The Hungarian–Romanian Agreement, 1991

On 11 May 1991 the Hungarian and Romanian governments met in Bucharest to sign the Hungarian–Romanian Agreement on the Establishment of an Open Skies regime. This was an important agreement designed to promote confidence in both states that neither was preparing a military attack upon the other. Such conflict was, at the time, seen to be a credible possibility. For over forty years, Hungarian–Romanian tensions over their respective borders, and the treatment of the large Hungarian minority in

Romania, had been disguised by the pressures of the cold war, and Soviet management of relations between the states of Eastern Europe. With the emergence of non-communist governments in the region in 1989 and 1990, concerns grew that with the elimination of the 'restraining' influence of the Soviet Union, the states of the region might seek to redress that which some elements of society in many of the countries concerned interpreted as historical wrongs. One of these wrongs was seen by some to be the position of the Hungarian minority in Romania.

In the aftermath of the First World War, the signing of the Treaty of Trianon in 1920 led to the vast reduction of the land area of Hungary (by some 71 per cent, along with 60 per cent of its population), and placed some 1.8 million Hungarians outside the boundaries of the new Hungarian state, particularly in Transylvania, but also in Vojvodina in what became the new state of Yugoslavia, and in Slovakia in the new Czechoslovakia.[6] This caused much political tension in the Inter-War period, and was a contributory factor to the Hungarian alliance with Hitler, through which Hungary regained control of many of these lands through the Vienna Awards of 1938 and 1940.

Thus concern about the resurfacing of Hungarian–Romanian tension in the early 1990s did not seem unreasonable.[7] Indeed, it was these fears that led many analysts to argue that NATO could not extend its membership to the East, for fear of becoming embroiled in such conflicts.[8] The states themselves, however, sought to take steps to enhance stability between them in order to reduce the likelihood of war breaking out at time of crisis. Initially, Hungary and Romania signed a joint military accord emphasising cooperation and exchanges of information and experience. This was to be followed by the Hungarian–Romanian Agreement on the Establishment of an Open Skies regime.

The agreement was negotiated very much within the general Open Skies framework (a negotiation and agreement that will be examined in Chapter Four), within the terms of the Conference on Security and Cooperation in Europe's 1990 Vienna Document of the Negotiations on Confidence- and Security-Building Measures in Europe. Thus, much of the context for the agreement was provided by a supportive arms control environment in Europe as a whole. The essence of the agreement was very simple. Each state would allow the other to overfly its territory in a regulated way in order to observe whether any concentrated military build-up of forces was occurring, or if any unusual military activities were taking place. Gathering such information, it was hoped, would alleviate the use of worst-case analysis in military relations between both sides, thus providing opportunities to prevent political crises from developing into military confrontations. Article II, 'Basic Rights and Obligations of the Parties', set out the main terms of this simple confidence-building arrangement: 'Each Party shall have the right to conduct Observation Flights ... Each Party undertakes to permit Observation Flights ... Each Party may conduct Observation Flights with its own Observation Aircraft or the Observation Aircraft of the other Party.'[9] Under Article III:

> For the purposes of fulfilling the objectives of this Agreement, each Party shall have the right to conduct and undertakes the obligation to accept an agreed number of Observation Flights ... The number of Observation Flights a Party shall be allowed to conduct shall be equal to the number of overflights it shall be required to accept.[10]

The agreement was in many ways quite deep in terms of detail, verification provisions, and regime formation. There was an attempt to provide detail and clarify meanings. Article I focused on narrowing the scope for misinterpretations, and provided agreed definitions for twenty-one items. Included in this list were descriptions of an Observation Aircraft and an Observation Flight. An Observation Aircraft was to be 'an unarmed, fixed wing aircraft, capable of carrying two Observed Party Flight Monitors in addition to its Aircrew members'.[11] An Observation Flight was to be 'a flight and any accompanying refuelling stops, conducted in accordance with the provisions and restrictions of this Agreement by an Observation Aircraft over the Territory of an Observed Party'.[12] Article IV set out further regulations concerning Observation Aircraft, Article V dealt with pre- and post-observation flight procedures, and Article VI outlined restrictions on flight plans and conduct of observations. Further regulations dealt with prohibition or curtailment of observation flights (Article XII) and with limitations on the uses that could be made of any information gathered (Article XV, in which it was stipulated that information obtained 'must not be used to the detriment of the other Party's security or other interests and must not be transferred to any third State'[13]). In addition, a series of further agreed statements were set out in attached annexes. For example, Annexe A recorded numbers of annual Observation Flights, Annexe B set out the airspace that could be used when flying between the two countries, Annexe C set out restrictions and duties relating to the inspections, Annexe D dealt with the rights and duties of Flight Monitors (individuals 'designated by the Observed Party to be on board the Observation Aircraft during the Observation Flight'),[14] Annexe E explained the nature of acceptable on-board equipment, and Annexe F set out the general provisions for the operation of the Open Skies Consultative Commission.

One of the key issues over which agreement was required was the definition of 'hazardous airspace'. The negotiations between the two states sought to obtain an agreement in which the whole territory of both states would be available for observation. However, there was a concern that access to certain areas might, for a variety of reasons, be prohibited. Thus a definition of 'hazardous airspace' was included in the terms of the agreement, and was deemed to 'include prohibited areas, restricted areas and danger areas, established in the interests of flight safety, public safety and environmental protection'.[15] Under Article VIII, the right to conduct Observation Flights 'anywhere over the Territory of the Observed Party' was reaffirmed.[16] However, where an overflight of hazardous airspace might prove dangerous, the Observed Party had to make public the reasons why. Following this, four alternatives were provided. First, the Observing Party might accept the restriction without further question. Second, the Observed Party might suggest a minimum altitude for an overflight of the hazardous area. Third, if no minimum altitude was consistent with safety, an alternative Flight Plan would be suggested by the Observed Party that would cover a route as close as possible to the hazardous area. Fourth, the Observed Party might suggest an alternative time for the Observation Flight, by which time the risk to safety would have been eliminated.[17] However, where none of these alternatives were deemed to be acceptable, and if:

> the Observing Party informs the Observed Party that denial of access to any portion of the Hazardous Airspace of the Observed Party was not justified on the basis of air safety considerations and in a further event that the matter is not resolved through diplomatic channels, the Observing Party may raise the matter for consideration in the Hungarian–Romanian Open Skies Consultative Commission.[18]

Through these various means, it was hoped that problems of access would be managed within a clear framework.

The Hungarian–Romanian Agreement was not one which was particularly suited to the creation of detailed verification provisions, for the agreement was seen in itself to be in large part an agreement over openness and verification. In the Preamble, it was noted that one of the purposes of the agreement was to 'improve the monitoring of, and thus promote compliance with, current or future arms control measures'.[19] However, there were still measures to ensure verification. The agreement stipulated three areas in which there were to be prohibitions: the flight path of the Observation Aircraft; activities in the Observation Aircraft when conducting Observation Flights; and the equipment of the Observation Aircraft. Under Articles V and VI, the point of entry and exit (i.e. the stipulated airfields) and the arrival and departure fixes (i.e. the point of entry into and exit from the Observed Party's airspace) had to be declared in advance, and compliance with these statements would be verified through national technical means. Under Article X, the Observed Party had the right to place Flight Monitors on board the Observation Aircraft, in order to ensure compliance with the agreement, with 'the right of access to all areas of the Observation Aircraft during the Observation Flight'.[20] Under Article IX:

> When an Observation Flight is conducted using an Observation Aircraft of the Observing Party, upon delivery of the Flight Plan, unless otherwise mutually agreed to by the Observed and Observing Party, the Inspection team of the Observed Party may inspect the Observation Aircraft, accompanied by Inspector Escorts of the Observing Party, to determine whether there is any Prohibited Equipment on the Observation Aircraft.[21]

Thus under the terms of the agreement, each state would have its own team of experts to verify that the behaviour of the other state was within the terms of the agreement.

In terms of regime formation, the agreement was also deep. It sought explicitly to create a regime, with reference to the formation of an Open Skies regime between Hungary and Romania made in three paragraphs of the Preamble. In addition, under Article XVI a joint Open Skies Consultative Commission was established in order to provide a forum for the discussion of complaints concerning compliance, update the annexes as required, and to provide a framework for agreement 'upon such technical and administrative measures, consistent with this Agreement, as may be necessary to ensure the viability and effectiveness of this Agreement'.[22]

The Hungarian–Romanian Agreement on the Establishment of an open skies regime was clearly designed to enhance stability between the two countries in order to reduce the likelihood of war breaking out at time of crisis. This focus on crisis stability was specified in the Preamble, which noted 'the possibility of employing the results of such overflights to improve openness and transparency, to enhance confidence and security building'.[23] The agreement was also a deep one, in which efforts were made to provide detail to which both sides could assent, with carefully drawn up verification provisions, and in the context of attempts to create a long-term regime. In this, the nature of the agreement that was finally settled upon was certainly aided by being within the context of the general negotiations at the end of the cold war, certainly CFE and the more widespread Open Skies talks.

Both the Indian and Pakistani Agreement on the Prohibition of Attack Against Nuclear Installations and Facilities and the Hungarian–Romanian Agreement on the Establishment of an Open Skies regime therefore sought to enhance crisis stability between pairs of states. However, there have also been agreements designed to strengthen arms race stability, and it is to this area that the analysis now turns.

Agreements to strengthen arms race stability

Agreements have been reached on many occasions in which states have sought to avoid a costly arms race in a particular field of weaponry, either by agreeing to prohibit certain forms of weaponry, or by restraining the size of their arsenals. Not only has this been designed in order to obviate the need for large-scale investment in weaponry, but also in order to lessen the degree of militarisation of relations between states, and thereby to reduce the likelihood of war breaking out amongst the parties at some stage in the future. There have been many examples of such agreements, such as the Argentine–Chilean Naval Limitation Convention of 1902, the Central American Arms Limitation Treaty of 1923, and the ABM Treaty of 1972. In the post-cold war period, a significant measure of this sort was agreed between Argentina and Brazil.

Argentine–Brazilian Declaration 1990

The Argentine–Brazilian Declaration on Common Nuclear Policy of Foz do Iguaçú, signed by Presidents Carlos Menem and Fernando Collor de Mello respectively on 28 November 1990, marked a departure from the approach to nuclear capabilities that both states had adopted up to that time. The Declaration has to be seen in the context of both countries' reticence towards the Treaty of Tlatelolco (on creating a nuclear weapons free zone in Latin America) and in terms of the decision of the Argentinians and Brazilians not to sign the Nuclear Non-Proliferation Treaty. However, the two countries had reached a series of joint agreements in the 1980s and 1990s on collaboration over political, economic and nuclear matters.

Neither Argentina nor Brazil had adhered to the Non-Proliferation Treaty nor to the Treaty of Tlatelolco. Both countries rejected membership of the NPT, along with Chile and Cuba, on several grounds: that it was a discriminatory treaty; that it did not address vertical proliferation; that it did not provide sufficient guarantees to the non-nuclear states that they would not be attacked by nuclear countries; and that it would hinder indigenous nuclear developments for civil purposes. Although both states signed the Treaty of Tlatelolco, neither nation had become full members; Argentina had not ratified the treaty, and although Brazil had ratified, it refused to implement the terms of the treaty until all states had ratified it. Further, in the 1970s, both Argentina and Brazil developed their indigenous nuclear programmes to a very great extent. Although there has rarely been conflict involving Argentina and Brazil, and few arguments between the two seemed to offer the possibility of conflict in the near future, international concern had been expressed over the failure of both nations to endorse global attempts to further nuclear non-proliferation. Despite the Peronist tradition in Argentina, which had stressed nationalism and rivalry with Brazil, the nuclear dilemma in the southern cone of Latin America did not appear, therefore, to be as tense as that in South Asia. Further, it was apparent that international advantages might have accrued to both Argentina and Brazil from making some movement on the nuclear non-proliferation issue.

The Declaration was a high point of a great deal of activity between Argentina and Brazil that originated at the very end of the 1970s. In 1979, the two countries signed a treaty concerning possible resolutions to arguments over energy issues and the exploitation of the River Plate basin region. The following year an agreement was reached whereby a Brazilian–German company would provide part of a new Argentine nuclear power reactor, and Argentina agreed to the transfer of nuclear fuels to Brazil. In 1985, the leaders of the two countries agreed that an eventual goal in the nuclear field would be the bilateral inspection of each other's nuclear facilities. In 1986 it was agreed that in the event of a nuclear accident, expertise from both countries would be pooled. Later in the year the development of a joint fast-breeder reactor was agreed. In 1987, a group of high ranking Brazilians led by the President and including representatives of the foreign ministry and the nuclear energy commission visited an Argentine nuclear facility; in 1988 a high level Argentine team visited a Brazilian facility. Thus the Declaration of 1990 has to be seen as a culmination of a series of joint efforts.

There was an important political and economic context to these agreements. Both countries faced growing debt problems from the early 1980s, and this accelerated financial pressures with general reductions in expenditure, including the nuclear field. Such pressures led to both countries working together to generate economic collaboration, a drive which reached a high point with the formation of the Southern Cone Common Market (MERCOSUR) in 1991. It also enlarged the sway of international pressure as financial and debt problems grew, with a consequent increase in the incentives to conform to global non-nuclear norms. This had an important link to the nuclear industry. Both countries faced the loss of nuclear collaborators because Argentina and Brazil stood outside the regime of safeguarded nuclear facilities. First the United States, then Canada, and in 1990 Germany, announced that they would only trade with states who had fully safeguarded facilities.[24]

Hence, for a variety of political and economic reasons, Argentina and Brazil reached an agreement in 1990 that would lead to the further development of arms race stability between the two. The Declaration stated clearly that both Argentina and Brazil renounced the military use of nuclear technology. In the Preamble, the Declaration emphasised 'The importance of the use of nuclear energy solely for peaceful purposes for the scientific, economic and social development of both countries.'[25] It further emphasised the importance of:

> The visits by the Presidents and technical experts of the two countries to each other's nuclear facilities, especially to the uranium enrichment plants at Pilcaniyeu and Iperó and the radiochemical process laboratories at Ezeiza, which are a clear indication of the level of mutual confidence achieved between Argentina and Brazil.[26]

Finally, the Preamble noted the importance of the joint work undertaken in order to establish criteria for the monitoring and 'classification of nuclear materials and facilities and the determination of their importance.'[27]

The Declaration itself covered four main points. First, it was agreed that a Joint Accounting and Control System would be adopted. Second, a series of activities would be carried out within forty-five days of the Declaration:

a.   The exchange of the respective lists describing all their nuclear facilities;
b.   The exchange of the statements of the initial inventories of nuclear material existing in each country;
c.   The first reciprocal inspections of centralised record systems;
d.   The presentation to the International Atomic Energy Agency of the records and reports system which is part of the Joint Accounting and Control System, with a view to bringing it into conformity with the records and reports which both countries submit to the Agency in accordance with the safeguards agreement in force.[28]

Third, both countries would enter into negotiations with the IAEA to try to obtain an agreement on safeguards based on the Joint Accounting and Control System. Finally, the Declaration stipulated that after successful negotiations with the IAEA, Argentina and Brazil would both take the necessary action to bring the Treaty of Tlatelolco fully into force for each country.

This agreement in itself was not particularly deep, but it was significant. Not a great deal of detail was provided, but the Declaration committed both sides to providing much information about their nuclear facilities and inventories of their nuclear materials. The verification provisions in the Declaration were not extensive, but drew upon existing practice and mandated further bilateral inspections, some of which were to happen within forty-five days. Subsequently, all the provisions of the Declaration were implemented within the time limit.

The key issue revolved around regime formation. As already elaborated, the Declaration was part of an ongoing series of developments in the field of nuclear policy between Argentina and Brazil. The Declaration went some way towards codifying that relationship into a regime, and much more in the way of codification was to follow with the Agreement for the Exclusively Peaceful Use of Nuclear Energy, signed by the Foreign Ministers of Argentina and Brazil in Guadalajara, Mexico, in July 1991.[29]

This important follow-up agreement developed further the commitments entered into at Foz do Iguaçú in three important ways.[30] First, the Agreement established the Joint System for Accounting and Control of Nuclear Materials (SCCC).[31] Under Article V, the function of the Common System was to operate so that there would be verification that nuclear materials in all nuclear activities were not diverted into any activities prohibited by the agreement; specifically, of course, nuclear weapons. This verification would take place through initiating a system of records and reports, by taking physical inventories, and by implementing measuring systems and inspections. The second important contribution of the Agreement for the Exclusively Peaceful Use of Nuclear Energy was in the formal establishment of the Argentine–Brazilian Agency for Accounting and Control of Nuclear Materials, with the acronym ABACC.[32] The ABACC, under Articles VI and VII, was to be a joint agency with a legal identity to administer and implement the accounting and control system, the SCCC. Under Article XII, ABACC was to have a Commission which was to be an executive, made up of two representatives from each country, and a Secretariat which would implement the directives of the Commission, designate inspectors from the central list drawn up by the Commission, represent the ABACC in its relations with the states and third parties, and draw up the budget for approval by the Commission. Third, for the first time, Argentina and Brazil rejected the right to carry out peaceful nuclear explosions since, under Article 1.3, 'no technical distinction can be made between nuclear explosive devices for peaceful purposes and those for military purposes'.[33]

Developing this framework further, Argentina and Brazil were able to continue negotiating with the IAEA, as stipulated in the Foz do Iguaçú Declaration, and agreement was reached in December 1991.[34] The agreement, signed by ABACC, Argentina, Brazil and the IAEA meant that full-scope safeguards would operate over the entire nuclear programmes of Argentina and Brazil. The ABACC would implement the SCCC, and the IAEA would apply its safeguards to verify the findings of the ABACC, as well as conducting independent measurements and observations. This agreement was almost identical to the 1957 agreement between the IAEA, EURATOM (European Atomic Energy Commission), and the European non-nuclear weapon states that were members of EURATOM.

The quadripartite agreement between ABACC, Argentina, Brazil and the IAEA was in many ways a culmination of over a decade of growing rapprochement between Argentina and Brazil in political, economic and security matters. In the series of statements and agreements between the two during the 1980s and early 1990s, the Declaration was the key document in the transition from the growing process of Argentine–Brazilian mutual reassurance over their respective nuclear programmes and joint cooperation in the civil nuclear field into a fully developed regime in which both countries were to be associated with global safeguard measures against nuclear proliferation. The regime that Argentina and Brazil developed was a sub-set of the global non-proliferation regime.

In August 1992, these measures allowed both Argentina and Brazil (along with Chile) to introduce amendments to the Treaty of Tlatelolco, and therefore to argue that there should be a movement towards the full implementation of the treaty, and thereby the full introduction of a nuclear weapons-free zone in Latin America.[35] In these important ways, both countries were able to conclusively avoid a nuclear arms race between each other, thus enhancing arms race stability. They were also able to produce something more positive and tangible in creating a good deal of cooperation between themselves in the context of greater efforts at regional economic integration.

One of the most interesting features about the Argentine–Brazilian agreements over nuclear weapons, facilities and materials was that a deep regime was created by a series of agreements. The Declaration was certainly important in this, but it was not sufficient in its own right for the purposes of Argentina and Brazil. The Declaration consolidated a series of measures and provided a framework for further development of a joint regime; in a similar way, the START II Treaty consolidated a series of previous declarations by the Russians and Americans. It is to this treaty that the analysis now turns.

Arms control to enhance both crisis and arms race stability

This chapter has thus far examined arms control treaties that enhanced strategic stability between states either through emphasising crisis stability or arms race stability. The fourth case study of this chapter considers a treaty in which the objective and outcome was to enhance both crisis and arms race stability.

The START II Treaty

The START II Treaty was similar to the Argentine–Brazilian Declaration on Common Nuclear Policy in three respects. First, like the Argentine–Brazilian Declaration, START II sought to replace competition with cooperation. Second, as the Declaration was part of an ongoing process bringing about enhancements to the strategic relationship between Argentina and Brazil, so START II was part of a series of unilateral statements and agreements that sought to strengthen strategic stability between Russia and the United States. Third, as in the Latin American agreement, START II was an agreement that was designed to enhance arms race stability. For START II, enhancing arms race stability had two aspects. The first was to reduce the level of expenditure on nuclear weapons. As President Bush declared in a speech outlining the scale of American cuts, 'The reductions I have approved will save us an additional 50 billion dollars over the next five years ... These cuts are deep, and you must know my resolve: This deep, and no deeper. To do less would be insensible to progress – but to do more would be ignorant of history.'[36] If this was important to the United States, it was even more important to Russia, given the level of economic transformation in the country. Second, START II was designed to create a stability at a lower level of forces that would dramatically reduce the likelihood of war breaking out between the United States and Russia at some stage in the future. As American Secretary of Defense Cheney argued, 'there's a level there that we want to hold at ... It's important to preserve an adequate level in terms of the numbers of submarines we have. I think that's stabilizing, not destabilising'.[37] In addition, the nature of the START II agreement, particularly deMIRVing ICBMs, meant that the treaty also enhanced crisis stability.[38]

START II was thus an important example of an arms control agreement that sought to strengthen strategic stability. Its purpose and scope, therefore, differed to that of START I, which was an example of arms control at the end of major conflict. Whereas START I was in the framework of the end of the cold war, START II was negotiated and signed as Russia and the United States were seeking to develop new stable relations between themselves and amongst the states of the former Soviet Union. In addition, whereas START I produced advantages for the United States as the predominant power at the end of the cold war confrontation, START II was a much more equal treaty. The United States, for example, made major concessions on the size of its bomber and SLBM forces. Although some in Russia rejected START II as unequal, (for the United States would probably be able to deploy a larger number of weapons than Russia), one might assess START II to be more favourable to Russia than had been START I.

This new arms control process between the United States and Russia, refocused upon issues of strategic stability, moved through three stages. First, in January 1992 the United States and Russia announced unilateral reductions. Second, in June1992, Presidents Bush and Yeltsin met in Washington DC and consolidated these announcements into a new framework for reductions. Finally, in January 1993, the START II Treaty was signed which legalised that framework. This section will examine each of these stages.

The first stage of this new process took place in January 1992 when Presidents Bush and Yeltsin announced a series of unilateral reductions, and made a series of offers to the other nation. Bush's announcement was made in his State of the Union address on 28 January 1992. There were two categories in this announcement: immediate and unilateral American moves; and proposals for further reductions should the proposals be accepted in the former Soviet Union. In the first category, Bush declared several changes:

> After completing twenty planes for which we have begun procurement, we will shut down further production of the B–2 bomber. We will cancel the small ICBM program. We will cease production of new warheads for our sea-based ballistic missiles. We will stop all new production of the Peacekeeper missile. And we will not purchase any more advanced cruise missiles.[39]

Bush also made a proposal for a grand bargain. The United States had long feared the power of the Soviet ICBM force and to obtain a reduction in that element of Russian/Commonwealth of Independent States' (CIS's) strategic arsenal, the United States would make further reductions. If the Russians/Commonwealth of Independent States would eliminate all land-based multiple warhead ballistic missiles (i.e., deMIRV its ICBMs), then the United States would:

> eliminate all Peacekeeper missiles. We will reduce the number of warheads on Minuteman missiles to one, and reduce the number of warheads on our sea-based missiles by about one-third. And we will convert a substantial portion of our strategic bombers to primarily conventional use.[40]

President Yeltsin responded the following day, also offering immediate reductions and proposals for further reductions. In terms of immediate disarmament, Yeltsin announced that production of the TU–160 Blackjack and TU–95MS Bear bombers would cease, as would production of existing types of air-launched and sea-launched cruise missiles (ALCMs and SLCMs), and no new types of SLCMs would be developed. Military exercises with large numbers of strategic bombers would be stopped. Air-launched tactical nuclear weapons stockpiles would be halved. In terms of proposals, these fell into two categories: immediate trading of reductions on a bilateral basis; and a future framework for cuts. Yeltsin offered the renunciation of creating new types of ALCMs, renunciation of combat patrols of submarines carrying strategic nuclear weapons, the elimination of all nuclear SLCMs if the United States would agree, and he proposed that all air-launched tactical nuclear weapons should be placed in a central storage area. In addition, he proposed the ending of the two sides targeting each other with nuclear weapons. In terms of creating a framework for future arms control, Yeltsin put forward several ideas. These included new limits of 2000 to 2500 nuclear weapons for each state as a next step, the elimination of anti-satellite systems and the introduction of a ban on such weapons. Yeltsin also suggested that both sides jointly develop and operate a global ballistic missile defence system, agree on ending all nuclear tests, and agree an end to the production of fissile material for nuclear weapons.[41]

The Russian agenda for arms control had been much more wide ranging than the American. In his speech, Yeltsin had included comments on biological, chemical and conventional arms control as well as reductions in nuclear weapons. Subsequently, the Russians also emphasised the importance of including the other nuclear powers in discussions over new global levels of nuclear weapons. In the period before the opening of the second stage with the June 1992 understanding, however, most discussion revolved around the nature of further nuclear reductions at the strategic level between Russia/Commonwealth of Independent States and the United

States. The Americans were successful in ensuring that the arms control agenda remained sufficiently tight so that credible arms control proposals might emerge and be implemented. However, two areas of disagreement emerged. First, the Russians sought reductions to between 2000 and 2500 strategic nuclear warheads; the Americans only to some 4500 to 4700. Second, the Americans sought an agreement over the deMIRVing of the ICBM fleets, whereas the Russians sought the deMIRVing of both the ICBM and SLBM fleets.[42]

These disagreements were resolved in the middle of 1992 through compromise with the Joint Russian–United States Understanding agreed in Washington DC between Presidents Bush and Yeltsin. The Understanding represented an agreement in three major areas. The main part related to further reductions in strategic nuclear arsenals, which were to be implemented in two phases:

> In the first phase, to be completed by the end of the START Treaty's seven-year implementation period, each side will reduce its forces until it deploys no more than 3,800-4,250 strategic nuclear weapons (warheads and bombs). Of this total, no more than 2,160 warheads can be deployed on SLBMs, no more than 1,200 on multiple-warhead ICBMs, and no more than 650 on heavy ICBMs.[43]

The second phase was to be completed by the year 2003, or by the end of 2000 if the United States could assist Russia with the elimination process. In this phase, the total number of strategic nuclear warheads would have to be in the range 3000 to 3500. MIRVed ICBMs were to be completely eliminated, and a maximum of 1750 warheads could be deployed on SLBMs.[44] In the second significant part of the agreement, the START counting rules for bombers was changed. Under START I, each bomber was effectively counted as carrying only one warhead, even though it would be capable of carrying significantly more. Under the revised counting rules, bombers would be counted as having 'the number of nuclear weapons that they are actually equipped to carry'.[45] These reductions, along with this change in counting rules, meant that the real reductions in nuclear weapons would have been a total of two-thirds from START I levels. The third and final major part of the agreement related to strategic defences. Both states agreed to cooperate with each other and any interested allies in developing a global protection scheme against limited ballistic missile attacks, and acknowledged that any movement towards deployment of such asystem might require 'changes to existing treaties', above all the 1972 Anti Ballistic Missile Treaty.[46]

Despite the progress towards the Joint Understanding from the two Presidents' statements in early January, it was to take the rest of the year to complete an agreed text for START II. Partly, this was due to the time consumed by the American Presidential election, and particularly by the resignation of Secretary of State Baker in August in order to manage Bush's re-election campaign. Partly, this was also due to the strength of opposition in Moscow to the Joint Understanding and to the nature of the outline START II Treaty. Opponents argued that providing a range of warhead numbers, and losing the SS–18 while only reducing the strength of the American SLBM force, would mean an end to strategic parity and the emergence of Russian strategic inferiority.

These factors led to a series of compromises in the terms of the START II Treaty that was finally signed by Presidents Bush and Yeltsin in Moscow on 3 January 1993. The Treaty Between the United States of America and the Russian Federation on Further Reduction and Elimination of Strategic Offensive Arms contained eight articles, plus three protocols.

The heart of the treaty was Article I as can be seen in Table 3.1. Both sides agreed to a series of reductions in two phases. The first phase was to be completed within seven years of the entry into force of the START Treaty. The second phase was to be completed no later than 1 January 2003, or by 31 December 2000, provided that the states could agree 'a programme of assistance', which was interpreted as American finance for the elimination of Russian weapons.[47]

Table 3.1   *Warhead limits under START II*

	Aggregate warheads	*SLBMs*	*MIRVed ICBMs*	*Heavy ICBMs*
Phase 1	3800-4250	2160	1200	650
Phase 2	3000-3500	1700-1750	0	0

Source: Compiled by the author from the terms of Article I, reproduced in "START II Supplement' *Arms Control Today* January/February 1993, p. 5.

The START II Treaty reflected a series of compromises between the United States and Russia over the two states' views of their vital interests and over their declared aims. The United States gained concessions over the SS–18, which in Phase II was to be entirely eliminated under Article I; and under Article IV each side could apportion 100 strategic bombers to conventional roles, therefore outside the treaty, as long as they had never been equipped with ALCMs, and were based separately from areas where there were nuclear armed bombers and nuclear weapons. Russia gained concessions over the silos for the SS–18 under Article II, with 90 out of 154 being available for adaption to smaller missiles (an SS–25 type) rather than being destroyed; whereas the maximum warheads that could be removed from a missile was four under START I, it was five under Article III of START II, thus allowing the Russians to keep 105 deMIRVed SS–19s; and a once-only inspection of the American B–2 bomber was authorised in an associated protocol.

START II sought to build upon START I, and the additional level of depth was limited to three significant areas. First, whereas under START I, deployed ballistic missile could be removed from the arsenal by destroying or converting *launchers* (silos for fixed ICBMs, mobile launchers for mobile ICBMs and missile tubes for SLBMs) START II, under Article II, stipulated that the missiles for the SS–18 also had to be destroyed. Further detail was provided in the Protocol on the Elimination of Heavy ICBMs and Conversion of Silo Launchers. Second, Article III altered the START Treaty's rules in allowing each state 'to reduce by more than four warheads, but not more than five warheads attributed to each ICBM out of no more than 105 ICBMs of one existing type of ICBM'.[48] In addition:

> Notwithstanding the number of warheads attributed to a type of ICBM or SLBM inaccordance with the START Treaty, each Party undertakes not to:
> (a) produce, flight test, or deploy an ICBM or SLBM with a number of reentry vehicles greater than the number of warheads attributed to it under this Treaty; and
> (b) to increase the number of warheads attributed to an ICBM or SLBM that has had the number of warheads attributed to it reduced in accordance with the provisions of this Article.[49]

Finally, under Article IV (the longest article, with fourteen paragraphs), new bomber rules were introduced in order to count the number of weapons with which an aircraft was actually equipped, rather than set figures as under START I. Such detail was expanded upon in the Protocol on Heavy Bomber Inspections, and the Memorandum of Understanding on Number of Warheads Attributed to Deployed Heavy Bombers Other than Heavy Bombers Reoriented to a Conventional Role.

In terms of verification, the START II Treaty did not have the depth of START I. There were three reasons for this.[50] First, there was a concern that negotiating more precise verification restrictions would take too long, and an implicit assumption was that speed was still more important than verification depth. Second, any verification regime would have to be mutual, and there was concern in the United States that this might lead to the proliferation of secret information or weapons design information. Third, although an agreed formula for monitoring declared weapons and facilities could be devised, it would have to be very intrusive for it to be effective in ensuring full compliance with the terms of the treaty. Thus, START II relied upon the verification procedures of START I, as made clear in Article V, paragraph 1: 'the provisions of the START Treaty, including the verification provisions, shall be used for implementation of this Treaty'.[51] However, in verification terms, regardless of the political logic for this solution, this was not an ideal arrangement. Many of the reductions would be brought about not through destruction, but by reducing the numbers of warheads deployed on missiles, known as downloading, and by reorienting bombers to conventional roles. Although the political climate made it unlikely, there would therefore be scope for either side to threaten a sizeable breakout capability from the Treaty. Extra measures – such as 'verified commitments to dismantle excess warheads and use the resulting fissile material for peaceful purposes' – were excluded for reasons of speed and cost.[52] However, this meant that the verification provisions of START II were in some senses quite shallow compared to START I.

The commitment to the START regime initiated by START I was very clear in START II. Under Article VI, START II would 'remain in force so long as the START Treaty remains in force'.[53] However, given the expansion of the START Treaty from two parties to five, an issue examined in Chapter Five, a bilateral commitment to the continuation of the regime essentially between the United States and Russia was given in Article V, which stated:

> To promote the objectives and implementation of the provisions of this Treaty, the Parties hereby establish the Bilateral Implementation Commission. The Parties agree that, if either Party so requests, they shall meet within the framework of the Bilateral Commission to:
> (a) resolve questions relating to compliance with the obligations assumed; and
> (b) agree upon such additional measures as may be necessary to improve the viability and effectiveness of this Treaty.[54]

Further commitment towards the development of a regime in this area was evident in the Preamble, in which it was agreed that the furthering of nuclear disarmament and the strengthening of strategic stability contained within the treaty would 'help lay a solid foundation for a world order built on democratic values that would preclude the outbreak of war'.[55]

The START II Treaty produced an agreement that in many ways was more equitable than START I, although it was greeted with more overt hostility in Moscow than the earlier treaty had been.[56] Each side would have to give up weapons in categories which it valued the most, although the effect of the implementation of START II would probably lead to the United States deploying 3500 warheads, and Russia around 3000.[57] However, the United States had made significant concessions, for the change in the bomber counting rules would mean that the real reductions between START I and START II would be greater for the United States, while the United States would also have to reduce its valued SLBM fleet by one half, rather than the one-third which American military leaders had hoped for.

START II was clearly a treaty designed to enhance strategic stability between two states. Unlike the other agreements examined in this section, however, START II enhanced both arms race stability and crisis stability. In terms of arms race stability, START II allowed both Russia and the United States to create a framework for limiting any arms race between themselves, and also a framework for disarmament in which real financial savings would be made. The Congressional Budget Office estimated that START II might save the United States up to $3.5 billion in addition to savings from unilateral cuts and the START I Treaty.[58] Savings of a large magnitude would also be likely in Russia, although there would be real costs involved in terms of the destruction of nuclear weapons. The implication of this was that the political process of enhancing cooperative security relations between the two states would be enhanced. START II also strengthened crisis stability. The ban on MIRVed ICBMs contained in Article I had been sought by many in the United States for two decades, convinced that they were the most destabilising systems. MIRVed missiles could threaten a variety of targets, and were therefore lucrative targets in their own right. Above all, fixed ICBMs were vulnerable and desirable targets, while themselves offering high levels of accuracy and destructiveness. In a crisis, temptations to pre-empt the MIRVed element of the opponent's arsenal could, thus, be high. Hence, agreement to eliminate this portion of both the American and Russian fleets would remove tempting targets should a military crisis occur between the two. The aim of START II, according to the Preamble, was to 'enhance strategic stability and predictability, and, in doing so, to reduce further strategic offensive arms'.[59] Yet as seen above, the means selected for achieving this end were relatively shallow. The emphasis on speed over depth was, however, only possible in the context of building upon the regime initiated by the first START Treaty.

Conclusion

The agreements examined in this chapter illustrate the significance of enhancing strategic stability in adversarial relationships. It illuminates also the dissimilarities in the nature of various relationships. India and Pakistan, and to a lesser extent, Hungary and Romania, were concerned about crisis instability, and thus sought to gain reassurance from arms control agreements. On the other hand, given different political relations, Argentina and Brazil were clearly not concerned by crisis instability, but the insecurities inherent in a potential arms race. Finally, the START II Treaty between Russia and the United States demonstrated a relationship in which both crisis and arms race instability were concerns.

The four agreements examined in this chapter all demonstrated significant differences. In terms of depth, the Indian–Pakistani Agreement was very shallow, START II shallow (certainly in comparison with START I),

political tension reducing

and the Argentine–Brazilian Declaration and subsequent agreements very deep. The Hungarian–Romanian Agreement was different in that it was about verification and transparency, and yet even within those terms it was a fairly deep arrangement. Much of this can be understood by the context. The conditions for the Indian–Pakistani Agreement were not very supportive. It was the first agreement between the states for sixteen years, and the two states were not party to other multilateral negotiations over nuclear assurances. In contrast, although the history of Hungarian–Romanian collaboration did not appear to be strong, the agreement over an open skies regime took place in a much more supportive multilateral environment, in which regional arms control was both dynamic and at the point of producing substantial agreements. Argentina and Brazil were able to work towards agreement in the context of work already undertaken at the IAEA, and through the Treaty of Tlatelolco. Thus arms control is clearly more viable, and appears to be capable of producing greater depth, when there is a generally supportive environment of arms control either at the regional or global level.

Notes

1   For a review of Indian–Pakistani relations in this period see, for example, Barry Buzan, Gowher Rizvi and Rosemary Foot *South Asian Insecurity and the Great Powers* London: Macmillan, 1986; Edmundo Fujita 'The Prevention of the Geographical Spread of Nuclear Weapons: Nuclear Weapons Free Zones and Zones of Peace in the Southern Hemisphere' *UNIDIR Research Report 4* New York, 1989; Helen Leigh-Phippard 'Nuclear Weapons Free Zones: Problems and Prospects' *Arms Control: Contemporary Security Policy* Vol. 14, No. 2, 1993; Shekhar Gupta 'India Redefines its Role' *Adelphi Paper 293* OUP for IISS, 1995; Paul Dibb 'Towards a New Balance of Power in Asia' *Adelphi Paper 295* OUP for IISS, 1995; George H. Quester 'Some Pakistani Problems and a Nuclear Non-Solution' *The Journal of Strategic Studies* Vol. 8, No. 4, December 1985; Ashok Kapur *Pakistan's Nuclear Development* London: Croom Helm, 1987; Zalmay Khalilzad 'India's Bomb and the Stability of South Asia' *Asian Affairs* Vol. 5, No. 2 1977; Leonard S. Spector with Jaqueline Smith *Nuclear Ambitions: The Spread of Nuclear Weapons 1989–90* Boulder, CO: Westview 1990; and K. Subrahmanyam *India and the Nuclear Challenge* New Delhi: Lancer, 1986.
2   The text of the agreement is reproduced in Newsbrief, No. 6, University of Southampton: Programme for Promoting Nuclear Non-Proliferation, July 1989.
3   *Ibid.*
4   *Ibid.*
5   See Susan M. Burns 'South Asia: India and Pakistan' in Richard D. Burns (editor) *Encyclopedia of Arms Control* New York: Charles Scribner, 1993.
6   See Erik Goldstein *Wars and Peace Treaties 1816–1991* London: Routledge, 1992, pp. 47–8.
7   On Hungarian–Romanian relations during the cold war and in its immediate

aftermath, see, for example, Gerard Holden *The Warsaw Pact: Soviet Security and Bloc Politics* Oxford: Basil Blackwell, 1991; Jonathan Eyal (editor) *The Warsaw Pact and the Balkans* London: Macmillan for RUSI, 1989; Jonathan Eyal 'Central and Eastern Europe' in Alex Pravda (editor) *Yearbook of Soviet Foreign Relations: 1991 Edition* London: I. B. Taurus, 1991; and Istvan Gyarmati 'A Hungarian Security Policy for the 1990s' *Defense and Disarmament Alternatives* Vol. 3, No. 4, 1990.

8 See, for example, Adrian Hyde-Price 'East Central Europe in the 1990s' *Arms Control: Contemporary Security Policy* Vol. 12, No. 2, 1991, especially pp. 292–7; more implicitly, see Trevor Taylor 'NATO and Central Europe' *NATO Review* Vol. 39, No. 5, 1991.

9 Article II, paragraphs 1, 2 and 3. The text of the agreement is reproduced in Richard D. Burns *Encyclopedia*, pp. 1537–42.

10 Article III, paragraphs 1 and 2. *Ibid.*

11 Article I, paragraph 11. *Ibid.*

12 Article I, paragraph 12. *Ibid.*

13 *Ibid.*

14 *Ibid.*

15 Article I paragraph 5. *Ibid.*

16 Article VIII paragraph 1. *Ibid.*

17 Article VIII, paragraphs 5, 6 and 7. *Ibid.*

18 Article VIII, paragraph 8. *Ibid.*

19 *Ibid.*

20 *Ibid.*

21 Observing Parties could either use their own aircraft, or an aircraft of the Observed Party. *Ibid.*

22 Article XVI, paragraph 4(a). *Ibid.*

23 *Ibid.*

24 There is a great deal of material on the nuclear relationship between Argentina and Brazil. Much of this section is drawn from the following: Ruth Stanley 'Cooperation and Control: The New Approach to Nuclear Non-proliferation in Argentina and Brazil' *Arms Control: Contemporary Security Policy* Vol. 13, No. 2, 1992; Virginia Gamba-Stonehouse 'Argentina and Brazil' in Regina Cowen Karp (editor) *Security with Nuclear Weapons? Different Perspectives on National Security* Oxford University Press for SIPRI, 1991; John Redick 'Argentina and Brazil: An Evolving Nuclear Relationship' *PPNN Occasional Paper* University of Southampton: Programme for Promoting Nuclear Non-Proliferation, July 1990; John Redick 'Nuclear Restraint in Latin America: Argentina and Brazil' *PPNN Occasional Paper* University of Southampton: Programme for Promoting Nuclear Non-Proliferation, June 1988; J. Goldemberg 'Brazil' in Joseph Goldblat (editor) *Nuclear Proliferation: The Why and the Wherefore* London: Taylor and Francis, 1985; M. Hirst and H. E. Bocco 'Nuclear Cooperation in the Context of the Programme for Argentine–Brazilian Integration and Cooperation' in P. Leventhal and S. Tanzer (editors) *Averting a Latin American Nuclear Arms Race* Macmillan in association with the Nuclear Control Institute, 1992; and David Albright 'Brazil comes in from the cold' *Arms Control Today* December 1990.

25 The text is reproduced in Richard D. Burns *Encyclopedia*, p. 1473.

26 *Ibid.*
27 *Ibid.*
28 *Ibid.*
29 The text of this agreement is reproduced in IAEA, INFCIRC/395, 26 November 1991.
30 On this, see Ruth Stanley 'Co-operation', pp. 192–4.
31 The SCCC referred to Sistema Commún de Contabilidad y Control de Materiales Nucleares.
32 ABACC stands for Agencia Brasileño-Argentina de Contabilidad y Control de Materiales Nucleares.
33 Quoted in Ruth Stanley 'Co-operation', p. 193.
34 For the text of the agreement, see UN Conference on Disarmament, CD/1118, 22 January 1992.
35 See *Strategic Survey 1992–1993* London: International Institute for Strategic Studies, May 1993, p. 217.
36 The text of the speech is excerpted in 'President George Bush's State of the Union Address' *Survival* Vol. 34, No. 2, 1992, p. 121.
37 Quoted in Ivo H. Daalder and Terry Terriff 'Nuclear Arms Control: Finishing the Cold War Agenda' in a special issue of *Arms Control: Contemporary Security Policy* entitled *Rethinking the Unthinkable: New Directions for Nuclear Arms Control*, Vol. 14, No. 1, 1993, p. 18.
38 DeMIRVing referred to reducing the number of warheads on each missile to one.
39 See Bush's State of the Union Address *Survival*.
40 *Ibid.*
41 See 'Russian Arms Control Initiatives, 29 January 1992' in *Survival*, pp. 122–4.
42 See, for example, 'Baker, Kozyrev Discuss Deep Cuts' *Arms Control Today* Vol. 22, No. 2, 1992 and Ivo H. Daalder and Terry Terriff 'Nuclear Arms Control'.
43 'US–Russian Joint Understanding on Strategic Offensive Arms' *Survival* Vol. 34, No. 3, 1992, pp. 136–7.
44 *Ibid.*
45 *Ibid.*
46 See 'US–Russian Statement on a Global Protection System' *Survival* Vol. 34, No. 3, 1992, p. 137.
47 The Treaty is reproduced in 'START II Supplement' *Arms Control Today* January/February 1993, pp. 5–8. This quotation comes from Article I, paragraph 6: *ibid.*, p. 5. On interpretation, see, for example, 'START II Executive Summary', *ibid.*, p. 3.
48 Article III, paragraph 2 (c); *ibid.*, p. 6.
49 Article III, paragraph 3; *ibid.*
50 See Ivo H. Daalder and Terry Terriff 'Nuclear Arms Control'.
51 *Ibid.*
52 Dunbar Lockwood 'Strategic Nuclear Forces under START II' *Arms Control Today* December 1992, p. 13.
53 Article VI, paragraph 3; *ibid.*
54 Article V, paragraph 2; *ibid.*

55 Preamble; *ibid.*, p. 5.
56 See, for example, Dunbar Lockwood 'The Penchant for Peace' *Bulletin of the Atomic Scientists* Vol. 48, No. 8, 1992; Ivo H. Daalder and Terry Terriff 'Nuclear Arms Control', pp. 18–20; George Leopold 'Russian Military May Hamper START' *Defense News* 7–13 September 1992; Dunbar Lockwood 'Bush, Yeltsin sign START II' *Arms Control Today* January/February 1993, p. 19; Sergey M. Rogov 'The Evolution of Strategic Stability and the Future of Nuclear Weapons' *Arms Control: Contemporary Security Policy* Vol. 14, No. 2, 1993.
57 For an assessment of the post-START II force posture, see *The Military Balance 1992–1993* London: International Institute for Strategic Studies, 1992, especially p. 226; and Dunbar Lockwood 'Strategic Nuclear Forces under START II', especially p. 13.
58 This included measures that although not mandated by the Treaty, might be seen as consistent with the Treaty: for example, reducing the size of the Department of Energy's warhead production along with intelligence capabilities. See Dunbar Lockwood 'Strategic Nuclear Forces under START II', p. 14.
59 Preamble; *ibid.*, p. 5.

4

Arms control to create norms of behaviour

Introduction

In Chapter 1 it was argued that over the past thousand years a number of agreements and treaties can be identified that have sought to create or modify norms in international relations, particularly as they affected the use of arms. It was further argued that these agreements may be divided into three categories relating to: prohibitions on certain uncivilised types of weapons; norms protecting and defining non-combatants; and prohibitions on the resort to warfare in certain geographically defined areas.

In the first case, efforts can be identified that have sought to contain the destructive effect of warfare by prohibiting the use of certain weapons. This has itself taken two forms. In the majority of cases, there has been a focus on a particular type of weapon, the use of which has been deemed to be unacceptable, or uncivilised. Examples of prohibitions on the use of such weapons might include the Declaration of St Petersburg in 1868 and the 1925 Geneva Protocol. Less common have been attempts to define not just the use of certain types of weapons as unacceptable or uncivilised, but to go much further and prohibit any recourse to armed conflict, as in the Fourth Lateran Council of 1215, the Kellogg–Briand Pact of 1928 and the Saavedra Lamas Treaty of 1933.

In the second category, policy-makers have sought to create rules for the identification and treatment of non-combatants. Over time, the definition of non-combatants expanded and developed from a focus on the clergy in the early medieval period, to later include merchants and women, to rules governing the conduct of an occupying army, and the proclamation of norms governing the treatment of wounded soldiers and prisoners of war. Examples of such agreements would include the Peace of God, proclaimed by Guy of Anjou in 990, the Hague Conventions of 1899 and 1907, the Red Cross Convention of 1929 on the Amelioration of the Condition of the Wounded and Sick of Armies in the Field, and the

Convention on Treatment of Prisoners of War of 1929.

Finally, the third form of arms control designed to create norms of behaviour related to the identification of areas in which conflict is deemed to be illegitimate. This originated in medieval Europe with ecclesiastical declarations on protecting church property. Later examples would include the Clayton–Bulwer Treaty of 1850, and the 1881 Straits of Magellan Treaty.

Across a long period of history, human agency has sought to place limitations on the nature of warfare, through the definition of acceptable targets that may be attacked with those which are deemed to be acceptable weapons. Despite the bitterness of the East–West conflict and the intensity of the ideological dispute throughout the cold war period these prohibitions were extended and developed further.

Developments during the cold war

During the cold war, arms control agreements were reached in all these various categories. In terms of prohibitions of weapons types, three examples may be given from the cold war era. First, United Nations General Assembly Resolution 1,653 of 24 November 1961, which prohibited the use of nuclear weapons. Second, in 1972 the Biological Weapons Convention was signed.[1] In the Preamble, the Convention declared that the signatories were:

> Determined, for the sake of all mankind, to exclude completely the possibility of bacteriological (biological) agents and toxins being used as weapons,
> Convinced that such use would be repugnant to the conscience of mankind and that no effort should be spared to minimize this risk.[2]

Having declared biological weapons to be uncivilised, Article I prohibited states from developing, stockpiling or producing biological agents or weapons, and Article II committed states to destroy any previously existing stockpiles of such items. A final example would be the United Nations Convention on Restricting Excessively Injurious or Indiscriminate Conventional Weapons of 1981.[3] This Convention stipulated in the Preamble that:

> the civilian population and the combatants shall at all times remain under the protection and authority of the principles of international law derived from established custom, from the principles of humanity and from the dictates of public conscience ... Reaffirming the need to continue the codification and progressive development of the rules of international law applicable in armed conflict.[4]

The Convention, in a series of Protocols, prohibited the use of weapons which threatened to leave non-detectable fragments, and set restrictions on the use of mines, booby traps, and incendiary weapons. However, during the cold war, unlike the inter-war period, and indeed the medieval period, there were no clear prohibitions on the recourse to warfare itself.

In the second category, further restrictions were placed around the treatment of non-combatants. The most important of these agreements were the Geneva Conventions of 1949 on Wounded and Sick in the Armed Forces in the Field, on the Amelioration of the Condition of Wounded, Sick and Shipwrecked Members of Armed Forces at Sea, on the Treatment of Prisoners of War, and on the Protection of Civilian Persons in Time of War.[5] Further examples related to United Nations General Assembly Resolutions in 1968 on the necessity of applying basic humanitarian principles in all armed conflicts (Resolution 2444), and in 1970 on the protection of civilians in conflict (Resolution 2675).[6]

The third and final category, relating to prohibitions on the use of weapons and resort to conflict in specified geographical areas, was also advanced during the cold war period, with one example being the Antarctic Treaty of 1959. Other examples include the Outer Space Treaty of 1967, in which under Article IV states agreed 'not to place in orbit around the Earth any objects carrying nuclear weapons or any other kinds of weapons of mass destruction, install such weapons on celestial bodies, or station such weapons in outer space in any other manner'.[7] As a final example, under Article I of the Seabed Treaty of 1971, states agreed:

> not to emplant or emplace on the seabed and the ocean floor and in the subsoil thereof beyond the outer limit of a seabed zone ... any nuclear weapons or any other types of weapons of mass destruction as well as structures, launching installations or any other facilities specifically designed for storing, testing or using such weapons.[8]

Thus, during the cold war period, norms of behaviour relating to the control of arms were continued and developed along the lines of the historical development of the rules of war. However, there was one important area in which these rules and norms developed in a way different to previous experience. Arms control practice during the cold war not only continued the deepening of arms control designed to create norms of behaviour, it also widened those norms into a new area: confidence- and security-building measures (CSBMs).

The purpose of CSBMs has been to create confidence either bilaterally or multilaterally that mechanisms exist to illustrate to potential adversaries that military activities are defensive, and for the provision of information regarding the defensive nature of the military activities of any adversary. That is, the aim of confidence- and security-building measures has been to create expectations that a state or group of states can gain sufficient advance notification of the military activities of the potential adversary that fears of a surprise attack would be significantly reduced over a period of time. In addition, if the leaders of a state calculate that their adversary has misinterpreted their actions, CSBMs would create a possibility for direct communication, thus reducing fears on all sides. Over time, the successful introduction of confidence- and security-building measures should, therefore, reduce the intensity in relations characterised by deep political rivalry. CSBMs thereby provide reassurance to a state about the behaviour of its potential adversary; allow that state to reassure its adversary that its intentions are not aggressive; and provide reassurance to all states involved that there are mechanisms for communication to prevent accidents and misunderstandings from escalating into direct conflict. Confidence- and security-building measures have, therefore, been concerned with creating a war avoidance regime between states. It has not been assumed that they could prevent a premeditated aggressor from attacking its neighbours; rather, a CSBM regime would give those neighbours prior warning of adverse military activities, and allow them an opportunity to clarify with the potential aggressor whether its actions were deliberate or miscalculated.[9] These CSBMs can be divided into three groups: the provision of information; the establishment of rules of conduct; and creation of modes of direct communication. During the cold war, agreements were reached in each of these categories.

First, three cold war agreements can be identified in terms of CSBMs designed to provide information that adversaries are not preparing to launch a surprise attack, and to establish assurances that accidents would not escalate into a major war. Part of both the Agreement Between the United States and Soviet Union on the Prevention of Incidents On and Over the High Sea of 1972, and the United Kingdom–Soviet Union Agreement on the Prevention of Incidents at Sea Beyond the Territorial Sea of 1986 were, in part, concerned with providing information. Article VI, paragraph 1, of the American–Soviet Agreement, and Article VI of the British–Soviet Agreement stipulated that the Parties to the agreements had to give between three and five days advance notification of actions 'which represent a danger to navigation or to aircraft in flight'.[10] Under Article VII of both agreements 'The Parties shall exchange in a timely manner appropriate information concerning instances of collisions, incidents which result in damage, [and/or] other incidents at sea between ships and aircraft of the Parties.'[11]

The most far-reaching version of this form of agreement was the Document of the Stockholm Conference on Confidence and Security Building Measures and Disarmament in Europe of 1986. The purpose of the Document, as stated in paragraph ninety-nine, was to produce CSBMs which would 'reduce the dangers of armed conflict and misunderstanding or miscalculation of military activities.'[12] This extensive agreement stipulated that states in NATO and the Warsaw Pact had to provide prior notification of certain military activities. In the zone of application, defined in Annexe I to cover the land and air-space of Europe along with adjoining sea areas, states had to give forty-two days advance notice of movements of military forces of at least 13,000 troops including support forces, or at least 300 battle tanks.[13] Further, military exercises of over 40,000 troops had to be notified by 15 November of the previous calendar year to the one in which the exercise was planned. Should military manoeuvres of this magnitude be carried out, all other states could send observers to witness all notifiable military activities. The agreement included thirty-five paragraphs on verification and compliance. The extensive Stockholm Document was one of the most significant arms control achievements of the cold war period. It allowed for a deep level of detailed on-site inspection, on which agreement had not previously been thought possible. The Stockholm Document also created an environment in which it would have been extraordinarily difficult for any state or group of states to build up sufficient forces to threaten an invasion of another state without that target state being alerted to the danger.

The second function of confidence- and security-building measures is to create rules of conduct. To a certain extent, this was a part of both the Agreement Between the United States and Soviet Union on the Prevention of Incidents On and Over the High Sea of 1972, and the United Kingdom–Soviet Union Agreement on the Prevention of Incidents at Sea Beyond the Territorial Sea of 1986. Both agreements sought to strengthen 'rules of the road' in order to minimise risks of naval confrontations through misjudgements. Four other agreements also fit into this category of confidence- and security-building measures. In 1971 the United States and Soviet Union signed the Agreement on Measures to Reduce the Risk of Outbreak of Nuclear War. Article II of this Agreement stipulated that each state would notify the other 'in the event of an accidental, unauthorized or any other unexplained incident involving the possible detonation of a nuclear weapon which could create a risk of outbreak of nuclear war'.[14] Under Article III, 'The Parties undertake to notify each other immediately in the event of detection by missile warning systems of unidentified objects.'[15] Under Article IV, 'Each Party undertakes to notify the other Party in advance of any planned missile launches if such launches will extend beyond its national territory in the direction of the other Party.'[16] Finally, under Article V, 'Each Party, in other situations involving unexplained nuclear incidents, undertakes to act in such a manner as to reduce the possibility of its actions being misinterpreted by the other Party.'[17] The United Kingdom–Soviet Union Agreement on the Prevention of Accidental Nuclear War of 1977 was a similar, although shorter, document.[18] The United States–Soviet Union Agreement on the Prevention of Nuclear War in 1973 was, if anything, less specific. It was a declaration that both states sought to avoid a nuclear war between them, would renounce the use of force in their diplomatic relations, and seek consultations should a crisis occur.[19] In the Agreement Between France and the Soviet Union on the Prevention of the Accidental or Unauthorised Launch of Nuclear Weapons, effected by an exchange of letters on 16 July 1976, both states agreed to notify the other in the event of nuclear accidents that could or had led to nuclear explosion, and to take steps to lessen the possibilities for misunderstanding.[20] All of these agreements sought in some way to establish or strengthen guidelines for security policy.

The third category of confidence- and security-building measures developed during the cold war concerned the creation of direct lines of communication and explanation. Most famously, this related to the establishment of 'Hot Lines'. The first of these agreements was the United States-Soviet Union Memorandum of Understanding Regarding the Establishment of a Direct Communications Link, signed in 1963.[21] A similar agreement was signed by France and the Soviet Union in 1966.[22] A further agreement was reached by the United Kingdom and Soviet Union in 1967.[23] In 1971, the United States–Soviet Union Agreement on Measures to Improve the Direct Communications Link was signed, adding satellite communications to the telegraph system established by the 1963 Agreement.[24] A further upgrading of the link was agreed upon in the 1984 United States–Soviet Union Memorandum of Understanding on the Direct Communications Link.[25] Finally, the United States–Soviet Union Nuclear Risk Reduction Centers Agreement of 1987 established Centres in both Washington DC and Moscow to transmit information required by the 1972 Prevention of Incidents On and Over the High Seas Agreement and the 1971 Agreement on Measures to Reduce the Risk of Outbreak of Nuclear War.[26] Protocol II attached to the agreement set out technical specifications of the requirements of the two centres so as to maximise the ability to exchange information.

During the cold war, therefore, not only did the traditional forms of arms control designed to create norms of behaviour develop further, but an additional type – the CSBM – was added. The rest of this chapter will examine the nature of arms control agreements that have sought to develop norms of behaviour in the post-cold war environment.

Arms control, norms of behaviour and the post-cold war world

Relatively few agreements were signed in the immediate post-cold war period that were directly concerned with creating and strengthening norms of behaviour. Indeed, only five agreements are immediately apparent: the 1989 United States–Soviet Union Agreement on the Prevention of Dangerous Military Activities; the 1989 United States–Soviet Union Agreement on the Notification of Strategic Exercises; the 1992 Open Skies Treaty; the 1992 CFE 1A Agreement; and the Vienna Documents of the CSCE. What is clear from these agreements is that the arms control activity in this sphere at the beginning of the post-cold war period was very narrow. None of these agreements had any connection with the traditional agenda – relating to prohibitions on certain uncivilised types of weapons, to norms protecting and defining non-combatants, and to prohibitions on the resort to warfare in certain geographically defined areas. Instead, these agreements were concerned with the cold war innovation – CSBMs. Further, it is apparent that four of these agreements – the 1989 United States–Soviet Union Agreement on the Notification of Strategic Exercises; the 1992 Open Skies Treaty; the 1992 CFE 1A Agreement; and the Vienna Documents – were concerned with CSBMs relating to the provision of information through greater openness. The 1989 United States–Soviet Union Agreement on the Prevention of Dangerous Military Activities was related to CSBMs designed to create or strengthen rules of conduct. None of these agreements related to the creation of modes of direct communication. In the remaining section of this chapter, each of these agreements will be examined in turn.

The US–Soviet Agreement on Strategic Exercises

The United States–Soviet Union Agreement on the Notification of Strategic Exercises was signed in September 1989, and, under Article VI, came into force on 1 January 1990.[27] The essence of the agreement was in Article I, which stated that 'On the basis of reciprocity, each Party shall notify the other Party no less than fourteen days in advance about the beginning of one major strategic force exercise which includes the participation of heavy bomber aircraft to be held during each calendar year.'[28]

The agreement was a short and shallow one, comprising only six brief articles. Information was to be provided through the Nuclear Risk Reduction Centres, which had been agreed upon two years previously. Article III committed both states to consultations over future developments, and under Article V was to be of unlimited duration.

That this limited agreement was concerned with CSBMs in terms of the provision of information was entirely clear from its terms and the Preamble, which stated that the governments sought this agreement in order to affirm 'their desire to reduce and ultimately eliminate the risk of outbreak of nuclear war, in particular as a result of misinterpretation, miscalculation or accident'.[29] But if this was a brief and shallow agreement, the same could certainly not be said of the Open Skies Treaty.

Treaty on Open Skies

In 1955 at the Geneva Conference of Heads of Government President Eisenhower had suggested that an agreement should be reached that would allow the United States and Soviet Union the ability to engage in unimpeded aerial reconnaissance over the territory of the other superpower. For Eisenhower, this would:

convince the world that we are providing as between ourselves against the possibility of great surprise attack, thus lessening the danger and relaxing tension. Likewise we will make more easily attainable a comprehensive and effective system of inspection and disarmament, because what I propose, I assure you, would be but a beginning.[30]

However, this beginning was dismissed by the Soviet Union as representing American designs for greater espionage.

Thirty-four years later an American President again proposed an agreement to produce Open Skies as a new beginning. Two clear advantages seemed to accompany such an initiative. First, although both superpowers possessed sophisticated surveillance satellites, those satellites were less manoeuvrable and reactive than aircraft. Thus, more information could be provided, and the agreement could act to enhance confidence much as Eisenhower had suggested. Second, sophisticated surveillance satellites were essentially limited to the capabilities of the two major military powers. If more states in Europe could obtain sophisticated information, it might stabilise relations between states that, with the ending of the cold war, could otherwise be tempted to worry greatly about the military activity of their neighbours.

Negotiations began in early 1990. They were given a boost by the speedy completion of the CFE Treaty, which lacked any aerial inspection regime, as well as the unification of Germany which did much to clear some of the agenda to allow a focus on Open Skies. Equally significantly, the importance of aerial inspections became clear over the winter of 1990-1 as it became apparent that before the signing of the CFE Treaty, the Soviet Union had moved vast amounts of material east of the Urals and, thereby, beyond the scope of the CFE regime. For many NATO countries, an Open Skies regime would have proved greatly reassuring in being able to monitor the shape and configuration of the Soviet military beyond the Urals.[31]

The course of the negotiations over the next eighteen months reflected the increasing desire of the NATO countries to obtain an agreement in this area, and the growing difficulty of producing a treaty as the Soviet Union began its final and terminal collapse. The NATO countries made three important concessions. First, NATO countries accepted the desirability of sharing raw data with all countries in the regime, rather than limit it to themselves. Second, they agreed to restrain the technological capabilities of the sensors that would implement the monitoring, as some states feared that the Western countries would be able to gain more information due to the higher quality of their equipment. Third, the NATO countries agreed that when an overflight was being carried out, the host nations' aircraft could be used. This was designed to reassure the Soviet Union, who feared that otherwise secret monitoring devices could be placed on the observation aircraft. Despite further difficulties over negotiations, the delay caused by the collapse of the Soviet Union, and then the haste to complete within the deadline of 24 March 1992, these compromises proved to be the basis of a long and complex treaty.

The Treaty on Open Skies commits all the signatories to accept intrusive overflights at short notice – a minimum of seventy-two hours – of its entire territory, with any information generated available to all the signatories. The national allocations are indicated in Table 4.1. The area to be covered was more extensive than that envisaged in the CFE Treaty. Whereas CFE covered the zone from the Atlantic to the Urals, Open Skies covered the area from Vancouver to Vladivostok. States could engage in observation flights (the active quota) within the limits of those flights it had to receive from other states (the passive quota). However, states could transfer their active quota to others, subject to general agreement, and no individual state could use 50 per cent of its active quota in overflying one other state. Section II of the treaty allowed states to form groups for the purposes of the Open Skies regime. Three groups were formed, with varying degrees of integration: Russia and Belarus; the countries of the West European Union; and Belgium, Luxembourg and the Netherlands, which formed a very tight group with a single point of entry for flights over their territory.[32]

Table 4.1   *Open Skies allocation of passive quotas*[a]

State	Quota	State	Quota
United States	42	Russia–Belarus	42
Canada	12	France	12
Germany	12	Italy	12
Turkey	12	Ukraine	12
United Kingdom	12	Norway	7
Benelux[b]	6	Denmark	6
Poland	6	Romania	6
Bulgaria	4	Czech & Slovak	4
Greece	4	Hungary	4
Iceland	4	Spain	4
Portugal	2	Georgia[c]	—

Notes:

[a] Figures upon full implementation; only 75 per cent valid during first three years.

[b] Belgium, Luxembourg and the Netherlands.

[c] Quota decided after signature of the treaty.

Source: From Peter Jones 'Open Skies: A New Era of Transparency' *Arms Control Today* May 1992, p. 13.

The Open Skies Treaty was a very deep arms control agreement. There was a large amount of detail – the total text of the treaty, including annexes, ran to over 100 pages – with much technical information and many definitions. This was particularly important as the technical information was vital to obtaining agreement, and to limiting the amount of information that could be obtained through the Open Skies regime. The treaty stipulated the nature of the sensors to be acceptable under the regime in Article IV, thus limiting the amount of information that could be gathered under the technical maximum. States could use their own aircraft for observations, although if the recipient country insisted, the observing party would have to use an aircraft belonging to the hosts. In any case, observation aircraft had to be designated as such in advance.

The verification provisions of the Open Skies Treaty in a sense relate to the whole treaty, for as the Preamble stated, all saw 'the possibility of employing such a regime to improve openness and transparency, to facilitate the monitoring of compliance with existing or future arms control agreements'.[33] The central verification provisions related to the aircraft, sensors and personnel that would conduct the observation. The aircraft had to be designated in advance, and there was much technical information on the general provisions relating to the sensors, including the output, in Articles IV and IX along with the appendices. Section IV of Article IX stipulated that:

> Each State Party shall have the right to request and receive from the observing Party copies of data collected by sensors during an observation flight. Such copies will be in the form of first generation duplicates produced from the original data collected by the sensors during an observation flight.[34]

However, the nature of the sensors was stipulated, thus limiting the amount of information that could be gathered by the more technologically advanced states: only optical panoramic and framing cameras; video cameras with real-time display; infra-red, line-scanning devices; and synthetic aperture radars could be used.[35]

Once the observing party arrived, a mission plan had to be submitted including the route and distances involved. Within twenty-four hours the mission was to begin, and it was to be completed within ninety-six hours. Importantly, 'The mission plan may provide for an observation flight that allows for the observation of any point on the entire territory of the observed Party, including areas designated by the observed Party as hazardous airspace.'[36] No part of the territory of a state could be placed out of bounds to observation.

One of the most important aspects of the treaty was the creation of a regime. This was made explicit in Article I, paragraph 1, which stated that 'This Treaty establishes the regime, to be known as the Open Skies regime, for the conduct of observation flights by States Parties over the territories of other States Parties, and sets forth the rights and obligations of the States Parties relating thereto.'[37] In order to ensure the smooth working and development of the regime, the Open Skies Consultative Commission was set up through Article X. The role of the Commission was to:

(A) consider questions relating to compliance with the provisions of the Treaty; (B) seek to resolve ambiguities and differences of interpretation that may become apparent in the way this Treaty is implemented; (C) consider and take decisions on applications for accession to this Treaty; and (D) agree as to those technical and administrative measures, pursuant to the provisions of this Treaty, deemed necessary following the accession to this Treaty by other states.[38]

However, the Commission had two other important roles. First, the Commission itself could propose amendments to the treaty under Article X paragraph 5, in accordance with Article XVI. Second, under Section IV of Annexe L, if proposed by one of the States Parties, consideration could be given in the Commission 'for the use of the Open Skies regime in additional specific fields, such as the environment'.[39] Thus the Commission was given an important role not only in ensuring that the regime operated effectively, but also in extending the scope of the regime into new areas.

The Treaty on Open Skies was thus concerned with confidence and security building in terms of the provision of information. Although only a modest addition to the capabilities of Russia and the United States, it would provide enormous opportunities for other countries in Europe not only in that these other countries would be able to carry out observation flights themselves, but also in that they would be able to gain access to the raw data of other states' observations. Particularly for the post-communist and post-Soviet states of central and eastern Europe, this offered significant CSBM possibilities. One of the key features was the short-notice provisions for observation flights. Although seventy-two hours notice had to be given (this would allow possible coordination if more than one overflight was planned at the same time, since simultaneous overflights were not permitted), only twenty-four hours notice of the intended route had to be given. This would be sufficient time to verify that the observation aircraft met the provisions of the Treaty, but insufficient time to hide any large concentrations of military forces. Thus, the ability to observe military preparations throughout a large area was expected to further lessen tensions between states.

The CFE 1A Agreement

The CFE 1A negotiations over personnel levels began on 14 February 1991, and an agreement was signed at the Helsinki meeting of the Conference on Security and Cooperation in Europe (CSCE) on 10 July 1992. Originally, it had been thought that some agreement on personnel might be included within the CFE Treaty; however, this had not proved possible, and talks were put off until after the signing of CFE. Yet this led to the CFE 1A talks being slowed by the arguments over the implementation of the CFE Treaty, particularly disputes over data, the movement of Soviet Treaty Limited Equipment and the resubordination issue during the winter and spring of 1990-1. The solution of these immediate problems concerning ratification in the first half of 1991 seemed to clear the way for progress on CFE 1A. The North Atlantic Council communique issued after the meeting in Copenhagen on 6 and 7 June 1991 welcomed the resolution of the CFE problems, and stated that agreement over CFE would 'open the way for substantive work at the CFE 1A negotiations in Vienna and will enable us to introduce negotiating proposals on limits on military manpower in Europe during the present round'.[40]

The nature of the talks seemed fairly clear in four areas. First, they would be about national rather than alliance limits.[41] Second, the talks had to be concluded for signing at the Helsinki CSCE in the summer of 1992. Such a timetable would, inevitably, limit the possibility of creating a deep agreement. Third, the coverage would be the personnel who normally operated the equipment limited in the CFE Treaty. Fourth, the area of application would be the same as that for the CFE Treaty; that was, from the Atlantic to the Urals. However, this still left room for disagreement in three important areas: the definition of manpower; the legal status of the agreement; and the influence of other states on nationally declared levels.

First, the key argument was over the definition of manpower. The NATO position was that the definition of manpower should be:

all full-time military personnel of land, air and air-defence forces, together with personnel in all other formations or units based on land which hold battle tanks, ACVs, artillery, combat aircraft, or attack helicopters ... and reservists called up for more than 90 days in any period of 12 months.[42]

However, in contrast – and continuing the arguments put forward after the signing of the CFE Treaty – the Soviet Union proposed a definition that would include land forces, air forces and air defence forces, but would specifically exclude forces subordinated to the navy and would exclude Strategic Rocket Forces. This position was maintained by the Russian Federation after the collapse of the Soviet Union until a compromise was agreed immediately before the Helsinki meeting. All forces except paramilitary ones would be included in the limits; however, a comprehensive information exchange about all forces would be created which would include paramilitary forces. These forces would thus not be formally limited, but information on their size and disposition would be exchanged.

Second, there was disagreement over whether the agreement should take the form of a politically or legally binding document. Germany, in particular, sought a legally binding treaty, disliking the singularisation of the limitations on the size of German armed forces decided upon during the negotiations over German unification, and added as an Annexe to the CFE Treaty. Other countries, and in particular the United States, sought politically binding declarations of limits rather than a treaty, since the problems of ratification and verification seemed to them to be insoluble. It was this latter position that was ultimately accepted.

Third, Poland, Hungary, the Czech and Slovak Federal Republic, and Turkey argued that states should obtain explicit approval from others, and especially their neighbours, before declaring personnel levels. Due to complexity, time constraints, the fact that all states were reducing forces, and the collapse of the Soviet Union, this position was dropped just before the Helsinki meeting. The format of the negotiations and the agreement was to be that each state would declare its own level, then react to a discussion in which other states would comment on the acceptability of the proposal.[43]

The CFE 1A Agreement was signed in Helsinki at the CSCE meeting on 10 July 1992. It involved politically binding limitations on troop levels by twenty-nine countries. However, since several countries involved were at that time engaged in wars, not all countries were able to set limits (Armenia, Azerbaijan and Moldova). It was agreed that the ceilings announced could not be modified except by the consensual agreement of the other signatories. The limits are set out in Table 4.2.

The CFE 1A Agreement was of variable depth. It was not a very detailed agreement, and was not legally binding. However, in terms of verification, the agreement did include provision for an extensive verification exchange to provide increasingly detailed and more precise information. The purpose of this was twofold: to obtain greater insights into the overall size and posture of armed forces; and to gain precise information about military personnel down to the level of brigade or its equivalent. The agreement also required states to provide prior notification of increases in the strength of units, on any reorganisation of forces, and on the mobilisation of reserves. Finally, the agreement allowed for information on the nature of personnel levels to be provided for during inspections mandated under the CFE Treaty. This inspection would include those units present who did not possess equipment limited under the CFE Treaty. Thus, with regard to on-site inspections, the CFE 1A Agreement developed further the verification provisions of the CFE Treaty.

In terms of regime formation, the CFE 1A Agreement was clearly closely tied to the CFE Treaty, and its full implementation by the end of 1995 would be largely dependent on the progress of the modified CFE Treaty. However, CFE 1A was seen to bring the CFE process to a close, and to allow other avenues to be explored. There had been discussion in 1989, 1990 and 1991 about the development of a possible CFE II framework for further negotiations on conventional armed forces in Europe. However, by the time of the Helsinki CSCE summit it was clear that if there was an immediate future for conventional arms control in Europe, it would have to take place in a new forum. This forum was to be called the CSCE Forum for Security Cooperation. Yet this would have little to do with the CFE 1A process, for three main reasons. First, there seemed little prospect of other states joining the CFE 1A Agreement. Yugoslavia was in the midst of bloody collapse; Sweden and Switzerland's large militia forces made their accession difficult; while other states, such as Malta and Cyprus, seemed disinterested.[44] Second, with a CSCE membership of fifty-two states, the creation of an overarching framework for further discussions seemed to be implausible. Third, most states were in any case reducing the levels of their armed forces to below those stipulated in the CFE 1A Agreement. Thus the CFE 1A regime seemed to have little scope for further expansion or deepening.

Table 4.2   *The CFE 1A Agreement*

State	Level	State	Level
Armenia	—[a]	Kazakhstan	0[c]
Azerbaijan	—[a]	Luxembourg	900
Belarus	100,000	Moldova	—[a]
Belgium	70,000	Netherlands	80,000
Bulgaria	104,000	Norway	32,000
Canada	10,660	Poland	234,000
Czeck/Slovak	140,000	Portugal	75,000
Denmark	39,000	Romania	230,000
France	325,000	Russia	1,450,000
Georgia	40,000	Spain	300,000
Germany	345,000	Turkey	530,000
Greece	158,621	Ukraine	450,000
Hungary	100,000	UK	260,000
Iceland	0[b]	USA	250,000
Italy	315,000		

Notes

[a]   No levels declared at time of the signing of the agreement.
[b]   No armed forces.
[c]   No armed forces to be held within the Atlantic to the Urals region. (Only a relatively small part of the country lay within the region.)

●   This includes all land based forces including armies, air forces and those reservists called up for more than ninety days.
●   The United States limits applied to its forces in Europe. It declared a level of

250,000 even though at the same time planning a reduction to 150,000 by 1995.
- Canadian limitations applied only to their forces deployed in the Atlantic to the Urals region.
- Russian planned reductions did not expect to go below 2.5 million by 1995, reaching the CFE 1A level of 1,450,000 after the turn of the century.

Source: Concluding Act of the Negotiation on Personnel Strength of Conventional Armed Forces in Europe, p. 5. Also see 'Signing of CFE 1A Agreement in Helsinki' *Atlantic News* No. 2,443, 14 July 1992, pp. 1–2; 'ATTU Troop Strengths Agreed' *Jane's Defence Weekly* 18 July 1990, p. 5.

CFE 1A sought to further confidence and security building through the provision of detailed information on the levels of forces in particular states, and thus sought to further reduce fears and tensions in post-cold war Europe.

The Vienna Documents of the CSCE

Following agreement on the Stockholm Document in 1986, it was agreed that further arms control within the CSCE should take place through two parallel negotiations. The first was the CFE talks between the then twenty-three members of the two cold war alliances. The second was to be negotiations on CSBMs amongst the then thirty-five members of the CSCE. The latter negotiations produced the Vienna Document of 1990; and this Document was updated in 1992.

The Vienna Document of 1990 was negotiated alongside the CFE Treaty; however, despite the short period from March of 1989 when the talks began to the signing of the agreements in November 1990, the Vienna CSBM talks proved the easier and, from time to time, were slowed by difficulties in the CFE talks.

The Vienna CSBM talks were characterised by much common ground between the NATO and Warsaw Pact positions from the beginning. Following the Stockholm Document agenda, it was agreed that the Vienna Document should include new measures for the provision of information, improve opportunities for observations, and set new limits for notifiable and observable military activity. The only major area of disagreement was the desire of the Soviet Union to include naval activity within the remit of the Vienna talks, an argument which was repeatedly rejected by the Western nations.[45]

On 17 November 1990 the Vienna Document was signed.[46] It covered essentially four areas. First, military exercises over 40,000 troops had to be notified two years in advance, and alert activities were to be kept to a minimum. Second, an information measure was added. All states would have to submit a detailed report and account of their military forces each year, explaining organisation down to brigade or regiment level: location, troop levels and equipment holdings. In addition, states had to provide information on defence expenditure. Third, the verification provisions of the Stockholm Document were to be deepened, particularly as it related to the evaluation of the above information. This evaluation provision was designed to verify the accuracy of officially supplied data. In order to do this, states were obliged to accept one on-site inspection for every sixty deployed reporting units, which were defined as the brigade or regiment or equivalent, up to a maximum of fifteen per year. Fourth, there were a series of smaller measures, including the establishment of cooperation and consultation mechanisms in the event of unusual military activities, a requirement to invite visitors from other states to visit an air base every five years, and the establishment of a direct communication network between the capitals of all the states in the CSCE.

The Vienna Document of 1990, therefore, deepened the confidence- and security-building measures of the Stockholm Document. However, almost immediately after the signing of the 1990 Document, follow-on negotiations began. Despite the negotiations taking place in the context of the turbulence in European security issues during 1991, the talks moved forward with relative speed and ease towards completion by 25 February 1992.

The Vienna Document of 1992 further developed the CSBMs in the Stockholm and 1990 Vienna Documents. The 1992 Vienna Document made three main contributions relating to thresholds for notification and observation of military activity, the exchange of military information, and the development of risk reduction activities.

With regard to thresholds for notification and observation of military activity, the 1992 Vienna Document made several alterations and additions to the previous regime. States were allowed only one major military activity, defined as over 40,000 troops or 900 tanks, every two years with two years notification. Further, states could only conduct six smaller exercises per year, defined as being in the range from 13,000 to 40,000 troops or 300 to 900 tanks, while only three of these exercises could be of over 25,000 troops or 400 tanks. A military activity could be observed if it involved 13,000 troops (previously 17,000) or 300 tanks, or 3500 (previously 5000) amphibious or parachute assault troops. Forty-two days advance notification was required for exercises or movements of 9000 troops or 250 tanks, reduced from 13,000 troops and 300 tanks.

The second development in the 1992 Vienna Document increased the amount of military information that states had to provide. One of the concerns expressed about the 1990 Vienna Document was that information regarding low strength and non-active units would be insufficient. The 1992 Vienna Document obliged states to provide more information on units of this sort if they were expected to have their personnel levels increased for periods of more than twenty-one days. Further, states had to supply extra information, including photographs, relating to specific equipment and weapons systems.

The third improvement on previous arrangements related to risk reduction activities. Although there had previously been provision for voluntary hosting of visits from other states to allow them to conduct air or ground observation to dispel any fears, this was formalised into a mechanism in the 1992 Vienna Document. This mechanism was to be operated through the Conflict Prevention Centre of the CSCE, which had been set up in Vienna after the signing of the 1990 Paris Charter. In addition, under the 'contacts' portion of the Document, states were required to provide demonstrations of new military equipment, including weapons systems.

Taken as a whole, the CSCE Vienna Documents represented a very deep arms control process. A great deal of detail and information was provided, and, in particular, the 1992 Vienna Document created a large amount of information through requiring states to provide detailed information about a specified range of equipment. For example, states had to declare whether tanks were equipped with night vision, and the gun calibres of artillery pieces. Further, states were required to exchange a wide range of military information regarding size and organisation of military formations, and the nature of the equipment deployed with such groups. In addition, detailed annual calendars requiring extensive information regarding notifiable activities were mandated. The compliance and verification provisions were also substantial, providing for short warning inspections to problematic sites and activities, and also visits to confirm the veracity of official information. Taken together, these procedures and Documents created a very full regime. That regime was supported through certain institutions mandated by the Documents. A system of communications between all the member states was established for the distribution of notifications and requests for information, while certain contacts between military officers of the member states were provided for. Finally, emphasis was placed on risk reduction, through the Conflict Prevention Centre, which would allow for discussion about unusual military activities and other developments that might cause concern.

The Vienna Documents, in requiring states to provide large amounts of military information to one another, thus represented one of the deepest sets of arms control provisions related to confidence- and security-building measures in the post-cold war world.

US–Soviet Agreement on Prevention of Dangerous Activities

The United States–Soviet Union Agreement on the Prevention of Dangerous Military Activities was signed in 1989 and came into force on 1 January 1990. It represents the only example of CSBMs explicitly designed to develop rules of conduct in the immediate post-cold war period. The origins of the agreement were in the concerns in both countries that certain events might lead to an escalation of responses. Examples included the Soviet shooting down of a Korean Airlines flight in 1983, the Soviet assumption that any territorial incursions were hostile, and worries over Soviet and American forces operating in close proximity in the Persian Gulf. The purpose of the Agreement was, therefore, to try to ensure that the armed forces of the two states did not come into contact with each other through misjudgement and, if that did happen, to create channels for dealing with the crisis. Neither state wanted to take the risk that a limited engagement might escalate into a more serious exchange.

The agreement sought to ensure that:

> each Party ... take the necessary measures directed toward preventing dangerous military activities, which are the following activities of personnel and equipment of its armed forces when operating in proximity to personnel and equipment of the armed forces of the other Party during peace-time.[47]

There were four such activities listed. First, 'entering by personnel and equipment of the armed forces of one party into the national territory of the other Party owing to circumstances brought about by *force majeure*, or as a result of unintentional actions by such personnel'.[48] Second, using a laser in a way which could lead to injury to the personnel or damage to the equipment of the other state. Third, interfering with the activities of the personnel or equipment of the other state in a Special Caution Area which could lead to injury or damage. Special Caution Areas were defined as 'a region, designated mutually by the parties, in which personnel and equipment of their armed forces are present and, due to circumstances in the region, in which special measures shall be undertaken in accordance with this Agreement'.[49] Fourth, interfering with command and control networks.

This agreement was fairly deep. Care was taken to produce definitions of terms such as armed forces, personnel, equipment, ship, aircraft, ground hardware, laser, special caution area and interference with command and control networks. Under Annexe 1, procedures were established for maintaining communications, including the identification of the point of contact for such negotiations (the relevant commander), relevant radio frequencies, and signals to be used. In addition, efforts were made to institutionalise the agreement into a regime. Article IX set up a Joint Military Commission, which had three functions. The agreement stated that it was to consider:

> (a) Compliance with the obligations assumed under this Agreement;
> (b) Possible ways to ensure a higher level of safety for the personnel and equipment of their armed forces; and
> (c) Other measures as may be necessary to improve the viability and effectiveness of this Agreement.[50]

The Joint Military Commission would be the forum within which the states would exchange information about dangerous military activities, and within which solutions to any infringements of the agreement would be discussed.

Conclusion

Arms control to create norms of behaviour widened significantly during the cold war period. In previous periods, such arms control agreements could be divided into three categories. These related to prohibitions on certain uncivilised types of weapons, to norms protecting and defining non-combatants, and to prohibitions on the resort to warfare in certain geographically defined areas. However, adding to this list, in the period after 1945, CSBMs were developed and agreed upon.

The purpose of confidence- and security-building measures has been to clarify military intentions, rather than to bring about reductions in the levels of forces. These CSBMs have been subdivided into three areas in this Chapter: agreements over the provision of information regarding the size, status and equipment levels of military forces; agreements over codes of conduct of military forces between states; and the creation of direct lines of communication to be used to clarify misunderstandings.

In the sphere of arms control to create norms of behaviour, agreements during the post-cold war era have been extremely limited. The only activity was in the field of CSBMs and, with the exception of the United States–Soviet Union Agreement on the Prevention of Dangerous Military Activities, limited to agreements over the provision of information regarding the size, status and equipment levels of military forces. This is not to underestimate the importance of agreements such as those over Open Skies, or the Vienna Documents. However, it is to suggest that despite the significant and successful conclusion of deep agreements such as those just mentioned, arms control to create norms of behaviour has been very narrow in the post-cold war world not only conceptually but, as all of these agreements relate to the Northern half of the planet, also geographically. In contrast, arms control efforts focused on managing the proliferation of weapons has been much more related to North–South activities, as well as to the management of weapons in the North.

Notes

1   The text of the Convention is reproduced in Richard D. Burns (editor) *Encyclopedia of Arms Control and Disarmament* New York: Charles Scribner, 1993, pp. 1394–7.
2   *Ibid.*, p. 1395.
3   The text of the Convention may be found in *ibid.*, pp. 1520–7.

4   Reproduced in *ibid.*, p. 1521.
5   The text of these four Conventions is reproduced in Leon Friedman (editor) *The Law of War Volume I*, New York: Random House, 1972 pp. 525–691.
6   Texts to both resolutions are reproduced in *ibid.*, pp. 699–700 and 755–6 respectively.
7   Text reproduced in Richard D. Burns *Encyclopedia*, pp. 1345–7.
8   The text is reprinted in *ibid.*, pp. 1357–9.
9   For a conceptual treatment of confidence- and security-building measures, see Jonathan Alford (editor) *The Future of Arms Control, Part III: Confidence-Building Measures* London: International Institute for Strategic Studies, 1979; Johan Jorgen Holst 'European Security- and Confidence-Building Measures' *Survival* July–August 1977; and James MacIntosh *Confidence (and Security) Building Measures and the Arms Control Process* Ottawa, 1985.
10 The wording is identical in both Agreements. The text of the American–Soviet Agreement is published in Richard D. Burns *Encyclopedia*, pp. 1575–6, and that of the British–Soviet Agreement in *ibid.*, pp. 1577–8.
11 *Ibid.* The word 'or' in the American–Soviet Agreement is replaced with 'and' in the British–Soviet Agreement.
12 The Stockholm Document is reproduced in *ibid.*, pp. 1594–1603.
13 *Ibid.* This information is drawn from Annexe I (p. 1602), paragraph 29 (pp. 1595–6) and paragraph 31 (p. 1596).
14 For the text, see *ibid.*, pp. 1568–9.
15 *Ibid.*, p. 1568.
16 *Ibid.*
17 *Ibid.*
18 For the text, see *ibid.*, pp. 1570–1.
19 For the text, see *ibid.*, pp. 1569–70.
20 For the text, see Jozef Goldblat (editor) *Agreements for Arms Control* London: Taylor and Francis for SIPRI, 1982, pp. 227–228.
21 The text is reproduced in Richard D. Burns *Encyclopedia*, pp. 1558–9.
22 For the text, see Jozef Goldblat *Agreements*, p. 159.
23 Quoted in Richard D. Burns *Encyclopidia*, pp. 1564–5.
24 See *ibid.*, pp. 1560–2.
25 For the text, see *ibid.*, pp. 1562–4.
26 The text is reprinted in *ibid.*, pp. 1571–3.
27 The text is reproduced in *Arms Control Today* October 1989, p. 25.
28 *Ibid.*
29 *Ibid.*
30 The text is reprinted in Trevor Dupuy and Gay Hammerman *A Documentary History of Arms Control and Disarmament* New York: R. R. Bowker Co., 1973 pp. 379–81.
31 See Peter Jones 'Open Skies: A New Era of Transparency' *Arms Control Today* May 1992, pp. 10–11.
32 The treaty is excerpted in Richard D. Burns *Encyclopedia*, pp. 1543–52.
33 Richard D. Burns *Encyclopedia*, p. 1543.
34 *Ibid.*, p. 1550.
35 Article IX, Section 1, paragraph 1; *ibid.*, p. 1549.

36 Article VI, Section II, paragraph 2; *ibid.*, p. 1548.
37 *Ibid.*, p. 1543.
38 Article X, paragraph 4; *ibid.*, p. 1550.
39 Under paragraph 1; *ibid.*, p. 1552.
40 See 'CFE Allies satisfied with resolution of problems' *Atlantic News* No. 2328, 7 June 1991.
41 See 'CFE 1A Three Proposals' *Atlantic News* No. 2338, 9 July 1991, pp. 1–2.
42 This quote comes from the tabling of a proposal on behalf of NATO by Luxembourg, proposing limits for each nation and categories of personnel within overall definitions. This took place on 4 July 1991. See *Focus on Vienna* No. 24, July 1991, p. 3.
43 See *BASIC Reports* No. 21, 10 April 1992, p. 3.
44 See P. Terence Hopmann 'From MBFR to CFE: Negotiating Conventional Arms Control in Europe' in Richard D. Burns (editor), *Encyclopedia* pp. 987–8.
45 On this, see, for example, James MacIntosh 'Confidence-Building Measures in Europe: 1975 to the Present' in Richard D. Burns *Encyclopedia*, pp. 929–45.
46 Part I, paragraphs 10–16, related to 'Annual Exchange of Military Information'; Part II, paragraphs 17–18, related to 'Risk Reduction'; Part III, paragraphs 19–35, related to 'Contacts'; Part IV, paragraphs 36–44, related to 'Prior Notification of Certain Military Activities'; Part V, paragraphs 45–64, related to 'Observation of Certain Military Activities'; Part VI, paragraphs 65–70, related to 'Annual Calendars'; Part VII, paragraphs 71–4, related to 'Constraining Provisions'; Part VIII, paragraphs 75–142, related to 'Compliance and Verification'; Part IX, paragraphs 143–50, related to 'Communications'; and Part X, paragraphs 151–4, related to 'Annual Implementation Assessment Meeting'.
47 The text is reprinted in Richard D. Burns *Encyclopedia*, pp. 1579–83. This is from Article II, paragraph 1, p. 1579.
48 *Ibid.*
49 *Ibid.*
50 In paragraph 1; *ibid.*, p. 1581.

5

Managing the proliferation
of weapons

Introduction

In Chapter 1 it was argued that three types of proliferation control may be identified. The first type may be described as defensive. The purpose of this form of proliferation control is to prevent arms from reaching direct enemies. Examples of this defensive form would be both the Third Lateran Council of 1179 and the Fourth Lateran Council of 1215 which sought to prevent military supplies, and especially naval materials and skills, from being sold to the Saracens; the *Confirmatio Tractatus Flandriae* of 1370 between the English King, Edward III, and the Count of Flanders; and the agreement between Great Britain and Spain in 1814 to limit the arms trade in Spain's American colonies. The second form would be the use of arms control to try to limit violence and the danger of war and escalation in a particular country or region. Useful examples of such an agreement would include the Restraining Sales of Armaments in China Agreement of 1919; the 1950 Tripartite Arms Declaration to limit instability in the Near East; the Treaty of Tlatelolco of 1967; and the South Pacific Nuclear-Free-Zone Treaty of 1985. Finally, arms control designed to control proliferation has been used in order to try to avoid dangerous imbalances in weapons occurring in the world in general. Examples of this form of arms control would include the 1919 Convention for the Control of the Trade in Arms and Ammunition; and the Nuclear Non-Proliferation Treaty of 1968.

This chapter will examine each of these categories in turn to assess the contribution of agreements in the post-cold war period to the widening and deepening of arms control related to the management of the proliferation of weapons.

Defensive proliferation control

One of the great differences between proliferation control in the twentieth century compared to previous periods has been the relative absence of arms control to prevent arms from reaching direct enemies. Before the twentieth century, it had been common for states to insert clauses into commercial treaties to prevent the sale or trade of weapons and their means of delivery to adversaries of the signatories. These clauses were later extended into sections forbidding one state from giving material assistance to another in the case of the latter's colonies being in revolt, or in case two or more countries sought to further their colonial exploitation of a particular continent.

In contrast, few of the agreements of the twentieth century have focused upon these forms of arrangements. Only two significant agreements of the cold war period stand out as examples of this form of arms control. The first is the Protocols to the Brussels Treaty of 1954, which was different from earlier forms of arms control mentioned above in that the limitations in the Protocols took the form of unilateral commitments by one state. The second example is the Co-ordinating Committee for East–West Trade Policy (CoCom) which unlike other arms control arrangements in this area, from 1949 created a regime to manage the trade in weaponry between NATO countries (excluding Iceland), Japan and Australia on the one hand, and the communist countries on the other.

The Protocols to the Brussels Treaty of 1954 modified the 1948 Brussels Treaty to allow the accession of the Federal Republic of Germany and Italy to the Western European Union and thereby into NATO. As part of the price for accession, and for German rearmament, the West German Chancellor made a series of unilateral commitments which were entered into the modified Treaty as Annexes I, II and III. Under Annexe I, the Federal Republic undertook 'not to manufacture in its territory any atomic weapons, chemical weapons or biological weapons.'[1] Annexe II provided definitions of each of these types of weapons, and Annexe III excused specific types of work in these fields for civilian and scientific purposes.

The CoCom regime was rather different in that it sought to maintain agreement between a group of states not to trade in high technology with a common adversary. It was a harmonisation of national policies towards the transfer of weapons and weapons-related technology, and was only an informal agreement, lacking legal authority and a treaty base. Through cooperation over the contents of the 'International List' the NATO countries, Japan and later Australia sought to prevent militarily useful knowledge and equipment from being transferred to the communist countries, in order to maintain the West's qualitative military advantages over the East.[2] The technologies placed on the CoCom embargo list were negotiated in secret amongst the parties to the agreement. Had all those states perceived a common threat from the adversary, the political incentives to trade would have been low, and CoCom would have been redundant. The difficulty lay when there were differences over the significance of particular items of trade, and when domestic economic interests seemed to imply that trade was beneficial; one of the largest disagreements came in the early 1980s over the Soviet Gas Pipeline.[3] However, despite the difficulties of the Pipeline dispute, CoCom was strengthened in the 1980s not only through the addition of extra finance for the Paris secretariat, but also through the voluntary association of Austria, Finland, Hong Kong, Indonesia, Malaysia, New Zealand, Singapore, South Korea, Sweden and Switzerland.

This cold war regime was modified throughout 1990. CoCom restrictions were reduced substantially on Western exports of technologies to the East that could be used for civilian as well as military purposes. Further, restrictions on sensitive technologies were also reduced for trade with Czechoslovakia, Poland and Hungary:[4]

> In place of restraint, the West suddenly discovered an interest in accelerating the transfer of computers, industrial and environmental technology to the new democracies. It was no longer unrestricted technology transfers to the East that threatened Western interests: the danger of economic and political instability came from insufficient technology transfer.[5]

Thus, in 1991, the International List was cut by some 65 per cent and restructured into a 'Core List' of nine categories. Moving further, in December 1992, the first meeting between CoCom countries and the ex-communist and ex-Soviet states was convened, in which greater access to Western technology was sanctioned in return for greater export controls on the part of the former Soviet bloc countries.[6] In these ways, the slow process began of reorienting CoCom from being a regime designed to limit the proliferation of weapons to the East, to one aimed at preventing weapons proliferation in the South.[7] As such, these efforts merged with other attempts to control global proliferation in the post-cold war world, which will be examined later in this chapter.

In the post-cold war period it is difficult to identify any agreements that were defensive in the sense that the purpose of this form of proliferation control was to prevent arms from reaching direct enemies. Reflecting the changes in the approach to defensive arms control during the cold war, the only possible example related to an agreement to update the commitments given as part of the Protocols to the Brussels Treaty. On 22 August 1990, a Joint Declaration was issued by the Federal Republic of Germany and the German Democratic Republic in which they reaffirmed 'their contractual and unilateral undertaking not to manufacture, possess or have control over nuclear, biological and chemical weapons. They declare that the united Germany, too, will abide by its obligations'.[8]

Defensive arms control has thus rarely been utilised in the twentieth century, let alone in the post-cold war world. The key example is surely CoCom, which in essence had much in common with both the Third Lateran Council of 1179 and the Fourth Lateran Council of 1215, and the *Confirmatio Tractatus Flandriae* of 1370, in terms of attempting to obtain international agreement on limiting the trade in weaponry to adversaries. Where this form of arms control has been practised elsewhere, it has been much more subtle than in the past. Instead of states imposing limitations on the arms of Germany, Germany itself has imposed self-restraint. Of course, in essence this has been a form of defensive arms control; Germany's allies and friends have not wanted it to develop nuclear, chemical and biological weapons, for fear of contributing to a resurgent and revanchist Germany. However, Germany's acts of self-restraint have also contributed to regional acts of proliferation restraint, and it to this field that the analysis now turns.

Regional proliferation control

The second form of arms control to manage the proliferation of weapons has been those agreements designed to limit violence and the danger of war and escalation in a particular country or region. Whereas the majority of examples of defensive proliferation control pre-dated the twentieth century, most examples of regional proliferation control emanate from the period after 1919. As already seen, these agreements have covered both conventional weapons (for example, the Restraining Sales of Armaments in China agreement of 1919 and the 1950 Tripartite Arms Declaration) and nuclear weapons (the Treaty of Tlatelolco of 1967 and the South Pacific Nuclear-Free-Zone Treaty of 1985). In the post-cold war period, two agreements related to regional proliferation control stand out: the START I Protocol, designed to prevent nuclear proliferation in the new states of the former Soviet Union; and the accession of the Republic of South Africa to the Nuclear Non-Proliferation Treaty. These examples will be examined in turn.

The START I Protocol

The START Treaty had been signed in 1991 by the United States and the Soviet Union. However, the Soviet Union ceased to exist before the treaty could be ratified. This created two important problems. First, a formula had to be arrived at to save the START Treaty from collapse by obtaining new ratification measures, rather as the CFE Treaty had to be saved through the work of the North Atlantic Co-operation Council, the Tashkent Agreement and the subsequent initialling of the modified CFE agreement in Helsinki. Second, the collapse of the Soviet Union meant that successor states were *de facto* nuclear weapon states. In order to ratify START, these states would also have to be included within the terms of the treaty, and in order to maintain the vitality of the Non-Proliferation Treaty, these states would have to be encouraged to surrender those nuclear weapons on their territory.

There were three aspects to the proliferation issue. First, up to nine of the post-Soviet states were in possession of tactical nuclear weapons (Russia, Ukraine, Kazakhstan, Belarus, Georgia, Turkmenistan, Uzbekistan, Moldova, Tadjikistan, and perhaps Kyrgyzstan).[9] However, in Article 6 of the Alma Ata Agreement of 21 December 1991 'By July 1, 1992, Byelorussia, Kazakhstan, and Ukraine will insure the withdrawal of tactical nuclear weapons to central factory premises for dismantling under joint supervision.'[10] This was widely interpreted as the withdrawal of tactical nuclear systems to Russia for eventual dismantling, thus confirming unilateral reductions announced the previous October by President Gorbachev on behalf of the Soviet Union. The second issue related to nuclear capabilities. Under the terms of the START Treaty, over twenty deployment, production and strategic nuclear sites were outside the territory of the Russian Federation. Thus, a number of post-Soviet states inherited significant nuclear capabilities, as indicated in Table 5.1. However, as Steven Miller has argued, 'None of the republics except Russia possesses anything close to a full nuclear complex capable of designing, producing, maintaining and modernising nuclear weapons.'[11]

Table 5.1   *Nuclear assets of post-Soviet states*

	1	2	3	4	5	6	7
Kazakhstan		Yes		?		Yes	Yes
Russia	Yes	Yes	Yes	Yes	Yes	Yes	Yes
Tajikistan		Yes			Yes		
Ukraine		Yes			Yes	Yes	
Uzbekistan		Yes	?			Yes	

Notes:

Azerbaijan, Lithuania, Moldova, Turkmenistan did not possess any of these facilities. Armenia, Belarus, Georgia and Latvia only possessed a research centre. Estonia and Kyrgyzstan only possessed uranium mining and milling facilities.

Source: Excerpted from William C. Potter 'Nuclear Exports from the former Soviet Union: What's New, What's True' *Arms Control Today* January 1993, p. 4.

Key:

1 weapons design;
2 uranium mining and milling;
3 uranium enrichment capability;
4 plutonium production and handling;
5 heavy water production;
6 nuclear research centre;
7 test site.

Thus the third proliferation aspect of the collapse of the Soviet Union became the most significant: how to manage the problem of those strategic nuclear weapons based outside Russia. The number of nuclear weapons involved were substantial, as set out in the START Memorandum of Understanding, illustrated in Table 5.2.

Table 5.2   *Strategic nuclear weapons in the former Soviet Union*

		Belarus	*Kazakhstan*	*Ukraine*
S–18	Missiles		104	
	Warheads		1,040	
SS–19	Missiles			130
	Warheads			780
SS–24	Missiles			46
	Warheads			460
SS–25	Missiles	54		
	Warheads	54		
Bear–H	Bombers		40	21
	Weapons		320	168
Blackjack	Bombers			13
	Weapons			104

Note: Weapons on bombers are under START counting rules.

Source: See Steven Miller 'Western Diplomacy and the Soviet Nuclear Legacy' *Survival* Vol. 34, No. 3 1992, p. 5; and 'Soviet Strategic Nuclear Weapons outside the Russian Republic' *Arms Control Today* December 1991, p. 29.

As many states had expressed their desire that Russia should be the successor state to the Soviet Union, and that therefore all other post-Soviet states should accede to the Non-Proliferation Treaty, this initially did not seem to pose a problem.[12] Indeed, along with the early resolution of the tactical nuclear weapons problem seemed to come a solution to the strategic nuclear weapons dilemma. At the Minsk summit on 30 December 1991 Belarus, Kazakhstan and Ukraine had verbally accepted the necessity to accede to the Non-Proliferation Treaty and thereby implicitly (or explicitly in the case of Ukraine) to disarm the nuclear weapons on their territory. In January 1992, Belarus, Kazakhstan and Ukraine agreed to eliminate their strategic nuclear forces to fulfil the START requirements.[13] Thus, all four post-Soviet states with strategic nuclear weapons on their territory declared that they would abide by the terms of the START I Treaty, yet the status of such declarations was unclear. Belarus, Kazakhstan and Ukraine were not nuclear powers, although they ostensibly shared in the joint control of the Commonwealth of Independent States' strategic nuclear weapons. These three states were unwilling to formally allow Russia to be the single successor to the Soviet Union's START obligations, for fear of strengthening Russia's position; yet neither Russia nor the United States wanted the other three states to become a party to the treaty for fear of strengthening their nuclear status.

After months of wrangling, a compromise on these positions was reached and codified in a Protocol to the START Treaty which would enable START to be ratified. This START Protocol was signed by the United States, Belarus, Kazakhstan, Russia and Ukraine in Lisbon. There were three important elements in the Protocol.[14] First, under Article I, 'The Republic of Belarus, the Republic of Kazakhstan, the Russian Federation, and Ukraine, as successor states of the former Union of Soviet Socialist Republics in connection with the treaty, shall assume the obligations of the former Union of Soviet Socialist Republics under the Treaty.'[15] Thus, if it is not a contradiction in terms, the bilateral partner of the United States was to be all four states. Second, under Article II, the four post-Soviet states had to 'make such arrangements among themselves as are required to implement the treaty's limits and restrictions; to allow functioning of the verification provisions of the Treaty; and to allocate costs.'[16] Third, under Article V, Belarus, Kazakhstan and Ukraine agreed to:

> adhere to the Treaty on the Non-Proliferation of Nuclear Weapons ... as non-nuclear weapons states Parties in the shortest possible time, and shall begin immediately to take all necessary actions to this end in accordance with their constitutional practices.[17]

Associated with this Protocol, the Presidents of Belarus, Kazakhstan and Ukraine sent letters to President Bush in which they committed their countries to completely eliminate nuclear weapons on their territory within the seven-year implementation period of the treaty.[18]

The Protocol was significant in providing a framework within which the START Treaty could be implemented. START offered a number of advantages to both the Americans and Russians, and they were anxious not to lose the fruits of a ten-year long negotiation; equally importantly to both states, START provided a framework within which further reductions could be brought about. Only one month after the signing of the Lisbon Protocol, Presidents Bush and Yeltsin met to agree a Joint Understanding on Offensive Arms which was to lay the groundwork for the START II Treaty. However, some elements in Ukraine especially, but also in Kazakhstan, argued that the denuclearisation required of their states in the Protocol did not enhance their security. The non-Russian post-Soviet states were able to extract some concessions from the Lisbon Protocol. First, although they were not recognised as equal to the United States under START, they did become parties to the treaty by simply confirming commitments that the governments of these states had already given, particularly with regard to acceding to the Non-Proliferation Treaty. Second, especially in the case of Ukraine, the terms of the Protocol allowed movement away from previous commitments. Ukraine had committed itself in December 1991 to removing all nuclear weapons from its territory by the end of 1994. However, the Protocol seemed to place strategic withdrawals into the context of the START implementation period – that was, seven years from ratification.

This change in the timing requirement for the denuclearisation of the non-Russian post-Soviet states – and, therefore, potentially a consequent delay in acceding to the Non-Proliferation Treaty – had a serious impact upon the whole denuclearisation process. The elongation of the timetable strengthened the hand of the nationalists who opposed the START process in Ukraine especially, but also in Kazakhstan. The Ukrainians stressed their security fears, and hinted that their political commitments did not necessarily ameliorate those concerns:

> The most important external threat [to Ukraine] remains the potential for imperialist ambitions on the part of Russia, and a claim to regional domination, born of a stubborn reluctance of the right wing and some democratic political circles in the Russian federation to recognise fully the existence of Ukraine as an independent, equal and sovereign state.[19]

The Ukrainians therefore seemed to look for more concessions to encourage them to fulfil their obligations. President Leonid Kravchuk stated in November 1992 that 'We must not link the ratification of START to conditions of some sort, but ... In order for Ukraine to complete its disarmament, we must have some material benefit and fixed guarantees for its security.'[20] The longer that it took to remove the strategic nuclear weapons, the stronger the nationalist opposition became. After all, the failure to withdraw the strategic nuclear weapons in the year after the signing of the Lisbon Protocol was political, not logistical, since 6500 tactical nuclear weapons were withdrawn in the first half of 1992, leaving less than 3000 strategic systems.[21]

The ratification of START I by Russia and the United States was insufficient for the implementation of the treaty, for through the Lisbon Protocol, the treaty required the ratification of Belarus, Kazakhstan and Ukraine. During 1992, Belarus and Kazakhstan completed the ratification process. However, this was not sufficient, for the Russians had insisted that all states must accede to the NPT.[22] Thus, the stubbornness of in particular the Ukrainians had further delayed START implementation, despite the signing of the Protocol. Given the seven-year implementation period, the longer ratification was delayed, the longer would be the conclusion of the denuclearisation period. From January 1993, the situation became even more difficult with the signing of START II, for that Treaty could not be implemented until START I came into force. In November 1993, the Ukrainian Verkhovna Rada, its parliament, ratified START I and the Lisbon Protocol. However, it did so under certain conditions, which included a rejection of Article V of the Lisbon Protocol, under which Ukraine would join the NPT as a non-nuclear power. Rather than resolve the difficulty, the ratification had actually complicated matters further.

Resolution of these problems, however, were to take only a few more months. In January 1994, the Presidents of Russia, the United States and Ukraine met in Moscow to issue a joint statement that was designed to end Ukrainian stubbornness. The Ukrainian President, Leonid Kravchuk, acceded to the principal Russo-American demand: acceptance of the urgency of denuclearisation. In the annexe to the statement, the Presidents agreed that 'All nuclear warheads will be transferred from the territory of Ukraine to Russia for the purpose of their subsequent dismantling in the shortest possible time.'[23] In addition, the statement noted that 'President Kravchuk reiterated his commitment that Ukraine accede to the nuclear non-proliferation treaty as a non-nuclear weapon state in the shortest possible time.'[24] In return, the Ukrainians gained the prestige of being a party to the Russo-American agreement; ten months fuel assemblies for nuclear power stations from Russia; and specific although limited security guarantees.[25]

It is not possible to assess the depth of the START I Protocol. Despite its importance, and its potential weaknesses, its sole function was to bring an existing arms control agreement into effect. Therefore, the Protocol had little detail, no specific verification requirements (instead drawing on the START I Agreement), and certainly did not seek to create a regime, for that would have implied the continuation of nuclear weapons in Belarus, Kazakhstan and Ukraine. However, throughout 1992 and early 1993, the Ukrainians in particular sought to extend the norms of the Protocol into a regime, thus delaying the time at which Ukraine would have to relinquish control of the strategic nuclear forces deployed on its territory. With the signing of the Tripartite Agreement in January 1994, the Ukrainian President signalled an end to that policy.

South African nuclear disarmament

During the 1970s and 1980s there was widespread suspicion that South Africa had developed nuclear weapons. There are abundant sources of uranium in South Africa, and the country had engaged in international collaboration in nuclear technology. On the commercial side, South Africa had collaborated with the United States over its Safari I plant, and with France over its Koeberg plant. On top of this imported knowledge, South African scientists had themselves developed the Safari II research reactor, and in

1978 began producing highly enriched uranium. South Africa was also suspected of working with Israel on nuclear weapons design.[26]

These suspicions were deepened by two seemingly related events in the
late 1970s. International evidence came to light that the South Africans
possessed an installation in the Kalahari Desert that reputedly could have
acted as a nuclear test site.[27] In September 1979, an American surveillance
satellite spotted a bright flash in the South Atlantic, which was interpreted
by some as representing evidence of a nuclear test.[28]

In 1991, South Africa acceded to the Nuclear Non-Proliferation Treaty
on 10 July and signed a safeguards agreement with the International
Atomic Energy Agency on 16 September. Over the following year, the
Agency conducted over one hundred inspections of seventy-seven sites.[29]
The inspections were particularly intensive and difficult, given the suspi-
cions about and capabilities for the development of nuclear weapons in
South Africa. During 1992, a report was issued suggesting that South
Africa might have produced as much as 400 kilograms of highly enriched
uranium which, if all had been allocated to a nuclear weapons programme,
could have produced up to twenty-five nuclear bombs.[30]

Despite these suspicions, President F. W. de Klerk's announcement on 24
March 1993 regarding the South African nuclear programme still caused
surprise. In a speech to Parliament on South Africa's accession to the Non-
Proliferation Treaty, de Klerk admitted that:

> South Africa did, indeed, develop a limited nuclear deterrent capability. The
> decision to develop this limited capability was taken as early as 1974, against
> the background of a Soviet expansionist threat in Southern Africa ... The build-
> up of the Cuban forces in Angola from 1975 onwards reinforced the percep-
> tion that a deterrent was necessary – as did South Africa's relative
> international isolation and the fact that it could not rely on outside assistance,
> should it be attacked.[31]

De Klerk further explained that the objective of the weapons programme
had been to assemble seven bombs; however, only six had actually been
produced. The purpose of the bombs was to create a strategy in which 'if
the situation in Southern Africa were to deteriorate seriously, a confidential
indication of the deterrent capability would be given to one or more of the
major powers, for example the United States, in an attempt to persuade
them to intervene'.[32] De Klerk also stressed that despite assumptions to the
contrary, South Africa had never conducted a nuclear test.

South Africa, therefore, became the first state to engage in full unilateral
nuclear disarmament. Given the settlement over Namibia and Angola in
1988 and 1989, the collapse of communism, and:

> The prospects of moving away from a confrontational relationship with the
> international community in general, and with our neighbours in Africa in par-

ticular ... a nuclear deterrent had become not only superfluous, but in fact an obstacle to the development of South Africa's international relations.[33]

In addition, accession to the Non-Proliferation Treaty opened up the prospects of trade and the lifting of nuclear-related sanctions by the United States in particular. Indeed, de Klerk announced that one of the reasons for South Africa's change of policy was that 'South Africa's present nuclear program, which is directed towards commercialisation, including the export of high technology products' was being 'harmed'.[34] With this in mind, the enrichment plant was closed in 1989, and the following year it was decided to destroy the six nuclear bombs, to return all nuclear materials to the civil cycle, to decontaminate relevant facilities, and to reorient Armscor (which had operated the programme) towards the sale of conventional weapons.

South Africa's act of unilateral nuclear disarmament was clearly related to regional proliferation control.[35] De Klerk emphasised the regional context repeatedly throughout his speech. South Africa had:

> become a member of the African Regional Co-operative Agreement, an organ-
> isation within the IAEA which co-ordinates peaceful nuclear projects and co-
> operation between African states in the nuclear field ... The prospects for
> further co-operation will be enhanced by the establishment of a nuclear
> weapons free zone in Africa ... South Africa will soon be taking an active part
> in the trans-continental discussion ... supported by the fact that South Africa
> acquired a nuclear capability and, in recognition of its new relationship with
> Africa ... abandoned it.[36]

Through accession to the Non-Proliferation Treaty, South Africa's act of unilateral nuclear disarmament was also very deep. Accession required the implementation of the full-scope safeguards regime, and the range of detailed requirements that went with the non-proliferation regime. South Africa's strengthening of regional stability also contributed to the global efforts at enhancing non-proliferation.

Global proliferation control

The third and final form of arms control to manage the proliferation of weapons has related to those agreements designed to limit violence and the danger of war and escalation globally. Whereas the majority of examples of regional proliferation control emanate from the period after 1919, it would be accurate to say that nearly all examples of global proliferation control have been in the period after 1945. This is not to argue that global prolif-eration measures have been common; in fact, they have been something of a rarity. As already seen, examples of these agreements have included the 1919 Convention for the Control of the Trade in Arms and Ammunition and the Nuclear Non-Proliferation Treaty of 1968. In the post-cold war period, three agreements related to global proliferation control stand out: the United Nations' Security Council Permanent Five (P5) members' Initiative on arms transfers and the United Nations Arms Register; the Chemical Weapons Convention; and moves to limit nuclear testing. These examples will be examined in turn.

P5 arms restraints and the Arms Register

Of the many areas affected by arms control, conventional arms transfers has been one of the most confused. Global restraints on the transfer of arms has been created through a combination of the creation of transparency in the global transfer of arms, and specific global agreements related to supplier restraint. Both of these strands will be examined before turning specifically to the agreements on supplier restraint by the P5 and the United Nations Arms Register.

Attempts to create transparency in the transfer of arms through the creation of a register dates at least to the mid-1960s.[37] Supporters, amongst them the Scandinavian countries, Malta and Japan, argued that a register might represent a global confidence- and security-building measure; opponents in the developing world, especially Egypt and India, argued that such a register would penalise non-arms producing states. However, in 1978, the United Nations General Assembly passed a resolution calling for negotiations on limiting the scale of the arms trade, which had increased enormously in the aftermath of the oil price increases of the early 1970s. Various countries raised the possibilities of talks thereafter, but no concrete progress was made.

Efforts to create supplier restraints can be dated to the mid- and late 1970s with the Conventional Arms Transfer Talks between the United States and the Soviet Union.[38] However, more serious efforts began in the mid-1980s. Western countries, given that agreement had not been reached on a register, and that the register would only provide information and not restraint in the short term, were especially concerned with the proliferation of ballistic missiles. The primary focus of concern was the Middle East, which had seen a massive increase in weaponry over the previous fifteen years and, with the prospect of large scale ballistic missile deployment, threatened nuclear, chemical and biological weapons arms races in the region.[39] Consequently, sponsored by the United States, the MTCR (Missile Technology Control Regime) was agreed in 1987 between the Americans and Germany, France, Italy, Japan and the United Kingdom.[40] The Agreement was designed to 'limit the risks of nuclear proliferation by controlling transfers that could make a contribution to nuclear weapons delivery systems other than manned aircraft'.[41] A detailed annexe set out the equipment and materials that were to be limited. Under paragraph 7, all states were asked to adhere to the guidelines. If they did so, they would be allowed access to advanced civil high technology and, with the accession of Argentina and Hungary in March 1993, twenty-five states had become full members.[42]

However, the MTCR had a limited impact, as so much equipment had already been transferred. The limits of the MTCR, and general concerns about the scale of the transfer of highly sophisticated weaponry, were highlighted and strengthened by the invasion of Kuwait by Iraq in 1990, and the multilateral war against Iraq in 1991. In the immediate aftermath of that war, the Permanent Five members of the United Nations Security Council sought to agree to restrain their supply of weapons to third parties.

The P5 countries met to review conventional arms transfers in Paris on 9 July 1991, and issued a joint statement. In this statement:

> They noted with concern the dangers associated with the excessive buildup of military capabilities, and confirmed they would not transfer conventional weapons in circumstances which would undermine stability ... They had a thorough and positive exchange of views on the basis of arms control initiatives ... which address these problems globally and as a matter of urgency in the Middle East.[43]

Paragraph 2 stressed the importance of states in the Middle East agreeing to and implementing restraints on the proliferation of ballistic missiles and nuclear and chemical weapons. Paragraph 4 set out the commitments of the P5, which were:

- when considering under their national control procedures conventional weapons transfers, they will observe rules of restraint. They will develop agreed guidelines on this basis;
- taking into account the special situation of the Middle East as a primary area of tension, they will develop modalities of consultation and of information exchanges concerning arms transfers to this region as a matter of priority;
- a group of experts will meet in September with a view to reaching agreement on this approach;
- another plenary meeting will be held in October in London;
- further meetings will be held periodically to review these issues.[44]

Representatives of the five countries met again in London on 18 October 1991. They agreed on several points. First, that they would exchange information on the transfer of major weapon systems to the Middle East. Second, they agreed to look for further ways of exchanging information, and to meet annually. Most significantly, they agreed on common guidelines for conventional weapons exports. They declared that:

> when considering under their national control procedures conventional arms transfers, they intend to observe rules of restraint, and to act in accordance with the following guidelines:

1. They will consider carefully whether proposed transfers will:

a) promote the capabilities of the recipient to meet needs for legitimate self-defense; b) serve as an appropriate and proportionate response to the security and military threats confronting the recipient country; c) enhance the capability of the recipient to participate in regional or other collective arrangements or other measures consistent with the Charter of the United Nations or requested by the United Nations;

2. They will avoid transfers which would be likely to:

a) prolong or aggravate an existing armed conflict; b) increase tension in a region or contribute to regional instability; c) introduce destabilising military capabilities in a region; d) contravene embargoes or other relevant internationally agreed restraints to which they are parties; e) be used other than for the legitimate defense and security needs of the recipient state; f) support or encourage international terrorism; g) be used to interfere with the internal affairs of sovereign states; h) seriously undermine the recipient state's economy.[45]

These 'Guidelines for Conventional Arms Transfers' were attached as an annexe to the Communiqué issued on 18 October.

As significant as this initiative was, it was also very limited. Even as an agreement of principles, the documents owed more to diplomatic writing skills than to substantial progress towards common restraints. Throughout 1991 and 1992, a series of meetings were unable to decide on how to implement these general statements. Thus verification was impossible, and the level of detail in the 'Guidelines' document designed to cover all conventional weapons was very weak, especially when compared to the level of detail in the MTCR guidelines which focused on only one type of weapons system. Finally, although the Paris document seemed to imply the creation of a regime, with follow-up meetings (which in fact were held), with the lack of agreement on implementation, no real regime could be instituted.

The P5 Initiative was, thus, very limited. It did, however, encourage progress on the United Nations arms register. In Paris, the P5 had:

> also agreed to support continued work in the United Nations on an arms transfers register to be established under the aegis of the UN Secretary General, on a non-discriminatory basis, as a step towards increased transparency on arms transfers and in general military matters.[46]

However, momentum towards the Register was evident before the coalition war against Iraq.[47] In 1989, the General Assembly of the United Nations adopted a Resolution mandating the Secretary General to initiate a study on the arms trade. In a general atmosphere of support for action on conventional weapons transfers expressed through organisations such as the European Community, the Non-Aligned Movement, the Conference on Security and Cooperation in Europe, and the OAS (Organisation of American States), the study reported in September 1991 in favour of the creation of a Register. On 9 December 1991, the General Assembly passed Resolution 46/36L mandating the establishment of a Register of Conventional Arms, by 150 votes to none, with two abstentions.[48]

The Register had two main parts.[48] First, states were to provide data on the number of items imported and exported in seven categories: battle tanks; armoured combat vehicles; artillery; combat aircraft; attack helicopters; warships (military vessels over 850 metric tonnes); and missiles and missile systems.[49] The data also had to include the name of the other state involved. Second, the Register had to include information on domestic weapons holdings and domestic production.

In terms of depth, the Register was very limited in relation to the level of detail provided and the verification provisions.[50] Although there was detail provided on the categories of weapons, it ignored many important weapons systems, in particular small arms and ammunition which would include portable anti-aircraft weapons. Further, the Register focused on quantitative indicators rather than qualitative; no information on the sophistication of weapons systems was required (unlike, for example, the 1992 Vienna Document) which, given that major weapons systems can be supplied in many variants, limited the utility of such a measure.[51] The reporting procedure was to be through a standardised one page form which, again, would limit the amount of useful information generated above and beyond that already available in the public domain through the activities of organisations such as the Stockholm International Peace Research Institute, Jane's, and the United States Arms Control and Disarmament Agency. However, a number of these bodies decided to alter their methodologies to take account of new information provided by the register. The verification provisions of the Register were non-existent. Compliance with the requirements of the Register were voluntary, and there was no means of taking up discrepancies, nor for verifying that officially supplied information was accurate. Of course, should state X declare a transfer to state Y, but state Y not report that transfer, then suspicions would be raised. However, there are no mechanisms associated with the Register to investigate those suspicions.

In terms of regime formation, the Register fared a little better. Information was to be sent to the United Nations by 30 April for each year, beginning with 1993. In its first two years of operation, some 106 countries participated.[52] The Register was seen as a global confidence- and security-building measure, and thus it had to begin in a fairly limited way. However, it might lay the foundation for a more comprehensive system of cooperative security arrangements.[53] Viewed from the complex confidence- and security-building measures developed in Europe, the Register seemed a poor document; seen from the perspective of the confidence- and security-building vacuum of, say, the Middle East, the Register – were it to develop – could make a more significant contribution.

Both the P5 Initiative and the United Nations' Register were, therefore, limited moves to create global arms control in the field of conventional weapons transfer. However, whereas the formation of a regime for the P5 Initiative seemed doomed almost from the start, the creation of a regime for the Register seemed more hopeful, even though the United Nations' requirement for states to provide details of their defence spending had been widely ignored, which was not a positive precedent.[54] However, in contrast to these limited moves, much greater and more dramatic progress was made in the control of chemical weapons.

The Chemical Weapons Convention

In the mid- and late 1960s, great international effort was made to produce global proliferation control over the weapons of mass destruction. Initial success came with the signing of the Nuclear Non-Proliferation Treaty in 1968. The following year, a report by the United Nations' Secretary General was supported by the General Assembly, which passed a Resolution agreeing with the report that:

> the prospects for general and complete disarmament under effective international control and hence for peace throughout the world would brighten significantly if the development, production and stockpiling of chemical and bacteriological (biological) agents for purposes of war were to end and if they were eliminated from all military arsenals[55]

Subsequently, negotiations began on conventions to produce a global ban on both chemical and biological weapons. Agreement on the Biological Weapons Convention was reached in 1972, and it entered into force in 1975. The essence of the agreement was contained in Article I:

> Each State Party to this Convention undertakes never in any circumstances to develop, produce, stockpile or otherwise acquire or retain:
> (1) Microbial or other biological agent, or toxins whatever their origin or method of production, of types and in quantities that have no justification for prophylactic, protective or other peaceful purposes;
> (2) Weapons, equipment or means of delivery designed to use such agents or toxins for hostile purposes or in armed conflict.[56]

Articles II, III and IV committed states to destroying or converting to peaceful use, and not to transfer, any prohibited item. Monitoring of the Convention and complaints were to be managed by the United Nations.

With major agreements on nuclear and biological weapons, attention turned to chemical weapons. Indeed, this was mandated in Article IX of the Biological Weapons Convention, which stated that:

> Each State party to this Convention affirms the recognised objective of effective prohibition of chemical weapons and, to this end, undertakes to continue nego-

tiations in good faith with a view to reaching early agreement on effective measures for the prohibition of their development, production and stockpiling and for their destruction, and on appropriate measures concerning equipment and means of delivery specifically designed for the production or use of chemical agents for weapons purposes.[57]

Yet the creation of a chemical weapons convention (CWC) was to take another twenty years. Of course, there was an important arms control treaty related to chemical weapons to which states widely adhered. However, the 1925 Geneva Protocol on Poisonous Gases only prohibited the first use of chemical weapons, not retaliatory use, nor their production and storage. Further, there were no verification provisions attached. The negotiations for the CWC sought to close these gaps.

While the negotiations for the CWC moved towards completion, other states signed up to bilateral and multilateral agreements. In 1990, the Soviet Union and United States signed a bilateral agreement, under which both states would stop producing chemical weapons, reduce stockpiles to 5000 agent tons by the end of 2002 (or 500 agent tons at the end of the eighth year of a CWC), cooperate over information for destroying weapons, and cooperate over developing inspection techniques.[58] However, details over inspections had not been clarified, and the agreement was overtaken first by the collapse of the Soviet Union, and second by the progress towards the CWC.[59] A further move came in September 1991 when Argentina, Brazil and Chile signed the Mendoza Commitment, banning chemical weapons (and biological weapons) from their countries; they were joined subsequently by Bolivia, Paraguay and Uruguay. In addition, they agreed that, until such time as the CWC entered into force, they would 'establish in their respective countries the appropriate inspection mechanisms for those substances defined as precursors of chemical warfare agents'.[60]

These limited agreements were subsumed into the general global obligations of the CWC when, after twenty years of negotiations, the CWC was agreed upon in 1992 and subsequently signed by over 150 states from January 1993.[61] It sought to prevent the further spread of chemical weapons by mandating the destruction of all existing chemical weapons. The CWC differed from the two other major global proliferation control treaties – the Non-Proliferation Treaty and the Biological Weapons Convention – by trying to draw on the strengths of each. The Nuclear Non-Proliferation Treaty provided for detailed verification, but also divided the world into 'haves' and 'have-nots'. The Biological Weapons Convention was completely non-discriminatory, but possessed almost no verification procedures. The CWC produced a non-discriminatory regime, but with detailed verification procedures.

The CWC was divided into twenty-four articles, but the essence of the Agreement was in Article I, which stated:

1. Each State Party to this Convention undertakes never under any circumstances:

(a) To develop, produce, otherwise acquire, stockpile or retain chemical weapons, or transfer, directly or indirectly, chemical weapons to anyone; (b) To use chemical weapons; (c) To engage in any military preparations to use chemical weapons; (d) To assist, encourage or induce, in any way, anyone to engage in any activity prohibited to a State Party under this Convention.

2. Each State Party undertakes to destroy chemical weapons it owns or possesses, or that are located in any place under its jurisdiction or control, in accordance with the provisions of this Convention.

3. Each State Party undertakes to destroy all chemical weapons if abandoned on the territory of another State Party, in accordance with the provisions of this Convention.

4. Each State Party undertakes to destroy any chemical weapons production facilities it owns or possesses, or that are located in any place under its jurisdiction or control, in accordance with the provisions of this Convention.

5. Each State Party undertakes not to use riot control agents as a method of warfare.[62]

States gain two major advantages from joining the CWC. First, under Article X, if a state is threatened with or actually suffers attack with chemical weapons or riot control agents, it is entitled to apply for assistance from other states. '"Assistance" means the coordination and delivery to States Parties of protection against chemical weapons'.[63] Second, under Article XI, states party to the CWC would be able to benefit economically from collaboration, and could 'participate in the fullest possible exchange of chemicals, equipment, and scientific and technical information'.[64] However, those who remained outside the CWC would be subject to prohibitions on the transfers of a range of specified chemicals.

Two key problems were associated with the CWC.[65] Some of the main parts of the CWC related to the destruction of prohibited weapons and chemicals in an environmentally safe manner within ten years, a particular problem for the United States and Russia who possessed the largest stockpiles. Of special concern was whether the Russians had the capabilities and finance to oversee the destruction of their arsenal, at a cost estimated in 1993 at some $10 billion, although the CWC allowed for the possibility of a five year extension.[66] The second problem related to universality.[67] Many Arab states made their adherence to the regime dependent on Israeli accession to the Nuclear Non-Proliferation Treaty which meant that states with chemical weapons capabilities – such as Egypt, Syria and Libya – would be outside the regime, along with North Korea, which also refused to sign.

However, despite these drawbacks, the CWC was a remarkable achievement. Further, in contrast to the 1925 Geneva Protocol and the 1972 Biological Weapons Convention, the CWC was in all respects a very deep treaty. It was extremely detailed. The CWC itself ran to forty-five pages; the Annexe on Chemicals to nine; the Annexe on Implementation and Verification to 113; the Annexe on the Protection of Confidential Information to six; and the text on the Preparatory Commission to fourteen. Article II provided a range of definitions and criteria, running to twelve paragraphs and including definitions of 'chemical weapons' and 'toxic chemicals'. Annexe I set out three lists, or schedules, of controlled chemicals. The lists related to different levels of verification. Although herbicides were not included at any point in the CWC, the Preamble reinforced the Environmental Modification Treaty's ban on 'the use of herbicides as a method of warfare'.[68]

The verification provisions of the CWC were remarkably deep for a global agreement which, by the middle of 1995, 159 nations were prepared to sign.[69] The precise detail was to be formulated after the signing of the treaty by the Preparation Committee, which was to operate in the period before the treaty came into force (after the instruments of ratification of the sixty-fifth state was deposited, or after two years) on implementation. However, the structure of the verification regime was clear in the terms of the treaty. Article III and Annexe 2 stipulated that within thirty days of the CWC entering into force, states would have to make extensive declarations regarding chemical weapons and production facilities, and their locations, along with a plan for their destruction. Further, lists of plants which could produce chemicals on the three Schedules above certain thresholds had to be declared, along with details of the possession of any riot control agents, and whether the state had received or transferred any chemical weapons (along with details) since January 1946.

Following the receipt of this information, an initial inspection would be carried out, followed by regular inspections on forty-eight hours notice to facilities within which inspectors would have free access. Inspections, at random, would also be carried out at facilities which were declared as producing Scheduled chemicals, with thresholds triggering inspections varying between the three Schedules. 'Thousands of plants will be subject to routine, systematic inspections under the CWC – exceeding the number of sites covered in all previous negotiated agreements combined.'[70] The CWC also provided for inspections to check on allegations of the use of chemical weapons. Finally on verification, states had the right to challenge inspections. These would allow inspectors to reach a designated perimeter of the site within forty-eight hours of providing notification, and access to the site within 120 hours. States under inspection could manage the access of the inspectors to guard sensitive sites and information, reflecting concerns about industrial espionage, but there should be sufficient access to determine whether there were breaches of the CWC.

In order to ensure the smooth operation of the CWC regime, the Convention set up a bureaucracy. The Organisation for the Prohibition of Chemical Weapons (OPCW) was established in Article VIII to administer the treaty, of which all parties to the Convention would be members. The OPCW would be divided into three sections. The Conference of States Parties would be the principal organ, meet once a year, and be able to discuss any issues, particularly related to verification procedures and compliance. The Executive Council, with a membership of forty-one states selected on a regional basis and with an emphasis on those with the most significant chemical industries, would oversee the operation of the CWC. The Technical Secretariat would be responsible for the inspections.

In contrast to conventional weapons transfers, the post-cold war period saw the creation of a deep agreement for the global proliferation control of chemical weapons.[71] A third area of global proliferation control related to the central method of mass destruction: nuclear weapons.

Controls over nuclear testing

During the cold war there was much debate over the value of a complete prohibition on nuclear tests. Many felt that such prohibitions were important to protect the environment, to slow the arms race, and to place technical barriers in the way of new states developing nuclear weapons. Others argued that limited numbers of tests were important for safety reasons in investigating nuclear stockpiles, and to enhance arms race stability by ensuring that no state could bring about a massive technical leap. Once the Nuclear Non-Proliferation Treaty was signed, non-nuclear weapons states demanded a comprehensive ban on tests to provide a first stage for the nuclear disarmament of the nuclear weapons states, thus ending the discriminatory nature of the regime. This insistence was contained by the pressures of the cold war; yet it did lead to three important cold war agreements: the Partial Test Ban Treaty; the Threshold Test Ban Treaty; and the Peaceful Nuclear Explosions Treaty.

The most important of these three treaties was certainly the Partial Test Ban Treaty of 1963. This Agreement, signed by the Soviet Union, the United Kingdom and the United States, committed these states:

> to prohibit, to prevent, and not to carry out any nuclear weapon test explosion, or any other nuclear explosion, at any place under its jurisdiction or control:
>
> (a) in the atmosphere; beyond its limits, including outer space; or under water, including territorial waters or high seas; or
>
> (b) in any other environment if such explosion causes radioactive debris to be present outside the territorial limits of the State under whose jurisdiction or control such explosion is conducted.[72]

Although the Partial Test Ban Treaty (PTBT) was able to reduce the amount of atmospheric pollution, it did not slow the number of nuclear tests (both the United States and the Soviet Union conducted more tests in the thirteen years after the signing of the PTBT than they had before), nor prevent the nuclear development and testing of France, China and India.[73]

The second of the cold war nuclear test treaties was the Threshold Test Ban Treaty (TTBT) of 1974, signed by the United States and the Soviet Union. In Article I, weapons tests over 150 kilotons were prohibited, and the two states agreed that they would limit 'the number of its underground nuclear tests to a minimum'.[74] However, this 150 kiloton limit was fairly high, in that it represented an explosion with a yield ten times larger than the one at Hiroshima. Nevertheless, it proved impossible to reach agreement on a verification protocol, and the TTBT remained unratified until the June 1990 Bush–Gorbachev summit, when agreement was reached and a decision taken to move forward to ratification.

The third cold war agreement was reached in 1976, when the United States and Soviet Union signed the Peaceful Nuclear Explosions Treaty. The treaty regulated explosions that might be carried out beyond the test sites which, therefore, had to be defined as peaceful. The Soviet Union, in particular, argued that peaceful nuclear explosions (PNE) had a number of useful engineering purposes.[75] A series of such explosions were reportedly carried out in the oil and gas industry, to create a canal between two rivers, and to irrigate arid land by reversing the flow of rivers.[76] However, such PNE could also provide information useful for weapons-test purposes, and to try to prevent such occurrences, the PNE Treaty was signed, which under Article III limited PNE to the same level as set out in the TTBT, that was 150 kiloton for one explosion, and 1500 megaton for 'group explosions'.[77] This detailed Treaty, with a Protocol giving additional definitions, aimed, through the Joint Consultative Commission set up through Article VI, to create a bilateral regime to strengthen the control of nuclear tests. However, as with the TTBT, a verification protocol was not agreed, and both states failed to ratify the Treaty until a settlement was reached at the Bush–Gorbachev summit of June 1990. The latter agreement, however, reflected an existing reality in that the United States had long since abandoned any interest in PNE, and the Soviet PNE programme was terminated in 1988.[78]

Pressure to bring about a full prohibition on nuclear testing failed, therefore, during the cold war. However, the post-cold war period saw a series of intensifying pressures, leading to unilateral restraints. The first of these pressures came from within the PTBT regime, while the second was located within the Nuclear Non-Proliferation regime. These pressures led to a series of unilateral gestures by the major nuclear powers.

The first of these pressures came from within the PTBT regime. The PTBT had stated in its Preamble that the signatories were:

Seeking to achieve the discontinuance of all test explosions of nuclear weapons for all time, determined to continue negotiations to this end, and desiring to put an end to the contamination of man's environment by radioactive substances.[79]

As seen above, little progress was made towards that end in the following quarter of a century. In the late 1980s a number of Non-Aligned countries, led by Indonesia, began to press the Depositary States (Britain, the Soviet Union and the United States) to hold a PTBT conference to consider an amendment to the PTBT which would turn it into a Comprehensive Test Ban Treaty (CTBT). The conference was held in January 1991 and although the amendment was not put to a vote, there was a vote on a proposal to continue the work of the Amendment Conference through the Conference President who would 'conduct consultations with a view to achieving progress on these issues and resuming the work of the Conference at an appropriate time'.[80] This resolution was passed with seventy-five votes in favour (including Denmark, Greece, Iceland, Norway, Australia, New Zealand and Sweden), nineteen abstentions (including Israel, Japan, Bulgaria, Czechoslovakia, Poland and Romania), and two votes against (the United Kingdom and the United States).[81] Whereas pressure for a CTBT had been focused in the Non Aligned Movement during the cold war, the vote indicated a growth of support for a CTBT in the developed world in the post-cold war period.

Yet even greater pressure was building up from within the Nuclear Non-Proliferation regime. Article VI of the Non-Proliferation Treaty had stated: 'Each of the Parties to the Treaty undertakes to pursue negotiations in good faith on effective measures relating to the cessation of the nuclear arms race at an early date and to nuclear disarmament'[82] For many, the symbol that this commitment was being taken seriously was the achievement of the CTBT. 'The conclusion of a CTBT is still seen by many NPT parties as part of the political "bargain" inherent in the Treaty: their acceptance of non-nuclear weapon status in return for the nuclear weapon states accepting parallel limitations.'[83] The Second Review Conference of the Non-Proliferation Treaty in 1980 failed to produce a final document largely over the CTBT issue. The Third Review Conference in 1985 reached a final document in which it was stated that:

The Conference except for certain States whose views are reflected in the following subparagraph deeply regretted that a comprehensive multilateral Nuclear Test Ban Treaty banning all tests by all States in all environments for all time had not been concluded so far and, therefore, called on the nuclear-weapon States Party to the treaty to resume trilateral negotiations in 1985 and called on all the nuclear-weapon States to participate in the urgent negotiation and conclusion of such a Treaty as a matter of the highest priority.[84]

157

In 1989 the Non-Aligned summit in Belgrade stated that concluding a CTBT was 'absolutely essential for the preservation of the nonproliferation regime'.[85] The Fourth Review Conference of the NPT in 1990 again failed to reach a final document, largely over the CTBT issue. The 1995 Conference would be even more important, since under Article X of the treaty, 'Twenty five years after the entry into force of the Treaty [ie, 1995], a conference shall be convened to decide whether the Treaty shall continue in force indefinitely, or shall be extended for an additional fixed period or periods. This decision shall be taken by a majority of Parties to the Treaty.'[86]

Thus, pressure to move on the CTBT issue grew greatly at the beginning of the post-cold war period. During the cold war, some efforts had been made to bring about a CTBT through negotiations. From 1958 to 1961, there had been American–British–Soviet talks over the CTBT, and these talks began again in 1977, being suspended in 1980. Further, the issue of the CTBT had been on the agenda of the United Nations' Conference on Disarmament and its predecessors from 1963.[87] However, the only significant progress came in terms of nuclear test moratoria, which were followed by the United Kingdom from 1965 to 1974, and by the Soviet Union in 1985–6.

In response to the growing pressure in the post-cold war world and the CTBT failures of the cold war period, the major nuclear powers again turned to the moratoria route, only this time three of the five declared nuclear states proclaimed what turned into a series of linked test moratoria. In the autumn of 1991, President Gorbachev announced a one year testing moratorium for the Soviet Union. This was confirmed on the collapse of the Soviet Union by Russian President Yeltsin, who also announced the closure of the Novaya Zemlya test site.[88] Yeltsin declared 'Russia is resolutely in favour of a ban on all nuclear arms testing ... we propose to the United States that bilateral talks on further limiting the testing of nuclear arms be resumed.'[89] On 8 April 1992, France announced a testing moratorium for twelve months.[90] President Mitterrand called for the other nuclear states to impose their own moratoria, and warned that if there was no progress, France would recommence nuclear tests in 1993.

Yet almost as quickly as events seemed to be moving towards a *de facto* CTBT, reverses began. President Bush declared that the United States had no plans to initiate its own moratorium, despite the call from the House of Representatives for the United States not to test for one year to match Russian restraint.[91] Hopes that China might move towards testing restraint were damaged by a 1 megaton test in May 1992, and another smaller test in September, the timing of which seemed to indicate 'that China has considered the technical benefits of testing to be more important than the political impact with respect to the Russian and French testing moratoria'.[92] The Commander of the Commonwealth of Independent States' armed forces called for renewed tests if other states did not stop their tests. President Mitterrand confirmed that this was also French policy. No movement on British testing was forthcoming.

Reflecting the fast changing nature of events, in September 1992, however, a dramatic advance in favour of a test ban was made with the announcement of the defence budget in the United States Senate. The Senate voted in favour of a proposal, enacted by President Bush on 2 October, for a nine-month American moratorium, the limitation to fifteen of all tests during the next three years, and an end to all tests after September 1996 unless Russia continued testing.[93] This dramatic move towards testing restraints had implications for the other declared nuclear powers. Under the American legislation the United Kingdom, which used American facilities for testing, was to be constrained to three tests in the period to 30 September 1996. On 19 October, in the light of the American decision, President Yeltsin announced an extension of the Russian moratorium until 1 July 1993. France announced that it would consider extension of its moratorium, and sought negotiations between the declared nuclear weapons states on testing. Even China, which had carried out two tests already, had also acceded to the Nuclear Non-Proliferation Treaty during 1992, and its Instrument of Accession had stated 'To attain the lofty goal of complete prohibition and thorough destruction of nuclear weapons, countries with the largest nuclear arsenals should earnestly fulfil their special obligations by taking the lead in halting the testing, production and deployment of nuclear weapons'[94] Movement continued during 1993. Presidents Clinton and Yeltsin met in Vancouver during April, and issued a joint statement declaring their agreement 'that negotiations on a multilateral nuclear test ban should commence at an early date'.[95] Clinton's announcement of an extension of the American moratorium was met with announcements in France and Russia that they would not break the test moratorium first.[96] However, problems remained with the fifth declared nuclear power, China, which, despite rhetoric to the contrary, had not indicated a full commitment to the process. Indeed, while other declared nuclear states were exercising restraint, China detonated a large device underground in October 1993.[97]

Conditions were developing for the initiation of negotiations for a Comprehensive Test Ban Treaty. In November, the UN General Assembly First Committee (which deals with disarmament issues) passed a resolution supporting the negotiation of a CTBT for the first time.[98] In January 1994, the Conference on Disarmament formally adopted a mandate for the Nuclear Test Ban Ad Hoc Committee to negotiate the CTBT. With the CTBT talks under way, some states in the developing world sought to create a linkage between the CTBT talks and the NPT review conference: no CTBT, no NPT. However, this was rejected by many of the states in the developed world.[99]

The CTBT issue was expected to be an important one at the NPT Review and Extension Conference in April and May 1995, but not a central one.[100] Indeed, the Conference agreed to the indefinite extension of the treaty. However, one of the principles adopted by the Conference was that the completion of a CTBT should be achieved 'no later than 1996. Pending the entry into force of a Comprehensive Test-Ban Treaty, the nuclear weapons States should exercise utmost restraint'.[101]

That the CTBT was not central to the Extension of the most successful-ever arms control treaty, the NPT, was due to the progress already made.[102] Significant progress in the Conference on Disarmament on the CTBT negotiations was made over the first fifteen months. However, the prospect of a final end to nuclear tests did not discourage a continuation of Chinese tests, with the forty-second test held just after the conclusion of the NPT Review and Extension Conference. One month later, French President Jacques Chirac announced a new series of tests, which began in the autumn, and were designed to be completed before the entry into force of a CTBT.

The development of arms control in the field of nuclear testing in the post-cold war world was thus highly unique. A limited cold war regime existed, but pressure to extend that regime into a CTBT (which during the cold war had not been decisive) became, in the early post-cold war period, much more significant. In the interests of furthering the global non-proliferation of nuclear weapons, the nuclear weapons states opted for a series of unilateral measures. Of course, these restraints were formally not deep. Declarations on the part of the Russians and French were more shallow than the United States, which had passed its moratorium into law. Nevertheless, all these restraints operated within a general global non-proliferation regime, were likely to be verifiable through national technical means, and they all relied on the strength of the norm of non-proliferation for their continued vitality. Pressures grew in each of the declared nuclear weapons states to conclude a final series of tests before the CTBT would come into effect, thus forcing states to rely upon simulations. However, with the advent of CTBT negotiations, the Americans, British, French and Russians all committed themselves to negotiate a very deep CTBT.

Conclusion

All three types of proliferation control identified in Chapter 1 have been present in the post-cold war world. However, clearly there are great differences in the significance of each category. Arms control to create norms of behaviour, as examined in the last chapter, in part sought to limit the use of weapons deemed to be uncivilised. Proliferation control sought to move further, and to prohibit not only the use but also the possession of such weapons. However, as international relations changed over the course of the twentieth century, arms control designed to create defensive proliferation control has been much reduced. In the post-cold war world, only the document confirming the obligations of the new Germany and the attempts to re-orient the direction of the cold war institution, CoCom, have been identified. Further, from the end of the cold war, regional proliferation agreements were designed not to create new regional arms control regimes, but rather to support existing regimes, as was clear with both the START I Protocol and the unilateral nuclear disarmament of the South Africans. Finally, globalisation in international relations has led to a greater emphasis on global proliferation management.

Global proliferation management in the post-cold war world has seen three major areas of development: conventional weapons transfers, chemical weapons development, and the testing of nuclear weapons. Limitations on conventional weapons transfers and restraints on nuclear testing have been shallow. However, the CWC has provided a particularly deep example in relation to detail, verification provisions and the creation of an arms control regime.

One of the most significant illustrations of the globalisation of international relations in the twentieth century has been the rise of the international organisation, which has moved into arms control increasingly as the century has progressed. It is to arms control by international organisation that the analysis now turns.

Notes

1 Protocols to the Brussels Treaty, reprinted in Richard D. Burns (editor) *Encyclopedia of Arms Control and Disarmament* New York: Charles Scribner, 1993 p. 1203.

2 See S. MacDonald *Technology and the Tyranny of Export Controls* London: Macmillan, 1990.

3 The controversial Yamal Gas Pipeline deal was a multilateral version of the gas-for-pipelines deals between the Soviet Union and the Federal Republic of Germany in the 1970s. Western pipes and compressors were sold to the East, financed by Western credits; this would be repaid over time through proceeds generated by gas sales. Whereas the Germans and other West Europeans saw this as commercially viable, and politically useful in giving the communist countries incentives to co-operate with the West, the United States argued that such arrangements would create a dependency on the Soviet Union. On this see, for example, Ernst-Otto Czempiel 'Germany–USA: Co-operation and Irritations' and 'America–Germany: A Particular Relationship *Aussenpolitik* Vol. 33, No. 1, 1982 and Vol. 34, No. 3, 1983, respectively; J. Dobrovolny 'East–West Trade in a Transition Period' *East European Quarterly* Fall 1983; P. Windsor 'Germany and the Western Alliance: Lessons of the 1980 Crises' *Adelphi Paper 170* London: International Institute for Strategic Studies, 1981; John Hardt

and Donna Gold 'Soviet Gas Pipeline: US Options' Washington DC: Congressional Research Service, 1983.

4   See Owen Greene 'Reforming the CoCom regime' in J. Poole (editor) *Verification Report 1991* London: Apex Press/Vertic 1991; and Aaron Karp 'Ballistic Missile Proliferation' in *SIPRI Yearbook 1991* Oxford: Oxford University Press for SIPRI, 1991.

5   International Institute for Strategic Studies *Strategic Survey 1991–1992* London: Brassey's for IISS, May 1992, p. 203.

6   See Carol Reed 'COCOM opens up to ex-WP nations' *Jane's Defence Weekly* 5 December 1992, p. 9.

7   On this, see Ian Anthony, Agnès Courades Allebeck, Gerd Hagmeyer-Gaverus, Paolo Miggiano and Herbert Wulf 'The Trade in Major Conventional Weapons' in *SIPRI Yearbook 1991*, pp. 220–2.

8   Joint Declaration of the Federal Republic of Germany and of the German Democratic Republic on Non-Proliferation of Nuclear, Chemical and Biological Weapons, reprinted in *Disarmament* Vol. 14, No. 1, 1991, p. 219.

9   See Steven Miller 'Western Diplomacy and the Soviet Nuclear Legacy' *Survival* Vol. 34, No. 3, 1992, p. 5.

10   The text is reproduced in *Newsbrief* No. 16 University of Southampton: Programme for Promoting Nuclear Non-Proliferation, Winter 1991/2, p. 15.

11   Steven Miller, 'Western Diplomacy' p. 4.

12   See Kurt M. Campbell, Ashton Carter, Steven Miller and Charles Zraket 'Soviet Nuclear Fission' *CSIA Studies in International Security* No. 1 Cambridge, MA: Center for Science and International Affairs, November 1991.

13   See Ivo H. Daalder and Terry Terriff 'Nuclear Arms Control: Finishing the Cold War Agenda' *Arms Control: Contemporary Security Policy* Vol. 14, No. 1, 1993, p. 8.

14   See Dunbar Lockwood 'US, Four Commonwealth States Sign START Protocol in Lisbon' *Arms Control Today* June 1992, pp. 18, 29.

15   Excerpted in 'Documentation' *Survival* Vol. 34, No. 3, 1992, p. 136.

16   *Ibid.*

17   *Ibid.*

18   The texts of the letters are reprinted in *Arms Control Today* June 1992, pp. 35–6.

19   A. N. Honcharenko and E. M. Lisitsyn 'Armed Forces of Ukraine and Problems of National Security' in Centre for Defence Studies *Brassey's Yearbook 1993* London: Brassey's 1993, p. 154.

20   From Serge Schmemann 'Ukraine may slow arms pact unless West sends more aid' *The New York Times*, 13 November 1992, in Ivo H. Daalder and Terry Terriff, 'Nuclear Arms Control" p. 10.

21   See Steven Miller, 'Western Diplomacy' p. 22.

22   Belarus acceded to the NPT in July 1993, Kazakhstan in February 1994, and Ukraine in November 1994.

23   The text is reproduced in Foreign and Commonwealth Office (FCO) *Arms Control and Disarmament Quarterly Review* No. 33, April 1994 (published in London by the Arms Control and Disarmament Research Unit of the FCO), p. 12.

24   *Ibid.*, p. 9.

25 However, these guarantees were merely restatements of existing commitments. Under the agreement Russia and America, subsequently joined by the United Kingdom (as a depository state of the NPT), affirmed that once Ukraine joined the NPT, it would have its borders respected, under the CSCE Final Act; confirmed that they would not use force against Ukraine, except in self-defence, under the UN Charter; agreed to refrain from economic coercion of Ukraine, again under the CSCE Final Act; confirmed that they would seek immediate action from the UN Security Council should Ukraine be threatened by a state with nuclear forces; and agreed not to use nuclear force against Ukraine, except in self-defence.

26 See Bernhard Rabert 'South Africa's Nuclear Weapons – A Defused Time Bomb?' *Aussenpolitik* Vol. 44, No. 3, 1993, pp. 232–242.

27 However, joint Soviet and American diplomatic pressure encouraged the South Africans to dismantle the facility. See Kenneth W.Grundy *South Africa: Domestic Crisis and Global Challenge* Boulder, Co: Westview, 1991, pp. 106–7.

28 *Ibid.* However, 'the conclusion of a special White House scientific panel [was] that "the signal was probably not from a nuclear explosion"'. 'South Africa Reveals it had Six Nuclear Weapons Until 1990' *Arms Control Today* April 1993, p. 23.

29 'IAEA Inspects South African Nuclear Program' *Arms Control Today* October 1992, p. 36.

30 See Mark Hibbs 'IAEA believes South Africa produced more than 200kg of high-enriched uranium' *Nuclear Fuel* Vol. 17, No. 20, September 1992.

31 Excerpts from de Klerk's speech are reprinted in 'Documents' *Arms Control Today* April 1993, pp. 27–8.

32 *Ibid.*

33 *Ibid.*

34 *Ibid.*

35 Although it is also difficult not to believe that movements towards full democracy and a majority government in South Africa did not play a part in the decisions of the white government.

36 See 'Documents' *Arms Control Today* April 1993.

37 On this, see Keith Krause 'Controlling the Arms Trade since 1945' in Richard D. Burns *Encyclopedia*, especially pp. 1029–32.

38 On this, see Barry Blechman and Janne Nolan *The US–Soviet Conventional Arms Transfer Negotiations* Washington DC: 1987.

39 See Thomas Ohlson (editor) *Arms Transfer Limitations and Third World Security* Oxford: Oxford University Press for SIPRI, 1988.

40 See Steve Fetter 'Ballistic Missiles and Weapons of Mass Destruction: What Is the Threat? What Should be Done?' *International Security* Summer 1991; and Martin Navias 'Ballistic Missile Proliferation in the Third World' *Adelphi Paper* 252 London: International Institute for Strategic Studies, 1990.

41 Paragraph 1: the agreement is excerpted in Richard D. Burns *Encyclopedia*, pp. 1474–80.

42 See 'Argentina Ships Condor Missiles for Destruction, Joins MTCR' *Arms Control Today* April 1993, p. 24.

43 The Statement of the Five Countries is excerpted in United States Arms Con-

trol and Disarmament Agency *World Military Expenditures and Arms Transfers 1990* Washington DC: 1991, pp. 23–24–B. This quote is drawn from paragraphs 1 and 2.

44   *Ibid.*

45   The text of the agreement is reproduced in J. B. Poole and R. Guthrie *Verification Report 1992* London: Vertic 1992, p. 299.

46   United States Arms Control and Disarmament Agency, op cit, pp. 23–24–B.

47   For a detailed review of the first year, and an examination of implications and future directions, see Malcolm Chalmers, Owen Greene, Edward J. Laurence and Herbert Wulf 'Developing the UN Register of Conventional Arms' *Bradford Arms Register Studies* No. 4 University of Bradford, 1994.

48   See Keith Krause, 'Controlling the Arms Trade' pp. 1030–2.

49   The specifications for the first five categories were based on the CFE Treaty.

50   A much more positive view is provided by Ambassador Hendrik Wagenmakers 'The UN Register of Conventional Arms: A New Instrument for Co-operative Security' *Arms Control Today* April 1993.

51   For more on these issues, see Keith Krause, 'Controlling the Arms Trade'.

52   See the excellent account of Malcolm Chalmers and Owen Greene 'The UN Arms Register' *Contemporary Security Policy* Vol. 15, No. 3, 1994, pp. 58–83.

53   For an argument in favour of further development, see Joanna Spear 'On the Desirability and Feasibility of Arms Transfer Regime Formation' *Contemporary Security Policy* Vol. 15, No. 3, 1994, pp. 84–111.

54   A point ably made by Keith Krause, 'Controlling the Arms Trade'.

55   The Secretary General's Report was entitled 'Chemical and Bacteriological (Biological) Weapons and the Effects of Their Possible Use'. The General Assembly Resolution, 2603(XXIV) 'Question of Chemical and Bacteriological (Biological) Weapons', was adopted on 16 December 1969. For the text, see Richard D. Burns *Encyclopedia*, pp. 1391–3.

56   For the text of the Convention, see *ibid.*, pp. 1394–7.

57   *Ibid.*

58   The text of the Agreement on Destruction and Non-Production of Chemical Weapons and on Measures to Facilitate the Multilateral Convention on Banning Chemical Weapons is reproduced in *SIPRI Yearbook 1991* Oxford: Oxford University Press for SIPRI, 1991, pp. 536–9.

59   See Charles C. Flowerree 'Chemical and Biological Weapons and Arms Control' in Richard D. Burns *Encyclopedia*, especially pp. 1016–17.

60   Paragraph 3. The text of the agreement is reproduced in J. B. Poole and R. Guthrie *Verification Report*, p. 300.

61   See Martine Letts, Robert Mathews, Tim McCormack and Chris Moraitis 'The Conclusion of the Chemical Weapons Convention: An Australian Perspective' *Arms Control: Contemporary Security Policy* Vol. 14, No. 3, December 1993; and Brad Roberts 'Chemical Disarmament and International Security' *Adelphi Paper* No. 267 London: Brassey's for the International Institute for Strategic Studies, Spring 1992.

62   The CWC is excerpted in *Arms Control Today* October 1992, CWC Supplement, pp. 5–16.

63   Paragraph 1; *ibid.*, p. 14.

64   *Ibid.*, p. 15.
65   For an elaboration of these points, see Oliver Thraenert 'The International Chemical Weapons Convention – Problems Involved' *Aussenpolitik* Vol. 44, No. 3, 1993, pp. 222–31.
66   See Lee Feinstein 'CWC Executive Summary' *Arms Control Today* October 1992.
67   See James F. Leonard 'Rolling Back Chemical Proliferation' *Arms Control Today* October 1992, pp. 13–18.
68   *Ibid.*, p. 5. This point is made by Lee Feinstein in 'CWC Executive Summary', p. 4.
69   For a discussion, see Gordon M. Burck 'The Chemical Weapons Convention Negotiations' in J. B. Poole and R. Guthrie *Verification Report*, pp. 122–30. For figures, see Foreign and Commonwealth Office *Notes on Security and Arms Control* No. 5, July 1995, p. 12.
70   Michael Krepon 'Verifying the Chemical Weapons Convention' *Arms Control Today* October 1992, p. 19.
71   On the possibilities of regime development, see Jessica Eve Stern 'Cooperative Security and the CWC' *Contemporary Security Policy* Vol. 15, No. 3, December 1994, pp. 30–57.
72   Under Article I. The treaty is reproduced in Jozef Goldblat (editor) *Agreements for Arms Control* London: Taylor and Francis for SIPRI, 1982 pp. 157–8.
73   See Jozef Goldblat *Agreements for Arms Control*, pp. 24–5. India was a party to the PTBT when it conducted its underground nuclear test/PNE in 1974.
74   Paragraph 2. See *ibid.*, pp. 211–12 for the full text.
75   According to reports in the *Daily Telegraph*, the Soviet Union detonated 116 PNE's (81 within Russia, 30 in Kazakhstan, and the rest in Turkmenistan, Ukraine and Uzbekistan). A number caused disastrous environmental devastation as radioactivity escaped into the air and poisoned water supplies. Cited in *Newsbrief* No. 30, University of Southampton, PPNN, 2nd quarter 1995, pp. 7–8.
76   *Nucleonics Week* 9 May 1991, reported in *Newsbrief* No. 14 University of Southampton: Programme for Promoting Nuclear Non-Proliferation, Summer 1991, p. 5.
77   The Treaty is reproduced in Jozef Goldblat *Agreements for Arms Control*, pp. 218–27.
78   See *Nucleonics Week* 9 May 1991.
79   Jozef Goldblat *Agreements for Arms Control*, p. 157.
80   Quoted in Patricia Lewis 'The PTBT Amendment Conference' in *Bulletin of Arms Control* No. 1, February 1991.
81   See idem, and *Newsbrief* No. 13 University of Southampton: Programme for Promoting Nuclear Non-Proliferation, Spring 1991, p. 1.
82   For the text, see Richard D. Burns *Encyclopedia*, pp. 1437–40.
83   Darryl Howlett and John Simpson 'The NPT and the CTBT: Linkages, Options and Opportunities' *Arms Control: Contemporary Security Policy* Vol. 13, No. 1, 1992, p. 86.
84   Reproduced in John Simpson and Darryl Howlett 'The Need for a Strong Nuclear Non-Proliferation Treaty: Issues at the Fourth NPT Review Conference' *Occasional Paper 8* University of Southampton: Programme for Promoting Nuclear Non-Proliferation, July 1990, p. 31.

85 'Nuclear Notebook' *Bulletin of the Atomic Scientists* March 1990, p. 48.

86 Paragraph 2: see Richard D. Burns *Encyclopedia*, p. 1440.

87 On these issues, see G. Allen Greb 'Survey of Past Test Ban Negotiations' in Jozef Goldblat and David Cox (editors) *Nuclear Weapon Tests: Prohibition or Limitation* Oxford: Oxford University Press for CIIPS and SIPRI, 1988.

88 See Sergei Kortunov 'The Deterrent Forces of the Commonwealth of Independent States' and Nikolai V. Kapranov 'A Russian Perspective on the Future of Nuclear Weapons' in Patrick J. Garrity and Steven A. Maaranen *Nuclear Weapons in the Changing World* New York: Plenum Press, 1992, pp. 68–9 and p. 87 respectively.

89 'Russian Arms Control Initiatives' *Survival* Vol. 34, No. 2, 1992 p. 123.

90 See Tom Zamora 'Mururoa-torium' *Bulletin of the Atomic Scientists* June 1992.

91 See *Newsbrief* No. 18 University of Southampton: Programme for Promoting Nuclear Non-Proliferation, Summer 1992, p. 3.

92 *Trust and Verify* No. 31, September 1992, p. 1.

93 See *Arms Control Today* September 1992, p. 24; 'US Begins Testing Moratorium' *Arms Control Today* October 1992, p. 32.

94 *Trust and Verify* No. 32, October 1992, pp. 1–2.

95 Quoted in George Bunn and Roland Timerbaev 'Avoiding the "Definition" Pitfall to a Comprehensive Test Ban' *Arms Control Today* May 1993, p. 15.

96 See *Newsbrief* No. 22 University of Southampton: Programme for Promoting Nuclear Non-Proliferation, 2nd Quarter 1993, pp. 6–7.

97 See FCO *Arms Control and Disarmament Quarterly Review* January 1994, pp. 11–12.

98 See Foreign and Commonwealth Office *Arms Control and Disarmament Quarterly Review* No. 32, January 1994, pp. 50–1.

99 See Foreign and Commonwealth Office *Notes on Security and Arms Control* No. 6, July 1994, pp. 9–10.

100 See John Simpson and Darryl Howlett 'The Future of Nuclear Non-Proliferation' *PPNN Study 6* Southampton: Mountbatten Centre for International Studies, April 1995, pp. 8–9.

101 Point 4(a) of the Principles and Objectives for Nuclear Non-Proliferation and Disarmament, reproduced from NPT/CONF.1995/32/DEC.2, cited in *Newsbrief*, No. 30, 2nd Quarter 1995, PPNN, Southampton, p. 23.

102 Successful in the sense that more states adhered to the NPT (178 signatories) than any other treaty.

6

Arms control
by international organisation

Introduction

In Chapter 1 it was argued that a new form of arms control has been developed during the twentieth century: arms control by international organisation. Furthermore, not only has arms control widened into this area, but the nature of arms control practice in this field has also widened. In the League of Nations, the major area of arms control with which international organisation was concerned was global controls on weapons. As already seen, the United Nations also did a great deal of work in this field during the cold war. In addition, the United Nations also instituted arms restraints on an individual member, and provided the forum for the provision of security guarantees to elicit an arms control agreement.

In the post-cold war period, arms control by international organisation has focused not on global controls, nor on providing a forum for security guarantees. However, there has been a great deal of activity in terms of imposing restraints on individual states. Recalling its activity in relation to Rhodesia (which faced sanctions from 1966 to 1977), and its proscriptions on arms trading with South Africa during the cold war, in the post-cold war period the United Nations instituted a series of arms embargoes. However, the Organisation also went further, and actively sought to bring about the disarmament of sections of a nation's arsenal, and of groups within states. This chapter will examine the development of United Nations activity in relation to arms control during the post-cold war period. Seven important examples of United Nations operations will be examined: in relation to arms embargoes on Libya and Haiti; peacekeeping operations in the former Yugoslavia; and disarmament work in Somalia, Cambodia, Mozambique and Iraq. These examples will illustrate the increased activity of the United Nations with regard to arms control in the post-cold war world.

167

The arms embargoes on Libya and Haiti

In order to put pressure on governments of states to comply with resolutions of the United Nations, the Security Council frequently resorted to the use of sanctions on those states. Of particular relevance to this study has been the increasing use of arms embargoes. Two particularly clear examples relate to Resolutions against Libya and Haiti.

In December 1988, a Pan Am aircraft was bombed by terrorists, and it disintegrated over the Scottish town of Lockerbie. After widespread international investigation, two individuals were identified and strongly suspected of being the perpetrators. These two individuals were Libyan nationals and great diplomatic pressure was put on the Libyan Government to surrender the accused for trial. Further, Libya was implicated in the bombing of the French flight UTA 772 over Africa. As a result, action was taken in the Security Council. Resolution 731 was passed on 21 January 1992, demanding information regarding Libyan involvement in both bombings. The failure to provide this information led to the passing of Resolution 748, on 31 March 1992, which stipulated:

> that all States shall:
> (a) Prohibit any provision to Libya by their nationals or from their territory of arms and related material of all types, including the sale or transfer of weapons and ammunition, military vehicles and equipment, paramilitary police equipment and spare parts for the aforementioned ...
> (b) Prohibit any provision to Libya by their nationals or from their territory of technical advice ...
> (c) Withdraw any of their officials or agents present in Libya to advise the Libyan authorities on military matters.[1]

Paragraph 9 of the Resolution set up a committee of the Council to monitor sanctions and Libya's response.

A similar Resolution was passed regarding the political crisis in Haiti when the military government prevented the return of the democratically elected President, Jean-Bertrand Aristide. Although not in power in Haiti itself, Aristide's government still held Haiti's seat in the OAS, and pressed for sanctions to bring about a change of government in Haiti. Having gained support in the OAS, the Haitian representative at the United Nations requested that the Security Council make sanctions on Haiti mandatory. In Resolution 841 on 16 June 1993, the Council supported the imposition of mandatory sanctions. Paragraph 5 included the imposition of an arms embargo, prohibiting the sale or supply of 'weapons and ammunition, military vehicles and equipment, police equipment and spare parts ... to any person or body in Haiti or to any person or body for the purpose of any business carried on in or operated from Haiti'.[2] Further, a blockade was ordered under paragraph 6, which prohibited 'any and all traffic from entering the territory or territorial sea of

Haiti' carrying the range of restricted goods, including military material.[3] The success of this Resolution was to be monitored by a Committee of the Security Council, established in paragraph 10.[4]

Of course, the use of an arms embargo in itself to attempt to enforce the will of the international community, or sections of it, was not novel. The League of Nations had, for example, voted in favour of a variety of sanctions – including an arms embargo – against Italy on 18 November 1935 in response to the invasion of Abyssinia.[5] Indeed, it became a standard response to the major crises of the post-cold war world in which the United Nations was involved: for example, the former Yugoslavia, Somalia, Cambodia and Iraq. However, in these other crises the United Nations was to become much more deeply involved. One such crisis was that in the former Yugoslavia.

The Yugoslav civil war

The Socialist Federal Republic of Yugoslavia moved from domestic political argument into bloody conflict in the summer of 1991 when the Yugoslav army and the Slovene militia began brief hostilities. Within weeks, the war spread with much greater violence to Croatia. By the spring of 1992, the war spread with even greater brutality and ferocity to Bosnia and Herzegovina. At the end of 1991, the Socialist Federal Republic of Yugoslavia dissolved into its constituent republics, with Serbia and Montenegro forming the core of what remained of Yugoslavia. The Security Council recommended the admission of Croatia, Slovenia and Bosnia to the United Nations under Resolutions 753, 754 and 755 respectively in May 1992.

The United Nations became involved in all manner of activities in the former Yugoslavia in the attempts to end the fighting, to create humanitarian action, and to facilitate negotiations. However, what is specifically at issue here is the activity of the United Nations as it related to arms control. Other United Nations activities and decisions as they related to the war in the former Yugoslavia will, therefore, not be the focus of this analysis.

United Nations' activity in relation to Yugoslavia can be divided into three areas. First, the United Nations sought to impose an international blockade on weapons, in order to limit the scale of violence and lay the foundations for a peace settlement. Second, as the violence grew, peacekeepers were sent to the former Yugoslavia, with a role in limiting the violence and collecting heavy weapons. (United Nations' activity in this connection was also concerned with protecting UN personnel). Third, as the war became more brutal, the United Nations developed its humanitarian concerns, seeking to enforce the treatment of civilians and prisoners of war set out in international humanitarian law. Each of these areas of activity will be examined in turn.[6]

The arms embargo

The United Nations first became directly involved in the war in the former Yugoslavia in September 1991. The Security Council unanimously adopted Resolution 713, which declared that the Council had decided:

> under Chapter VII of the Charter of the United Nations, that all States shall, for the purposes of establishing peace and stability in Yugoslavia, immediately implement a general and complete embargo on all deliveries of weapons and military equipment to Yugoslavia until the Security Council decides otherwise following consultations between the Secretary General and the Government of Yugoslavia.[7]

This was something of an unusual arms embargo, in that it was supported by the government of the state at which it was aimed. Given its control of the Yugoslav army, the embargo could only really damage the Slovene and Croatian attempts to create viable armed forces.

Expectations that this would help bring about a ceasefire that would not be violated were in vain. Resolution 724 of 15 December 1991 sought to tighten the embargo. The Council:

> (a) *Requests* all States to report to the Secretary General within 20 days on the measures they have instituted for meeting the obligations set out in paragraph 6 of resolution 713 [1991] to implement a general and complete embargo on all deliveries of weapons and military equipment to Yugoslavia;
> (b) *Decides* to establish ... a Committee of the Security Council ... to undertake the following tasks and to report on its work to the Council ... (i) To examine the reports submitted pursuant to sub-paragraph (a) above; (ii) To seek from all States further information regarding the action taken by them concerning the effective implementation of the embargo ... (iii) To consider any information ... concerning violation of the embargo ... (iv) To recommend appropriate measures in response to violations.[8]

These sanctions were to be deepened over the next eighteen months to include a variety of other products. However, rather than wait for sanctions to have greater effect, movement was made on the deployment of United Nations' personnel in the former Yugoslavia.

Peacekeeping and arms control

Tightening sanctions made no contribution to reducing the level of violence in the former Yugoslavia as the country collapsed, and the United Nations took the decision to deploy its own forces on the territory of the former Yugoslavia. From this point onwards, much of the United Nations arms control activity in this region was concerned with the attempt to use its forces to separate the warring parties and to disarm the combatants.

The Secretary General produced a peacekeeping plan on 11 December

1991 which was approved by the Security Council in Resolution 724, paragraph 1, accepting the view that 'the conditions for establishing a peacekeeping operation in Yugoslavia still do not exist'.[9] Resolution 727 approved the sending of 50 military liaison officers; Resolution 740 increased this to 75.[10] Resolution 743 established a United Nations Protection Force (UNPROFOR) to be based in Croatia for twelve months as 'an interim arrangement to create the conditions of peace and security required for the negotiation of an overall settlement of the Yugoslav crisis'.[11] Resolution 749 urged 'all parties and others concerned to take all action necessary to ensure complete freedom of aerial movement for UNPROFOR'; and called upon 'all parties and others concerned not to resort to violence, particularly in any area where UNPROFOR is to be based or deployed'.[12]

Resolution 752 in May 1992 demonstrated the concern of the United Nations to create an armistice. The Resolution demanded:

> that all forms of interference from outside Bosnia-Herzegovina, including by units of the Yugoslav People's Army as well as elements of the Croatian Army, cease immediately ...
>
> that those units of the Yugoslav People's Army and elements of the Croatian Army, now in Bosnia-Herzegovina must be either withdrawn, or be subject to the Government of Bosnia-Herzegovina, or be disbanded and disarmed with their weapons placed under effective international monitoring ...
>
> also that all irregular forces in Bosnia-Herzegovina be disbanded and disarmed.[13]

The United Nations' forces were to have a central role in managing the disbanding and disarming process. However, as with so many initiatives in the former Yugoslavia, little progress was made.

The problem was that it proved difficult to implement agreements. Skirmishes in Croatia and the war in Bosnia carried on with little regard to the positioning of United Nations forces. Security Council Resolution 762 demanded that 'the remaining units of the Yugoslav People's Army, the Serb territorial defence units in Croatia and others concerned to comply strictly with their obligations ... in particular with regard to the withdrawal and the disarming of all forces'.[14]

Yet progress did seem possible in July 1992, when the warring parties in Bosnia-Herzegovina agreed on the disarming of their heavy weapons under United Nations auspices. In a Statement by the Security Council President on 17 July, it was reported that:

> The Council has decided in principle to respond positively to the request for the United Nations to make arrangements for the supervision by the United Nations Protection Force of all heavy weapons (combat aircraft, armour, artillery, mortars, rocket-launchers etc.) in accordance with the agreement of 17 July 1992 [between the parties in Bosnia and Herzegovina].[15]

However, in a further Statement by the President, on 24 July, it was reported that:

> The Council concurs with the Secretary General's view that the conditions do not yet exist for the United Nations to supervise the heavy weapons in Bosnia and Herzegovina as envisaged ... The Council ... emphasizes in particular the need ... for them to declare immediately to the Force Commander of UNPROFOR the locations and quantities of the heavy weapons to be placed under supervision.[16]

Not only were the disarmament plans not coming to fruition, but UNPROFOR forces were increasingly becoming targets. On 4 August, the President of the Security Council was to report that 'The members of the Security Council condemn the recent cowardly attack on UNPROFOR positions in Sarajevo resulting in loss of life and injuries among the Ukrainian servicemen.'[17] Attempting to protect UNPROFOR forces and provide a new basis for negotiations, through Resolution 781 on 9 October 1992, the Security Council decided 'to establish a ban on military flights in the airspace of Bosnia and Herzegovina'.[18] However, the use of force was not authorised to enforce the ban.[19] This was reaffirmed in Resolution 786, which stressed the 'ban on military flights in the airspace of Bosnia and Herzegovina, which applies to all flights, whether of fixed-wing or rotary-wing aircraft'.[20]

However, there was to be yet another series of setbacks for the United Nations. Before the end of the mandate of the UNPROFOR forces in Croatia, conflict again broke out. Resolution 802 on 25 January 1993 had to appeal for 'the heavy weapons seized from the UNPROFOR-controlled storage areas be returned immediately to UNPROFOR'.[21] Resolution 807 on 19 February 1993 had to demand 'further that the parties and others concerned refrain from positioning their forces in the proximity of UNPROFOR's units'.[22]

In response to a mortar attack on a market in Sarajevo in early 1994, in which sixty-eight people were killed, Boutros Boutros-Ghali, the United Nation's Secretary General, wrote to the Secretary General of NATO, Manfred Wörner, to authorise the use of force under Resolution 836.[23] Three days later, on 9 February, NATO issued an ultimatum: either the Bosnian Serbs withdrew their heavy weapons 20 kilometres from Sarajevo, or submitted them to UN authority, or those weapons would be destroyed by NATO air attack within ten days.[24] When the Serb forces withdrew, within the time limit, some argued for an extension of the policy to the other cities that the UN had declared to be safe havens.[25] On 28 February, when four Bosnian Serb aircraft were identified by NATO in the no-fly zone contravening Resolution 816, they were destroyed by aircraft in the first use of force in NATO's history.[26] Six weeks later, when Bosnian Serb forces continued to attack Gorazde threatening United Nations' observers, NATO air forces retaliated on two successive days by striking against the Serb forces on the ground.[27] However, such actions were to remain extremely limited uses of force. Russia had been very hostile to the threat of NATO force in the Balkans. Able to persuade the Bosnian Serbs to withdraw from Sarajevo in February, the Russians did not expect to have to face such NATO threats against the region again. Most Western countries accepted this, fearing a new East–West division, and given the domestic vulnerability of President Yeltsin against more nationalist forces.[28] As a consequence, the momentum gained by the use of force by NATO on behalf of the United Nations in Bosnia was lost.[29]

There were repeated efforts to create a framework within which the United Nations forces could disarm the warring parties. Further, rather like the Somali case to be examined later in this chapter, there were moves to forcibly disarm the combatants. However, unlike the Somali case, these moves were very limited by the nature of the international balance of power. Although some heavy weapons were impounded, in Croatia as well as Bosnia, it made relatively little difference on the ground. Far from creating the grounds for a peace settlement, the peacekeepers became targets themselves. However, UNPROFOR did have some success in terms of providing humanitarian aid, and in keeping people alive. It is to these humanitarian concerns that the analysis turns next.

Humanitarian concerns

As the brutality of the war in the former Yugoslavia increased, the United Nations' Security Council attempted to remind the participants of the laws of war and, when that seemed to be inadequate, to take steps to impose the laws of war upon them. A particular concern was 'ethnic cleansing', and Resolution 752 in May 1992 called 'upon all parties and others concerned to ensure that forcible expulsions of persons from the areas where they live and any attempts to change the ethnic composition of the population, anywhere in the former Socialist Federal Republic of Yugoslavia, cease immediately'.[30] That same month, Resolution 757 noted that the demands of Resolution 752 had not been implemented, set out new sanctions, and demanded 'that all parties and others concerned create immediately the necessary conditions for unimpeded delivery of humanitarian supplies to Sarajevo and other destinations in Bosnia and Herzegovina, including the establishment of a security zone encompassing Sarajevo and its airport'.[31] This demand was repeated in Resolution 758 on 8 June, which extended the scope of the UNPROFOR action.

Throughout the early part of the summer of 1992, evidence emerged that the practice of 'ethnic cleansing' was not the only abuse of the laws of war. One military practice was to prevent the movement of humanitarian aid; another was the creation of prison camps with little reference to the Geneva Conventions. Resolution 764 of 13 July 1992 demanded:

that all parties and others concerned cooperate fully with UNPROFOR and international humanitarian agencies to facilitate the provision of humanitarian aid to other areas of Bosnia and Herzegovina which remain in desperate need of assistance.[32]

Further, the Security Council reaffirmed:

that all parties are bound to comply with the obligations under international humanitarian law and in particular the Geneva Conventions of 12 August 1949, and that persons who commit or order the commission of grave breaches of the Conventions are individually responsible in respect of such breaches.[33]

In a statement by the President of the Security Council on 4 August 1992, it was affirmed that

The Security Council is deeply concerned at the continuing reports of widespread violations of international humanitarian law ... The Council condemns any such violation and abuses ... The Council reaffirms that all parties are bound to comply with the obligations under international humanitarian law and in particular the Geneva Conventions of 12 August 1949.[34]

Resolution 769 of 7 August 1992 repeated the condemnation of 'the abuses committed against the civilian population, particularly on ethnic grounds'.[35] Resolution 770 of 13 August:

Demands that unimpeded and continuous access to all camps, prisons and detention centres be granted immediately to the International Committee of the Red Cross and other relevant humanitarian organisations and that all detainees therein receive humane treatment including adequate food, shelter and medical care.[36]

However, the parties largely ignored these requests, and consequently the next step was to clarify the United Nations position on abuses of the laws of war. In response to these events, the Security Council passed Resolution 776 on 14 September 1992 which 'Authorises ... the enlargement of UNPROFOR's mandate and strength in Bosnia and Herzegovina ... to perform the functions ... including the protection of convoys of released detainees if requested by the International Committee of the Red Cross'.[37] Resolution 771 on 13 August 1992 was largely focused on the question of the humanitarian law of war. It:

1) Reaffirms that all parties to the conflict are bound to comply with their obligations under international humanitarian law ...

2) Strongly condemns any violations of international humanitarian law including those involved in the practice of 'ethnic cleansing' ...

7) Decides, acting under Chapter VII of the Charter of the United Nations, that all parties and others concerned in the former Yugoslavia, and all military forces in Bosnia and Herzegovina, shall comply with the provisions of the present resolution, failing which the Council will need to take further measures under the Charter.[38]

On 6 October, Resolution 780 requested the Secretary General to set up a Commission of Experts to investigate breaches of international humanitarian law. Resolution 798 on 18 December strongly condemned the camps.

In early 1993, the Security Council decided to try to go further. In Resolution 808 on 22 February, it decided 'that an international tribunal shall be established for the prosecution of persons responsible for serious violations of international humanitarian law committed in the territory of the former Yugoslavia since 1991'.[39] On 25 May 1993, the Security Council passed Resolution 827, in which they decided:

> hereby to establish an international tribunal for the sole purpose of prosecuting persons responsible for serious violations of international humanitarian law committed in the territory of the former Yugoslavia between 1 January 1991 and a date to be determined by the Security Council upon the restoration of peace.[40]

While seeking to provide a legal framework for the punishment of the guilty, the United Nations also sought to establish protection for the innocent. Through Resolution 819 on 16 April 1993, the Security Council demanded 'that all parties and others concerned treat Srebrenica and its surroundings as a safe area which should be free from any armed attack or any other hostile act'.[41] Through Resolution 824, the Council demanded:

> that the capital city of the Republic of Bosnia and Herzegovina, Sarajevo, and other such threatened areas, in particular the towns of Tuzla, Zepa, Gorazde, Bihac, as well as Srebrenica, and their surroundings should be treated as safe areas by all parties concerned and should be free from armed attacks and from any other hostile act ... [and] The immediate cessation of armed attacks or any hostile act against these safe areas.[42]

However, as seen above, little military aid (even in Sarajevo) was provided to turn this declaration into reality.

United Nations' efforts at humanitarian relief sought to maintain the regime of the laws of war developed over many centuries. It sought to ensure that non-combatants were treated humanely; that rules were followed when laying siege to cities; that certain areas would be defined as illegitimate for fighting; that those who broke the laws would be punished.

Assessment

Few successes can be attributed to the United Nations' arms control efforts in the former Yugoslavia. An arms embargo was initiated and policed fairly successfully; however, the United Nations sought to go further. There was no real success in using UNPROFOR to disarm the warring parties, or even to impound the heavy weapons of the protagonists. Compounds with impounded weapons were frequently raided by the warring factions. There were many declarations regarding the sanctity of the laws of war, but little action. The most compelling evidence for this came in the summer of 1995, with the fall of the 'safe havens' of Srebrenica and Zepa to the Bosnian Serbs, with massive breaches of human rights and the 'disappearance' of thousands. Recourse to the use of force to impose the will of the United Nations was constrained by Russian (and Chinese) reticence. Over the two years from the first United Nations Security Council Resolution on Yugoslavia on 25 September 1991, there were nearly fifty Resolutions. Many more were to follow. So much diplomatic activity represented many words, but few deeds, and hence very little depth. No regime was created, and hence no verification or detailed provisions were drawn up. Indeed, the failure to support existing norms of behaviour in war may be said to have actually damaged the regimes designed to support those norms. Beyond the arms embargo, the activity of the global international institution in the war in the former Yugoslavia could only be described as an arms control failure.

Forcible disarmament in Somalia

The United Nations operation in Somalia as it related to the control of arms contrasted with that in the former Yugoslavia in two important and distinct ways. First, the United Nations Security Council passed some fifty Resolutions in two years in Yugoslavia related to an arms embargo, to attempts to disarm heavy weapons from the warring factions, and to efforts to impose the laws of war. These activities, as already seen, were unsuccessful. In contrast, in the eighteen months from January 1992, only eight Security Council Resolutions were passed concerning Somalia, focused in arms control terms on the disarmament of the factions and on the protection of non-combatants. Second, whereas UNPROFOR had no role in forcibly disarming the parties in Yugoslavia and Bosnia, UNOSOM (United Nations Operation in Somalia) were enabled to use military force to bring about a widespread disarmament.

The bloodshed in Somalia was exacerbated by the downfall of President Siad Barre in January 1991, as in the aftermath numerous factions – often but by no means exclusively centred around support for either Ali Mahdi Mohamed or Mohamed Farah Aidid, even in Mogadishu – fought for supremacy.[43] Within a year, an already poor nation was reduced to anarchy and starvation. Over half the population were threatened with famine and malnutrition, and one in eight Somalis fled the country.[44]

Peacekeeping and the deployment of forces

The United Nations became involved in December 1991 with efforts to negotiate a settlement. Resolution 733 of 23 January 1992 called for a ceasefire in Somalia and humanitarian assistance for the people. Under paragraph 5, the Security Council decided:

> under Chapter VII of the Charter of the United Nations, that all States shall, for the purposes of establishing peace and stability in Somalia immediately implement a general and complete embargo on all deliveries of weapons and military equipment to Somalia until the Security Council decides otherwise.[45]

Following this, negotiations were held from 12 to 14 February which produced a ceasefire, and an Agreement on the Implementation of a Ceasefire signed by Ali Mahdi Mohamed and Mohamed Farah Aidid on 3 March. This agreement included provision for the deployment of 20 military observers to monitor the ceasefire, and military protection of humanitarian convoys.[46] However, Security Council Resolution 746 of 17 March regretted 'that the factions have not yet abided by their commitment to implement the ceasefire'.[47] It also agreed to send a team to Mogadishu to prepare a monitoring mechanism, and to 'develop a high priority plan to establish mechanisms to ensure the unimpeded delivery of humanitarian assistance'.[48] In discussions with this team, Mohamed Farah Aidid and Ali Mahdi Mohamed exchanged Letters of Agreement on 27 and 28 March respectively on the ceasefire and the movement of humanitarian assistance.

On this basis, the Secretary General recommended to the Security Council on 21 April that UNOSOM be set up, which the Council approved in Resolution 751 on 24 April.[49] It also set up a Committee of the Security Council:

> (a) to seek from all States information regarding the action taken by them concerning the effective implementation of the embargo ...
> (b) to consider any information brought to its attention by States concerning violations of the embargo ...
> (c) to recommend appropriate measures in response to violations.[50]

Subsequently, as requested by the Council, the Secretary General sought agreement with the warring parties for fifty observers to be sent to monitor the ceasefire, and for military personnel to be sent to protect convoys of humanitarian aid from the airport and port of Mogadishu, as well as for the protection of United Nations' personnel. Agreement was reached on the deployment of monitors on 23 June, and they arrived in early July 1992. Resolution 767 was passed on 27 July urging 'the full respect of the security and safety of the personnel of the humanitarian organisations ... In the absence of such cooperation, the Security Council does not exclude other measures to deliver humanitarian assistance to Somalia'.[51] Agreement was reached with the Somali factions on the sending of a security force of 500 troops in mid-August, and they were deployed in mid-September. Following a report from the Secretary General on 24 August describing the problems of the humanitarian effort due to the lack of a ceasefire in the country, violence and a lack of law, the Council passed Resolution 775 and enlarged the

UNOSOM forces by an additional 750 troops.[52] Subsequently, UNOSOM was further enlarged, with a planned total of 4219 personnel.[53]

From peacekeeping to peacemaking

Despite these efforts, the situation deteriorated dramatically throughout Somalia during the rest of 1992. Aid arriving in Somalia was stolen by the factions; United Nations' personnel were fired upon; and many of the factions refused to allow the humanitarian convoys passage through their territory. Following reports by the Secretary General, and an offer from the United States to organise a mission to ensure the movement of humanitarian aid, the Security Council passed Resolution 794 which authorised the use of force. This extremely important Resolution set out the grounds for its action in the Preamble:

> *Expressing grave alarm* at continuing reports of widespread violations of international humanitarian law occurring in Somalia, including reports of violence and threats of violence against personnel participating lawfully in impartial humanitarian relief activities; deliberate attacks on non-combatants, relief consignments and vehicles, and medical and relief facilities; and impeding the delivery of food and medical supplies essential for the survival of the civilian population;
> *Dismayed* by the continuation of conditions that impede the delivery of humanitarian supplies to destinations within Somalia, and in particular reports of looting of relief supplies destined for starving people ...
> *Determined further* to restore peace, stability and law and order with a view to facilitating the process of a political settlement.[54]

The Security Council, noting the lead given by the United States and the need for the establishment of a unified command, authorised the use of force in paragraph 10:

> *Acting* under Chapter VII of the Charter of the United Nations, *authorises* the Secretary-General and Member States cooperating to ... use all necessary means to establish as soon as possible a secure environment for humanitarian relief operations in Somalia.[55]

The first units were deployed on 9 December, six days after the Resolution was passed.

One of the major operations of the force, and of central relevance to this analysis, was the disarmament of the local Somali factions. Following the agreements the Somali parties concluded at the 'Informal Preparatory Meeting on Somali Political Reconciliation in Addis Ababa on Implementing the Cease-fire and on Modalities of Disarmament', UNOSOM formed its disarmament concept. This would produce a 'continuous and irreversible' disarmament process, which would continue until a new Somali government was formed, and which in the meantime would be overseen by a United

Nations–Somali committee who would decide which heavy weapons would be stored for a new Somali army, and which destroyed.[56] The Somali parties would be informed and involved in the disarmament process, and any who failed to live up to their commitments 'would have their weapons and equipment confiscated and/or destroyed.'[57] In order to achieve this, cantonment sites would be established, where heavy weapons would be stored, and transition sites would be created, where factional forces would surrender their small arms and receive re-training. Factional forces would go first to the cantonments, then to the transition sites, and both sites would be separated by significant distances.

Resolution 814 of 26 March 1993 demanded full compliance by all the parties with the ceasefire and disarmament agreements. Paragraph 8 demanded 'that all Somali parties, including movements and factions, comply fully with the commitments they have undertaken in the agreements they concluded at the Informal Preparatory Meeting on Somali Political Reconciliation in Addis Ababa, and in particular with their Agreement on Implementing the Cease-fire and on Modalities of Disarmament'.[58] However, in the course of disarming the factions and groups, the United Nations forces came under attack from the United Somali Congress of Mohamed Farah Aidid. In the course of taking an inventory of militia weapons-storage sites in Mogadishu on 5 June, prohibited weapons such as TOW missiles, Milan missiles and SA–7s were discovered. In violence following the discovery of these weapons, 25 United Nations peacekeeping troops were killed and 57 wounded.

Forcible disarmament

In response to the violence against United Nations' forces, and the apparent failure to implement a peaceful disarmament of the Somali factions, the Security Council passed Resolution 837 on 6 June 1993. This Resolution:

> *Strongly condemn[ed]* the unprovoked attacks against the personnel of UNOSOM II on 5 June 1993, which appear to have been part of a calculated and premeditated series of ceasefire violations to prevent by intimidation UNOSOM II from carrying out its mandate as provided for in resolution 814 (1993) ...
> *Reemphasize[d]* the crucial importance of the early implementation of the disarmament of all Somali parties ...
> *Demand[ed]* once again that all Somali parties, including movements and factions, comply fully with the commitments they have undertaken ...in particular ... on implementing the ceasefire and on modalities of disarmament.[59]

With this mandate, UNOSOM II used force from 12 to 14 June in order to disarm all units in Mogadishu South, given that this was the base of Aidid, and that large numbers of weapons had apparently been hidden in the area.

Using air and ground strikes, and follow up sweeps, the UNOSOM II forces destroyed arms caches and ammunition dumps, and searched the area for other weapons, 'which included large numbers of tanks, artillery pieces, mortars, machine-guns, anti-aircraft guns, mines and ammunition'.[60] Following the attempt at the forcible disarmament of the Aidid forces, UNOSOM II conducted a sector-by-sector search of the entire city for weaponry. Disarmament was seen by the United Nations's Secretary General, Boutros Boutros-Ghali, as 'fundamental to the restoration of law and order and public safety, as well as to unimpeded progress in political reconciliation and national rehabilitation'.[61]

Assessment

In Yugoslavia and Bosnia, the United Nations had sought to control arms through embargo, negotiation and agreement. In Somalia, the United Nations again used an embargo but, when negotiation and agreement failed to bring about the control of the arms desired, UNOSOM II moved to forcible disarmament. The contrast could not be greater in relation to disarmament. For a long time, failure to obtain meaningful disarmament agreements in the former Yugoslavia did nothing in support of the norms of the rules of war. The forcible disarmament of the factions in Somalia at least led to the movement of humanitarian supplies. However, such activities made little contribution to ending the conflict in Somalia and, indeed, failed even to fully disarm the supporters of General Aidid. Further, the United Nation's use of force weakened the legitimacy of the Organisation in the country, while rallying nationalist as well as factional support behind Aidid.[62] Both Bosnia and in Somalia, in different ways, demonstrated the limits of arms control by international organisation. But what of the United Nations' role in Cambodia?

Disarmament and elections in Cambodia

Following decades of conflict and civil war, a peace process for Cambodia began in the late 1980s and, with the withdrawal of Vietnamese forces, led to a peace agreement signed in Paris at the Conference on Cambodia on 23 October 1991.[63] Through this agreement, and Security Council Resolution 717 of 16 October, a United Nations Transitional Authority in Cambodia (UNTAC) was to be set up with a mandate which included 'aspects relating to human rights, the organisation and conduct of free and fair general elections, military arrangements, civil administration, the maintenance of law and order, the repatriation and resettlement of the Cambodian refugees and displaced persons, and the rehabilitation of essential Cambodian infrastructures during the transitional period'.[64] The United Nations would work through the Supreme National Council of Cambodia which was established by the Paris Agreement to represent the sovereignty of Cambodia during the transition to an elected government, but which passed authority for the implementation of the Paris Agreement to the United Nations. Subsequently, Resolution 718 of 31 October 1991 welcomed the Paris Agreement, and requested information on the implementation plan for the United Nations, which led to the formal setting up of the United Nations Advance Mission in Cambodia (UNAMIC) to prepare the ground for UNTAC.[65] Thus, the work of the United Nations in Cambodia covered a large area; this brief analysis will focus only on the arms control aspects.[66]

The scope for disarmament in Cambodia

The Paris Agreement and subsequent United Nations' documents stipulated four areas which were to form the core military aspect of UNTAC's work.[67] These related to:

(a) Verification of the withdrawal and non-return of all categories of foreign forces and their arms and equipment;
(b) Supervision of the ceasefire and related measures, including regroupment, cantonment, disarming and demobilisation;
(c) Weapons control, including monitoring the cessation of outside military assistance, locating and confiscating the caches of weapons and military supplies throughout Cambodia, storing of the arms and equipment of the cantoned and the demobilised military forces;
(d) Assisting with mine-clearance, including training programmes and mine awareness programmes.[68]

Thus, as defined by the Paris Agreement, categories (b) and (c) were related to arms control.

In terms of the demobilisation required by category (b), the terms of the Paris Agreement stipulated that 70 per cent of the designated forces were to be demobilised prior to the end of the election registration period (i.e., by August 1992).[69] The size of this operation would be immense. As the Secretary General reported:

information provided by the four Cambodian parties revealed that their regular military forces totalled over 200,000, deployed in some 650 separate locations. In addition, militias, totalling some 250,000, operate in almost all villages throughout the country. These forces are armed with over 300,000 weapons of all types and some 80 million rounds of ammunition.[70]

Full demobilisation in cantons thus seemed almost impossible, and therefore UNTAC limited the extent of the disarmament and demobilisation that it was to bring about. UNTAC set itself the task of focusing on the regular forces, and creating mechanisms whereby the militias would simply surrender their weapons to UNTAC without being placed in cantons. Further, UNTAC set itself the task of achieving the regroupment of forces into cantonments for disarming and demobilising the troops, weapons, ammunition and equipment that the four parties had declared, rather than produce any independent assessment of force levels. In terms of the weapons control stipulated by category (c) in the UNTAC mandate, the United Nations' forces were to be responsible for destroying any reported arms caches. In addition, all surrendered weapons would have to be secured.

These arrangements, suggested by the Secretary General, were mandated by the Security Council in Resolution 745 of 28 February 1992. UNTAC was to be established for a maximum of eighteen months, and the elections were to be scheduled for May 1993.

Implementation problems

Problems with the arrangements emerged in the summer. In his First Special Report on UNTAC, the Secretary General noted that the Party of Democratic Kampuchea (PDK) was not complying with the terms of the Paris Agreement.[71] In his Second Report, the Secretary General noted that the PDK had 'still failed to comply with the Agreements and has refused to canton any of its forces'.[72] Further, UNTAC forces were denied access to areas controlled by the PDK. The PDK argued that foreign forces (ie the Vietnamese) were still able to enter Cambodia in breach of the Paris Agreements, and that UNTAC forces were not implementing the military aspect of their work as outlined in (a) above. This led to a massive delay in the cantonment process so that by 11 July (ie within four weeks of the beginning of Phase II of the Paris Agreement, by which time the regroupment and cantonment process should have been completed), barely 5 per cent of the declared military forces of all four groups had been cantoned. The Security Council, in Resolution 766, demanded 'that the Party that has failed so far to do so permit without delay the deployment of UNTAC in the areas under its control, and implement fully Phase II of the Plan as well as other aspects of the Paris Agreements'.[73] However, the PDK obstruction continued into the autumn, so that the Security Council was forced to repeat itself in Resolution 783 in October, deploring 'the fact that the PDK, ignoring the requests and demands contained in its resolution 766 (1992), has not yet complied with its obligations'; and demanding that the PDK 'fulfils immediately its obligations under the Paris Agreement; that it facilitate without delay full deployment of UNTAC in the areas under its control; and that it implement fully phase II of the plan, particularly cantonment and demobilisation'.[74]

In his Third Progress Report to the Security Council in January 1993, the Secretary General was forced to admit the failure of the arms control elements of the Paris Agreements. The non-compliance of the PDK 'meant the effective suspension of the cantonment, disarming and demobilisation of the armed forces of the four factions, with the result that those forces remain under arms in the field'.[75] Some 55,000 troops had been disarmed before the suspension; none belonged to the military arm of the PDK. In addition, cease-fire violations had increased since the onset of the dry season in November, with the military forces clearly searching for strategic advantages, while UNTAC members increasingly came under fire, especially after March 1993.

Assessment

The political activities of UNTAC in Cambodia were fairly successful. Elections were held in May 1993, with relatively little violence, and a high turnout.[76] The military component was also largely successful in its modified role of protecting the election process. However, in arms control terms, UNTAC failed. In any case, its mandate could have been criticised for not paying sufficient attention to the militias, and for accepting the information provided by the parties. This would perhaps have been harsh. The disarming and disbanding of 200,000 regular troops would have been a great arms control success. The policies of the PDK, however, made that impossible, and UNTAC did not have the resources and political support to engage in forcible disarmament. The United Nations faced similar intractable problems in Mozambique.

Delay and deferral over disarmament in Mozambique

Following its independence from Portugal in the mid-1970s, Mozambique descended into violent and bloody civil war. With government forces supported by Cuba, and rebels financed and armed by South Africa, Mozambique's internal problems became greatly magnified by external attention. However, as international actors interfered with and exacerbated the Mozambican crisis of the late 1970s and early 1980s, so the resolution of the Mozambican war was to be met by a measure of international indifference.[77]

On 4 October 1992, President Chissano of Mozambique and the President of the rebel Renamo (Resistência Nacional Moçambicana) forces, Afonso Dhlakama, signed a General Peace Agreement in Rome. This Agreement called for the implementation of a ceasefire (known as E–day) not later than 15 October, to be followed by a process of the separation of the two sides' military forces into specified cantonments, and the demobilisation of those forces that would not be integrated into a new Mozambican Defence Force. This demobilisation would take place within six months of E–day, while political parties would be formed in order that elections could be held not later than 15 October 1993.[78]

The General Agreement, ending fourteen years of war, comprised an agreement and seven protocols. Protocol IV related to military issues, V to guarantees, and VI to the ceasefire.[79] In addition, the overall agreement included the agreements of 10 July 1990, 1 December 1990, a Joint Declaration of 7 August 1992, and a declaration on guiding principles for humanitarian assistance of 16 July 1992. The United Nations was to take direct responsibility for certain functions in relation to the ceasefire, the elections and humanitarian assistance, and was to chair the body charged with supervising the implementation of the overall Agreement, the Supervisory and Monitoring Committee. Through Resolution 782 of 13 October 1992, the Security Council authorised the United Nations to perform these roles, and Resolution 797 in December authorised the establishment of the United Nations Operation in Mozambique, ONUMOZ.[80] This analysis will focus on the work of the United Nations in relation to the ceasefire, the separation of the two sides' forces, and the demobilisation process. It will examine first the requirements of the General Agreement on these points, then the difficulties of maintaining agreement amongst the Mozambican parties, the problems faced by the United Nations itself, and the implications of the many delays.

Requirements of the general agreement

The ceasefire was to be organised through the Ceasefire Commission (CFC), a subcommittee of the Supervisory and Monitoring Committee, which would have three regional headquarters, and representation in the assembly areas. Once the ceasefire had been established, the military forces of the two sides were to be taken to assembly points to be disarmed. Verification of this would take place in the forty-nine assembly areas identified for the separation and disarmament of the rival factions. The United Nations force would be represented at each site, but was to remain separate from the monitoring committees of the two Mozambican parties.

The disarmament process would be a major endeavour. Some 110,000 Mozambican troops from both sides were due to report to the 49 sites based in three military areas. They had to be disarmed, fed, demobilised and integrated into the new Mozambique. For this task, the United Nations was to have 354 military observers, 5 infantry battalions of 850 personnel each, an engineering battalion and 8 other companies and units with responsibility for logistics, headquarters, communications and including a medical unit and an air unit.

In the final part of the military sections of the General Agreement, the responsibility for the creation of new Mozambican Defence Forces was to lie with the Joint Commission for the Formation of the Mozambican Defence Forces (CCFADM), a subcommittee of the Supervisory and Monitoring Committee. Only a proportion of the two sides military was to form the new Forces, totalling 30,000 troops; the rest were to be integrated into Mozambican society. The United Nations was also to take overall monitoring responsibility for this activity.

Mozambican problems

Throughout 1993, the implementation of the General Agreement was bedevilled by arguments between the government and Renamo. Demobilisation was to have been completed within six months of E–day, according to the General Agreement. However, by the middle of 1993, little progress had been achieved. Resolution 850 on 9 July noted the delay with some concern.[81] Not only had there been ceasefire violations, but the assembly points had not yet all been identified. In the Secretary General's Report on 30 August, Boutros-Ghali noted that there had been 47 complaints of ceasefire violations reported to the CFC, while only 34 of the 49 assembly points had been found acceptable by both sides. Of these, only 8 were designated for Renamo forces out of the 20 that had been apportioned to Renamo. These problems led to a delay in the work of the CCFADM, which only met for the first time on 22 July, 3 months after its work should have been completed.

The problems in terms of the ceasefire, the identification of assembly points, and beginning the work of the CCFADM were due, essentially, to the suspicions between the government and Renamo over the good faith of the other. Renamo had refused to begin demobilisation fearing that it would lose control over its own territory. In July 1993, Renamo had complained that government forces had encroached into villages in Tete Province and on a Renamo base in Gaza Province. Under protest from the United Nations, the government claimed that it reserved the right to use force to reclaim territory. Renamo threatened retaliation; and the government refused to demobilise its troops until Renamo began.[82] Renamo were also unwilling to begin demobilisation until the full deployment of both ONUMOZ and the United Nations' police team. During this period, little progress was made towards elections, with bitter argument over the composition of the National Electoral Commission.

Such delays clearly required that a new timetable be devised. Proposals were reported by the Secretary General to the Security Council at the end of August. Under the new arrangements, elections were to be held no later than October 1994. Concentration of military forces would begin in September 1993, with demobilisation taking some eight or nine months. A total of 30,000 troops would be absorbed into the new army, half of which was to be operational by May 1994, the rest by September.

However, it took nearly two more months to reach agreement between Chissano and Dhlakama on points of dispute. In the 20 October agreement between the two, chaired by Boutros-Ghali, yet another new timetable was constructed. It set out the following schedule: concentration of troops to begin in November 1993; demobilisation to begin in January 1994, to be 50 per cent completed by March, and to be fully completed by May: training for the new army to begin in November 1993, to be completed by August 1994, and the new army was to be fully operational by September: elections to take place by the end of October.[83]

United Nations' problems

The United Nations responded slowly to its new responsibilities in Mozambique. It took until May 1993 to complete the deployment of the five battalions of infantry forces, seven months after E–day. It took another two months to complete the military deployments of ONUMOZ, while by the end of October 1993 only 303 of the required 354 military observers had arrived.[84]

The lack of observers was critical to the United Nations' commitment to Mozambique. The observers had to monitor the ceasefire; to prepare the assembly points; and to prepare for the disarmament of the Mozambican forces. In these activities, pivotal to the success of the General Agreement and over issues in which there was much disagreement between the government and Renamo, the United Nations had been unable to fulfil its commitment.

Further problems arose over the deployment of United Nations' police forces. In the Rome Agreement, 128 had been promised, to ensure impartiality in Mozambique's police force. Twelve months later, these officers had still not been recruited. Neither the finance was available to the United Nations, nor could they find 128 police officers who were qualified, willing, and who could speak Portuguese.[85] This failure allowed Renamo to delay the implementation of the peace agreement throughout much of 1993, arguing that the United Nations force was needed to monitor the activities of the Mozambican police. Renamo accepted the need to move forward in the 20 October 1993 agreement, but it was a good example of how the United Nations was unable to offer the reassurance promised in the General Agreement.[86]

In his Report to the Security Council in November 1993, the Secretary General described the nature of the expenditure being incurred by the organisation in Mozambique. To expand United Nations' activities to the committed level, Boutros Boutros-Ghali reported that an additional $6.5 million would be required each month.[87] Eventually, and with much reluctance, this level of expenditure was accepted by the Member States.

Delays into 1994[88]

Arguments between the Government and Renamo, and the problems faced by ONUMOZ, had led to a major delay in implementing the General Agreement. The 20 October agreement had set out a new timetable for the assembly of the armed forces, demobilisation and the construction of the new army. However, each aspect was to face yet further delays.

The concentration of forces into assembly points was due to begin in November 1993. This activity did begin on 30 November, but only on a limited basis. The Supervision and Monitoring Commission had been able to ratify the 'Declaration regarding the opening of assembly areas pursuant to the general peace agreement in Mozambique', but initially only on the basis of 20 of the 49 assembly points. By 20 December, 15 more sites were added, but delays continued over the final 14 due to arguments between the government and Renamo over control of locations for the proposed assembly sites. These problems were not resolved until 21 February 1994.

Utilisation of the assembly sites varied between the two sides. By 24 January 1994, 16,609 government troops (22 per cent of the declared total) and 6714 Renamo troops (58 per cent) had checked into the assembly sites. The percentages rose to 55 per cent of government forces and 81 per cent of Renamo by 18 April. However, from this point, further problems emerged. The Government had declared in the General Agreement that 61,638 troops would be sent to its twenty-nine assembly areas, with 14,767 registered outside those areas. On 21 April, the government revised its targets downwards, with 49,630 to be registered in the assembly areas, and 14,480 outside. Through one statement, the number of government soldiers in the assembly points rose from 55 per cent to 68 per cent. This was a position Renamo initially was unable to accept. However, under pressure from the United Nations both in New York (Resolution 916 of 5 May 1994 urged a speedy compromise) and in Mozambique, Renamo accepted the compromise brokered by the Ceasefire Commission, in which the government's argument that 13,776 soldiers had demobilised before the signing of the General Agreement was largely accepted. The government's new target figures were 49,638 in assembly areas, with 14,828 outside, which Renamo accepted on condition that these numbers were seen as a working estimate, to be verified by the Ceasefire Commission after the completion of the assembly of the government's troops. Although the concentration of forces into assembly areas could continue, there had been another significant delay.

Before the delay over figures, progress had begun with the demobilisation, but only on 10 March, ten weeks late. By 18 April, 12,195 government and 561 Renamo troops had been demobilised and transported home, corresponding to 20 per cent of government forces and 3 per cent of Renamo. This rose to 22,832 government (46 per cent) and 5,138 Renamo (54 per cent) troops by 4 July; but the likelihood of meeting the deadline of 15 August for complete demobilisation was low. In addition, the registration of those government troops that were not to be assembled was proceeding in a very tardy fashion. A final issue related to the government's paramilitary troops, which totalled some 155,600. The government delayed the deadline for the initiation of the dismantling of these forces until 12 January 1994, and progress thereafter was slow.

Problems also arose with the creation of the new Mozambican forces. The troops were to be selected from those in the assembly points. However, the delay in completing the concentration of forces led to overcrowding in those areas. Since it had been planned to manage the demobilisation in stages, the assembly areas were only designed to manage with between 30 to 50 per cent of the total troops at any one time. However, this staging system collapsed as the new timetable again fell behind schedule with some camps operating at 420 per cent of capacity, others at only 3 per cent. Overcrowding led to outbreaks of violence, and a decision to move some troops directly to training camps for the new army, without moving through the assembly sites. United Nations' military personnel had to be deployed around some cantonment bases to protect United Nations' staff. Further problems arose with a widespread unwillingness amongst soldiers to join the new Mozambican defence force. These difficulties, and the lack of finance for training purposes, led in April to a scaling back of the proposed size of the army to 15,000 before the elections in October. By July, it was clear that even this target was over-ambitious, as only 3000 troops had been trained.

Assessment

The United Nations had a particularly difficult task in implementing disarmament in Mozambique. The United Nations itself had not been a direct party to the creation of the General Agreement between the Mozambican Government and Renamo, and yet that Agreement made important demands of the United Nations. Most significantly, the initial six month timetable for the implementation of disarmament and demobilisation of the military forces, and for the creation of new Mozambican Forces, was hopelessly unrealistic. How could the United Nations have begun an operation in Mozambique, and overseen such an outcome in this period? Not enough ground work had been completed, for example in terms of identifying the assembly areas. The United Nations simply had to work within the terms of an unworkable Agreement.

However, these problems were greatly exacerbated by the disinterest shown by most of the member states of the United Nations. The delays in apportioning resources for ONUMOZ may have been decisive. The period immediately after the signing of the General Agreement was always going to be critical to the whole disarmament process. A successful start in the honeymoon post-agreement period was ruined, however, by the sloth of the United Nations in deploying its advisors and troops. This was a problem that bedevilled the United Nations' operation throughout its time in Mozambique, however, not just in the initial months. In July 1994, contributions to the

United Nations of some $153.2 million were outstanding for ONUMOZ, a figure which represented over 35 per cent of the total amount assessed on Member States for the operation. Further, the cost constraints led to pressure for early withdrawals. By April 1994, national components of ONUMOZ were beginning to be withdrawn, notably the infantry battalion from Italy. The size of ONUMOZ had always been smaller than planned: a maximum figure of 5914 had been achieved, against the planned total of 6979. Cost and other pressures had led to plans that the military presence of ONUMOZ would be scaled down from June 1994; however, it was clear that the demo-bilisation process would not be completed by that time.

Lessons seem apparent from the Mozambique case. The failures in Mozam-bique stem from the unrealistic nature of the General Agreement, and the inability of the United Nations to respond in a timely fashion. The United Nations had entered into commitments to impose deep disarmament on the warring factions; however, it had neither the resources nor the political framework to fully bring about that end. Timetables for military demobilisa-tion were never in tune with political or logistic reality. And yet a great deal had still been accomplished with, for example, 59,213 weapons collected from government troops, 15,645 from Renamo, and 37,622 from the gov-ernment's paramilitary forces by 4 July 1994. So much more could have been achieved had the United Nations been able to make the level of invest-ment that had been possible in Iraq after the Gulf War, let alone the level of physical and legal control possessed by UNSCOM in Iraq. It is to this Iraqi case that the analysis now turns.

The involuntary disarming of Iraq

Iraq's invasion of Kuwait on 2 August 1990 led the United Nations to pass Security Council Resolution 661 on 6 August 1990, which imposed full sanctions on Iraq, and in particular prohibited 'The sale or supply ... of any commodities or products, including weapons or any other miliary equipment ... to any body in Iraq or Kuwait'.[89] Iraq's failure to comply with Security Council instructions to withdraw from Kuwait led to the subsequent war with the Coalition forces, and the demand in Resolution 686 on 2 March 1991 for Iraq to accept terms for a ceasefire, which it did the following day.[90] These events were to lead to a series of decisions taken by the United Nations for the disarming of major Iraqi weapons systems.

The framework for Iraqi disarmament

The international framework for the disarming of Iraq was contained in Security Council Resolution 687. This Resolution contained a series of pro-visions for managing the relationship between Iraq and Kuwait, and between

Iraq and the international community. For the purposes of this analysis, only the sections which focused on Iraq's capabilities for the development and use of weapons of mass destruction will be examined.[91] The Council made clear that it was:

> *Conscious* ... of the statements by Iraq threatening to use weapons in violation of its obligations under the Geneva Protocol for the Prohibition of the Use in War of Asphyxiating, Poisonous or Other Gases, and of Bacteriological Methods of Warfare, signed at Geneva on 17 June 1925, and of its prior use of chemical weapons ...
> *Aware* of the use by Iraq of ballistic missiles in unprovoked attacks and therefore of the need to take specific measures in regard to such missiles located in Iraq ...
> *Concerned* by the reports in the hands of Member States that Iraq has attempted to acquire materials for a nuclear-weapons programme contrary to its obligations under the Treaty on the Non-Proliferation of Nuclear Weapons.[92]

This long Resolution reaffirmed the prohibition on the sale and supply of arms and related material to Iraq, and the continuation of sanctions, as set out in Resolution 660.[93] The heart of the new restrictions on Iraq were set out in Section C of the Resolution. Iraq had to:

> unconditionally accept the destruction, removal, or rendering harmless, under international supervision, of:
>   a) all chemical and biological weapons and all stocks of agents and all related subsystems and components and all research, development, support and manufacturing facilities;
>   b) all ballistic missiles with a range greater than 150 kilometres and related major parts, and repair and production facilities.[94]

To implement this requirement, Iraq had to submit 'a declaration of the locations, amounts and types of all items specified' within fifteen days.[95] Subsequently, the Secretary General was to produce a plan for the formation of a Special Commission 'which shall carry out immediate on-site-inspection of Iraq's biological, chemical and missile capabilities, based on Iraq's declarations and the designation of any additional locations by the Special Commission itself' and would oversee the supervision of the destruction of all such material.[96] This United Nations Special Commission (UNSCOM), with Rolf Ekeus in the chair, would work closely with the International Atomic Energy Agency (IAEA), which would conduct on-site inspection of nuclear facilities and would remove all nuclear weapons-usable materials.[97] Both bodies would be executive subsidiary organs of the Security Council itself.

UNSCOM and the IAEA were to operate a three stage disarmament process. First, on the evidence of the baseline information provided by Iraq, they were to take possession of prohibited weapons and substances. Second, they were to oversee the removal of certain items from Iraq and the destruction of the remaining prohibited items. Third, both UNSCOM and the IAEA were to prepare plans for the long-term monitoring of Iraqi weapons development. Within forty-five days, the two bodies were to submit a plan to the Security Council for the disarmament of Iraq, and were to carry it out within a further forty-five days after the approval of the plan. Within 120 days of Resolution 687, the bodies were to submit to the Council plans for the long-term monitoring of Iraq. The plans of UNSCOM and the IAEA in disarming Iraq in furtherance of Resolution 687 were approved in Resolution 699 of 17 June 1991, and in the face of difficulties in obtaining cooperation from Iraq, the Resolution extended the forty-five day implementation period so that the bodies could remain active in Iraq until their work was completed.

Problems with implementation[98]

Iraq was required to provide baseline information which would provide the basis for the UNSCOM and IAEA inspections. The first IAEA inspection took place from 15 to 21 May 1991, the first chemical inspection from 9 to 15 June, the first ballistic missile inspection from 30 June to 7 July, and the first biological weapons inspection from 2 to 8 August. However, these activities were met with Iraqi antagonism, animosity and hostility. Iraq failed to provide the level of information required by UNSCOM and the IAEA. Indeed, the baseline information provided by Iraq proved to be misleading and incomplete in the nuclear, chemical, biological and missile weapons fields. For example, by October 1991, UNSCOM had discovered a chemical weapons arsenal ten times the size of that initially declared by the Iraqis.[99] In addition, Iraq refused to open all of its weapons and production facilities to inspection.

The Security Council sought to keep up the pressure on Iraq to conform to the commitments entered into in Resolution 687. Resolution 700 had confirmed the continuation of the arms embargo and sanctions on Iraq.[100] Sanctions would only be lifted after Iraq had complied with the United Nations' requirement for the destruction of its weapons of mass destruction through cooperation with UNSCOM and the IAEA. Resolution 707 condemned:

> Iraq's serious violation of a number of its obligations under section C of resolution 687 (1991) and of its undertakings to co-operate with the Special Commission and the IAEA, which constitutes a material breach of the relevant provisions of resolution 687 which established a cease-fire and provided the conditions essential to the restoration of peace and security in the region.[101]

It also demanded Iraqi acquiescence with the activities of UNSCOM and the IAEA. The Security Council approved the plans of UNSCOM and the IAEA for ongoing verification and inspections of the various weapons and production sites in Iraq.[102]

A pattern of confrontation between the United Nations and Iraq, followed by Iraqi concessions, developed. There were many examples. In 1991, Iraq prevented an inspection of an army base while Iraqi forces crated and removed items; in 1992 Iraq refused inspectors entry into the Ministry of Agriculture and Irrigation Building where important documents relating to ballistic missiles were thought to be sited; in 1993, Iraq insisted that UNSCOM officials use Iraqi Airways aircraft exclusively instead of their own to enter into and depart from Iraq (which led to the American bombing attack on nuclear related sites of al-Rabiyah to try to force Iraqi compliance).[103] The Iraqis spent much of June and July 1991 unilaterally destroying materials and weapons, and in destroying evidence, making the work of UNSCOM much more difficult in the context of the ongoing Iraqi refusal to provide full detailed information regarding their weapons holdings. UNSCOM were forced to conduct wide searches for weapons, with, for example, the discovery in early 1992 of some one hundred artillery rockets hidden deeply in the desert sand, representing a 25 per cent increase on the number of such rockets declared by Iraq. Further, from initially declaring possession of only 62 ballistic missiles with ranges over 150 kilometres, in early 1992 Iraq confessed to still possessing another 92.[104]

Assessment

Criticisms of the United Nations' efforts to disarm Iraq could certainly be made. Without basic information from Iraq, and without any confidence in information that was provided, little assurance could be generated that the full disarmament of Iraq's weapons of mass destruction was, in fact, being totally implemented. However, there were some successes.[105] Iraq declared that it had no nuclear weapons programme in a letter from Foreign Minister Tariq Aziz to the Security Council on 8 April 1991.[106] Yet, 'By the end of September 1991, the main components of Iraq's multifaceted clandestine nuclear programme were uncovered: a program that involved 10,000 scientists and technicians working on projects with an estimated cost of several billion dollars.'[107] There were, however, clear limits to what could be achieved by UNSCOM and the IAEA. Chemical weapons were one area in which great progress was made.[108] However, the identification of all chemical agents would be extremely difficult in a country as large as Iraq, and even were they all to be discovered and destroyed, chemical programmes could be quickly reconstituted.[109]

Much of the activity of UNSCOM was new. After all, 'Iraq was ... the first sovereign state subject to unilateral disarmament measures at the direction of an international authority.'[110] However, Iraq was unwilling to be placed in this position, and through its own means was able to delay and confuse the disarmers. As the Advisor to UNSCOM's executive chairman argued:

Starting with the very first declarations and inspections, it became evident that Iraq was not acting in good faith, would use every possible pretext to reinterpret UNSCOM's inspection rights, and occasionally would use harassment tactics to make inspections as difficult as possible.[111]

The United Nations were able to put pressure on the Iraqis, not only through the passing of Security Council Resolutions, but also by continuing the sanctions and oil embargo (the costs of UNSCOM and IAEA activity were to be borne by Iraqi oil revenue), and by threatening and carrying out military strikes to compel Iraqi adherence to its obligations. In addition, in the light of inadequate information, UNSCOM itself had to develop far more intrusive measures of investigation and inspection than was originally anticipated.

An assessment of the disarmament efforts of the United Nations in Iraq would, therefore, be mixed. There was a great deal of activity. Fifty-three inspections were carried out in the first two years of the UNSCOM and IAEA mandate in Iraq.[112] Much material was identified and destroyed. However, Iraqi obstruction delayed the operation, and lessened confidence in its ability to totally eliminate all prescribed weapons. For former UNSCOM inspection leader David Kay, 'the UN inspectors have had to cope with an unparalleled level of deception, fraud, cheating and intimidation. The record of Iraqi activities designed to deceive and mislead inspectors runs from the subtle to the outrageous'.[113] Yet much was achieved, not only in terms of the actual disarming of large sections of the Iraqi arsenal of weapons of mass destruction, but also in terms of operating new techniques of arms control, such as:

zero-notice inspections, 'go anytime, anyplace, with anyone and anything' authority, right of unlimited aerial photography, the right to bring in all necessary inspection equipment without prior notice or the right of Iraqi inspection of it, unlimited sampling authority, freedom to mount helicopter flights for observation and movement and the right to operate without restriction open and encrypted communications.[114]

The involuntary disarmament of Iraq had its successes, but also demonstrated the problems inherent in coercive arms control.

Conclusion

This analysis has concentrated on examining the resolutions of the United Nations Security Council not only as representations of the will of the international community, but because those resolutions have had a direct impact on arms control. It was the Security Council Resolutions that created the structures for the arms control work in Somalia, Cambodia, Mozambique and Iraq. Further, when Resolutions were passed under Chapter 7 of the United Nations, as with Resolutions 687 and 707 in relation to Iraq, they were mandatory and could have been enforceable.

Whereas during the cold war, the United Nations was involved in creating global controls on weapons, imposing embargoes on individual countries and facilitating security guarantees, during the post-cold war period the United Nations focused purely on the limitations on the armaments of individual states. However, there has been a great increase in activity in this field. It would be accurate to say that the United Nations was more involved in arms control efforts and achievements in the first five years of the post-cold war period than in the whole of the previous forty or so years. And not only were there more examples of arms control by international organisation, those controls also became deeper.

These post-cold war activities of the United Nations can be grouped into four categories: concerns to support and strengthen the humanitarian laws of war; work to achieve the implementation of arms embargoes; efforts to bring about the creation of cantons for the disarmament of groups; and the initiation of arms control through compellance. Each will be briefly examined.

First, the United Nations issued proclamations that those engaged in fighting in the former Yugoslavia, Cambodia and Somalia should adhere to the laws of war. However, these declarations were weak in that there was no comprehensive monitoring arrangements, no means of enforcing penalties, and hence no regimes of humanitarian behaviour instituted or supported. Indeed, it may well be that the failure to take action following the issuing of declarations may have contributed to the weakening of the regime of the humanitarian laws of war, especially in Bosnia, where humanitarian norms were openly, repeatedly and deliberately flouted, leading to the use of NATO air power in August 1995.

Second, in six of the seven cases examined in this chapter, arms embargoes were instituted. This built upon the United Nations' experience during the cold war, in particular the embargoes imposed on both Southern Rhodesia and South Africa. However, in the post-cold war period this practice deepened, with the creation of machinery associated with the Security Council to oversee the implementation of the embargoes.

Third, the United Nations entered into agreements to manage the disarmament and disbandment of forces in Somalia, Cambodia and Mozambique. Arrangements of this sort had been entered into previously (for example, in the transition from white-ruled Rhodesia to majority-voting Zimbabwe) but not in such a comprehensive manner by the United Nations. It may be argued that these activities failed at different levels in Somalia, Cambodia and Mozambique; certainly the voluntary compliance on the part of the indigenous parties in these states although variable, was not as high as expected. However, the United Nations in this area was designed to provide a service, which was available to the groups if they wished to take advantage of it within the terms of the agreements into which they had entered.

The fourth and final area was the field in which the United Nations' arms control activities went much further than had ever been seen previously. The compulsory disarmament measures seen in Iraq and Somalia were very different exercises, reflecting the diverse nature of the two countries. Iraq was subjected to detailed investigation by civilian experts with regard to the elimination of sophisticated weapons of mass destruction. Even should that activity not eliminate all of those weapons, the United Nations' arms control work would certainly have eliminated a large amount of military material and capacity in Iraq. In Somalia, military forces were used to compel the warring parties to surrender their relatively low technology weapons. Again, a large amount of material was collected and destroyed by the United Nations' forces. In both cases military force was used to compel the parties to continue to adhere to their commitments. In both cases, substantial numbers of weapons were destroyed. However, only in Iraq was a regime instituted to try to ensure something more than a transitory arrangement and even here, doubts were raised about the long-term viability of monitoring.

The various arms control initiatives of the United Nations in the post-cold war world makes it clear that international organisation is an important category of arms control. That many of these efforts were failures does not, in itself, invalidate this category, for evaluations of success and failure were not criteria used in devising the typology presented in this book. Arms control has been a tool utilised for thousands of years. In the twentieth century, with the rise of the international organisation, it was perhaps inevitable that major institutions would also use this approach; or, perhaps more accurately, it was perhaps inevitable that states would seek to utilise arms control through international organisation. Certainly this has been the case with the United Nations since 1988. Perhaps the relative failure of UN arms control efforts since that time can be explained, at least in part, by the relatively recent development of this approach, and the paucity of conceptual development of arms control by international organisation.

Notes

1 Paragraph 5, Security Council Resolution 748 (1992), 31 March 1992; United Nations Document 92–14910 4192Z (E).
2 United Nations Document S/RES/841, 16 June 1993.
3 *Ibid.*
4 *Ibid.*
5 For a brief overview, see Erik Goldstein *Wars and Peace Treaties* London: Routledge 1992, pp. 164–6.
6 For more detailed examinations of these conflicts in the former Yugoslavia see, for example, J. Seroka and V. Pavlovic (editors) *The Tragedy of Yugoslavia* Armonk, NY: M. E. Sharp, 1992; A. B. Fetherston, O. Ramsbotham and T. Woodhouse 'UNPROFOR: Some Observations from a Conflict Resolution Per-

spective' *International Peacekeeping* Vol. 1, No. 2, 1995; Lenard J. Cohen *Broken Bonds: The Disintegration of Yugoslavia* Boulder, CO: Westview, 1993; and Age Eknes 'The United Nations' Predicament in the Former Yugoslavia' in Thomas G. Weiss (editor) *The United Nations and Civil Wars* Boulder, CO: Lynne Rienner, 1995, pp. 109–26. For an excellent examination of the historical background, see Ivo Banac *The National Question in Yugoslavia* Ithaca: Cornell University Press, 1984.

7   Paragraph 6: reproduced in 'The United Nations and the Situation in the Former Yugoslavia' United Nations Department of Public Information, reference DPI/1312, October 1992, p. 18.

8   Paragraph 5; *ibid.*, p. 19.

9   Paragraph 2; *ibid.*

10 Resolution 727, paragraph 3; *ibid.*, p. 20: and Resolution 740, paragraph 3; *ibid.*, p. 21.

11 Resolution 743, 21 February 1992, paragraphs 2, 3 and 5; *ibid.*, p. 22. Under paragraph 11, 'the embargo imposed by paragraph 6 of Security Council resolution 713 (1991) shall not apply to weapons and military equipment destined for the sole use of UNPROFOR'; *ibid.*

12 Resolution 749, paragraphs 4 and 5; *ibid.*, p. 23.

13 Resolution 752 of 15 May 1992, paragraphs 3, 4, 5 and 11; *ibid.*, p. 25.

14 Dated 30 June 1992; *ibid.*, p. 32.

15 For the text, see *ibid.*, p. 35.

16 *Ibid.*

17 For the text, see *ibid.*, p. 36. The loss of French soldiers was also condemned.

18 *Ibid.*, p. 42. China abstained.

19 See 'Weapons Monitors, "No-Fly" Zone Fail to Stem Bosnian Violence' *Arms Control Today* October 1992.

20 Adopted 10 November 1992; United Nations document 92–68974 4558Z (E).

21 Paragraph 3; United Nations document 92–82882 4846Z (E).

22 Paragraph 2; United Nations document 93–09542 4934Z (E).

23 Following these reverses, the United Nations made another effort to advance peacemaking efforts. On 4 June 1993, to support the Vance–Owen peace plan, Resolution 836

'Authorises UNPROFOR, in addition to the mandate defined in resolutions 770 (1992) or 13 August 1992 and 776 (1992), in carrying out the mandate ... acting in self-defence, to take the necessary measures, including the use of force, in reply to bombardments against the safe areas by any of the parties or to armed incursion into them or in the event of any deliberate obstruction in or around those areas to the freedom of movement of UNPROFOR or of protected humanitarian convoys;

Decides that, ... Member States, ... may take, under the authority of the Security Council and subject to close coordination with the Secretary General and UNPROFOR, all necessary measures, through the use of air power ... to support UNPROFOR in the performance of its mandate.' Paragraphs 9 and 10; United Nations document, no reference.

24 See 'Sarajevo Deaths Revive Debate over Response' *Financial Times* 8 February 1994; 'UN Row Brews over Bosnian Air Strikes' *Financial Times* 9 February

1994; and 'NATO Vows Air Raids in 10 Days unless Serbs Pull Back Artillery' *International Herald Tribune* 10 February 1994.

25　See Michael Evans 'NATO Air Commander Ready to Extend Strikes' *The Times* 22 February 1994; and Mark M. Nelson 'Success in Sarajevo Spurs New Efforts to End Conflict' *Wall Street Journal Europe* 23 February 1994.

26　See Edward Mortimer 'Western Military Alliance Fires Its First Shots in Anger' *Financial Times* 1 March 1994; Christopher Bellamy 'Serbian Aircraft Outclassed by NATO Operation' *The Independent* 1 March 1994; and Michael Evans 'Challenge to NATO Beaten Off in 19 Minutes' *The Times* 1 March 1994.

27　See 'NATO Air Strike Halts Serb Attack' *Financial Times* 11 April 1994; 'NATO Jet Fighters Attack Serb Positions in Gorazde' *Wall Street Journal Europe* 11 April 1994; Barbara Starr 'Serbs Feel Force from NATO's CAS Missions' *Jane's Defence Weekly* 16 April 1994, p. 3.

28　On this, see Andrew M. Dorman and Adrian Treacher *European Security: An Introduction to Security Issues in Post-Cold War Europe* Aldershot: Dartmouth, 1995, pp. 95–6.

29　See 'Russia Opposes Air Strikes' *Financial Times* 11 February 1994; 'Yeltsin Expresses Anger over Ultimatum by NATO' *Wall Street Journal* 16 February 1994; Helen Womack 'Russia Warns of All-Out War if Air Strikes Go Ahead' *The Independent* 19 February 1994; Laura Silber 'Serbs Still Believe They Hold Winning Cards' *Financial Times* 1 March 1994; and Bruce Clark 'Rift grows over UN action' *Financial Times* 12 April 1994. The momentum was built up 18 months later, with the NATO air assault on the Bosnian Serbs at the end of August 1995.

30　Resolution 752 of 15 May 1992, paragraphs 6; *ibid.*, p. 25.

31　Resolution 757, 30 May 1992, paragraph 17; *ibid.*, p. 30. China and Zimbabwe abstained on this vote.

32　Paragraphs 6 and 10; reproduced in 'The United Nations and the Situation in the Former Yugoslavia', pp. 33–4.

33　*Ibid.*

34　*Ibid.*, pp. 35–6.

35　*Ibid.*, p. 36.

36　*Ibid.*, p. 37.

37　*Ibid.*, p. 40. China, India and Zimbabwe abstained.

38　*Ibid.*, p. 38.

39　Paragraph 1; United Nations document 93–09821 4936Z (E).

40　Paragraph 2; United Nations Document, no reference.

41　Paragraph 1; United Nations Document SC/5390.

42　Paragraphs 3 and 4(a); United Nations Document, no reference.

43　See Jeffrey Clark 'Debacle in Somalia' *Foreign Affairs* Vol. 72, No. 1, 1993, pp. 109–23.

44　See 'The United Nations and the Situation in Somalia' United Nations Department of Public Information, December 1992, reference DP1/1321, p. 2.

45　*Ibid.*, p. 11.

46　For further details, see 'Report of the Secretary General', as mandated in Resolution 733, paragraph 10; United Nations document S/23693, 11 March 1992.

47　'The United Nations and the Situation in Somalia', p. 11. Also see R. Thakur

'From Peacekeeping to Peace-enforcement: The United Nations' Operation in Somalia' *Journal of Modern African Studies*, 1994.

48   Paragraph 7; 'The United Nations and the Situation in Somalia', p. 12.

49   Paragraph 2; *ibid.*, p. 13.

50   Paragraph 11; *ibid.*

51   Paragraph 3; *ibid.*, p. 14.

52   28 August 1992; paragraph 3; *ibid.*, p. 15.

53   See *ibid.*, p. 5.

54   *Ibid.*, p. 17.

55   *Ibid.*

56   'Further report of the Secretary General Submitted in Pursuance of Paragraphs 18 and 19 of Resolution 794 (1992)'; United Nations document S/25354, 3 March 1993, p. 14.

57   *Ibid.*

58   United Nations Document SC/5573, 26 March 1993.

59   Paragraphs 1, 3 and 4; 'Report of the Secretary General on the Implementation of Security Council Resolution 837 (1993) United Nations Document S/26022.

60   *Ibid.*, p. 8.

61   *Ibid.*

62   For a general critique of the UN role in Somalia, see Mohamed Sahnoun *Somalia: The Missed Opportunites* Washington DC: United States Institute for Peace, 1994.

63   On the United Nations' role in Cambodia, see Michael W. Doyle and Ayaka Suzuki 'Transitional Authority in Cambodia' in Thomas G. Weiss *The United Nations* pp. 127–49; and Michael W. Doyle and Nishkala Suntharalingam 'The UN in Cambodia: Lessons for Complex Peacekeeping' *International Peacekeeping* Vol. 1, No. 2, 1994, pp. 117–47.

64   'Report of the Secretary General on Cambodia' United Nations Document S/23613, 19 February 1992, p. 2.

65   United Nations Document 91–36366 3732Z (E).

66   On the broader issues, see Yasushi Akashi 'The Challenge of Peacekeeping in Cambodia' *International Peacekeeping* Vol. 1, No. 2, 1994.

67   In addition, UNTAC under the military component had to consider accusations of non-compliance with the Paris Agreement, the repatriation of prisoners of war, and the repatriation of refugees and displaced persons (all in Annexe 2 of the Paris Agreement, Articles X, XI and XII respectively).

68   Paragraph 54, 'Report of the Secretary General on Cambodia', p. 12.

69   Annexe 2, Article V, paragraph 1.

70   'Report of the Secretary General on Cambodia', p. 14. The four parties referred to were the Cambodian People's Armed Forces, the National Army of Democratic Kampuchea, the Khmer People's National Liberation Armed Forces, and the National Army of Independent Kampuchea.

71   See 'First Special Report of the Secretary General on the United Nations Transitional Authority in Cambodia' United Nations Document S/24090, 12 June 1992.

72   See 'Second Special Report of the Secretary General on the United Nations Transitional Authority in Cambodia' United Nations Document S/24286, 14 July

1992, p. 1.
73 United Nations Document 92–32926 4285Z (E), 21 July 1992.
74 Paragraphs 5 and 6; United Nations Document 92–49915 4403Z (E), p. 2.
75 'Third Progress Report of the Secretary General on the United Nations Transitional Authority in Cambodia' United Nations Document S/25124, 25 January 1993, pp. 1–2.
76 See 'Report of the Secretary General on the Conduct and Results of the Elections in Cambodia' United Nations Document S/25913, 1993.
77 See the sections on Mozambique in Stephen Hill and Shahin Malik *United Nations' Peacekeeping* Aldershot: Dartmouth, forthcoming 1996; and Raymond W. Copson *Africa's Wars and Prospects for Peace* Armonk, NY: M. E.Sharp, 1994.
78 See 'United Nations Operation in Mozambique' United Nations, 1993.
79 See 'United Nations Operation in Mozambique: Report of the Secretary-General' United Nations document S/24642, 9 October 1992.
80 United Nations' Documents 92–49921 4400Z(E) of 13 October 1992, and 92–82485 4837Z(E) respectively.
81 United Nations Document 93–39316(E), 9 July 1993.
82 See 'Report of the Secretary General on the United Nations Operation in Mozambique' United Nations Document S/26385, 30 August 1993.
83 'Report of the Secretary General on the United Nations Operation in Mozambique' United Nations Document S/26666, 1 November 1993.
84 See 'Report of the Secretary General on the United Nations Operation in Mozambique' 30 August 1993.
85 See 'Secretary General announces major breakthrough in Mozambican peace process' United Nations Document SG/SM/5133, 20 October 1993.
86 In October, Boutros-Ghali had admitted to the Government and Renamo that 'in the UN now we have problems due to the number of situations all over the world, due to the fact that we have a financial crisis, and we will not be able to provide immediately the police necessary in conformity with the agreement that was concluded in Rome'. United Nations' Document SG/SM/5133, 20 October 1993.
87 'Report of the Secretary General on the United Nations Operation in Mozambique' 1 November 1993, addendum.
88 Many of the details for this section have been drawn from official United Nations documentation: see 'Report of the Secretary General on the United Nations Operation in Mozambique', United Nations document S/1994/89, 28 January 1994; 'Report of the Secretary General on the United Nations Operation in Mozambique', United Nations document S/1994/511, 28 April 1994; and 'Report of the Secretary General on the United Nations Operation in Mozambique', United Nations document S/1994/803, 7 July 1994.
89 Paragraph 3 (c); 'United Nations Security Council Resolutions Relating to the Situation Between Iraq and Kuwait' United Nations, 1991, p. 9.
90 This was the thirteenth Resolution passed concerning the situation between Iraq and Kuwait.
91 The Resolution set up the United Nations Iraq–Kuwait Observation Mission (UNIKOM), the Iraq–Kuwait Boundary Demarcation Commission, and the United Nations Compensation Commission, as well as the disarmament initia-

tives described below.

92 From the Preamble; see 'United Nations Security Council Resolutions Relating to the Situation Between Iraq and Kuwait', pp. 20–1.

93 This was contained in paragraph 24; *ibid.*, pp. 24–5.

94 Paragraph 8; *ibid.*, p. 22.

95 Paragraph 9(a); *ibid.*

96 Paragraph 9 (b)(i); *ibid.*

97 Paragraphs 12 and 13; *ibid.*, p. 23.

98 One of the most detailed studies of the Iraqi case to date is Kathleen C. Bailey *The UN Inspections in Iraq: Lessons for On-Site Verification* Boulder CO: Westview, 1995.

99 See David Kay 'The Lessons of Intrusive Verification in Iraq' in Centre for Defence Studies *Brassey's Defence Yearbook 1993* London: Brassey's, 1993, p. 202.

100 17 June 1991; 'United Nations Security Council Resolutions Relating to the Situation Between Iraq and Kuwait', pp. 27–8.

101 Paragraph 1; *ibid.*, pp. 31–2.

102 11 October 1991; *ibid.*, pp. 34–5.

103 On these and other incidents, see Edmund Piasecki and Toby Trister Gati 'The United Nations and Disarmament' in Richard D. Burns (editor), *Encyclopedia of Arms Control and Disarmament* New York: Charles Scribner, 1993, especially pp. 766–7; 'UN, Iraq Reach Compromise; Avoid Renewed Warfare' *Arms Control Today* July/August 1992; and 'Allied Forces Bomb Iraq to Force Compliance with Demands' *Arms Control Today* January/February 1993.

104 See 'Ambassador Rolf Ekeus: Unearthing Iraq's Arsenal' *Arms Control Today* April 1992, pp. 6–10.

105 For an assessment of the activities in 1991, see Johan Molander 'The United Nations and Iraq: a Case of Enforced Verification and Disarmament?' in J. B. Poole and R. Guthrie, *Verification Report 1992* London: Vertic, 1992, pp. 241–8; for activities up to the end of 1992, see David Kay 'The Lessons of Intrusive Verification in Iraq', pp. 201–10.

106 See John Simpson 'The Iraqi Nuclear Programme and the Future of the IAEA Safeguards System', in *Verification Report 1992*, p. 249.

107 Maurizio Zifferero 'The IAEA: Neutralizing Iraq's Nuclear Weapons Potential' *Arms Control Today* April 1993, p. 7.

108 See 'Ambassador Rolf Ekeus: Unearthing Iraq's Arsenal'.

109 On this see, for example, Paul Doty 'The Challenge of Destroying Chemical Weapons' *Arms Control Today* October 1992, pp. 25–9.

110 Edmund Piasecki and Toby Trister Gati 'The United Nations and Disarmament', p. 766.

111 Tim Trevan 'UNSCOM Faces Entirely New Verification Challenges in Iraq' *Arms Control Today* April 1993, p. 11.

112 See 'IAEA and UNSCOM Inspection Teams in Iraq Since the Gulf War' *Arms Control Today* April 1993, p. 29.

113 David Kay 'The Lessons of Intrusive Verification in Iraq', pp. 203.

114 *Ibid.*, p. 205. UNSCOM even operated a U–2 spy plane over Iraq to increase its flow of independent information.

Conclusion

The first chapter of this book set out two theses with regard to arms control. The first thesis was that, over time, the nature of arms control has widened in scope from very limited functions to the broader comprehension of arms control employed in this book. The first task for this conclusion is, therefore, to examine the width of the arms control agreements in the post-cold war world. Were there significant agreements in all five types of arms control in the post-cold war world? Were any of these five categories particularly strengthened by that arms control activity? The second thesis was that particular arms control agreements can be assessed on the basis of a concept of the depth of that agreement. The second task for the conclusion is, therefore, to assess the depth of the various agreements in the post-cold war world. The final section of this conclusion will seek to place the widening and deepening concepts together in order to assess the nature of arms control agreements in the post-cold war world in historical perspective. This will enable some conclusions to be drawn as to whether arms control has a significant future in the latter half of the 1990s and beyond.

The width of arms control in the post-cold war world

Widening, it will be recalled, refers to the different types of arms control activity practised over the course of human history. Early arms control practice was fairly crude, with polities reaching agreements purely over the size, strength and disposition of their forces in two circumstances: at the end of conflicts, in order to formally create a new balance between them; and to create or perpetuate strategic stability between political entities that might have believed they were in between major conflicts. However, arms control widened during the Middle Ages, when agreements were reached over norms of behaviour in order to limit the scope, means and timing of inter-state violence. Further widening took place during the following centuries, for with the increasing sophistication of technology, growing attention was

201

placed on the problems of the proliferation of weaponry in various different forms. A fifth development came during the twentieth century, with the creation of a new form of arms control, one managed by global international organisation. Thus, conceptually, five types of arms control were identified as being in existence at the beginning of the post-cold war period: arms control at the conclusion of conflicts; arms control to further strategic stability; arms control to create norms of behaviour; arms control to manage the proliferation of weapons; and arms control by international organisation.

As has been seen in the successive chapters in this book, arms control agreements have been reached in the post-cold war era in all of these five conceptual categories. Two important issues need to be addressed in terms of widening. First, the existence of agreements in all five categories of arms control does not imply that there has been equal activity in each category, for in fact there has been a fairly uneven development across the board. Second, the concept of widening may be applied not only to the growth of different types of arms control, but also to a widening of forms of arms control *within* each conceptual category. Both of these issues will be addressed in turn.

First, there have been very uneven developments in relation to widening in the post-cold war world. It is possible to create a hierarchy amongst the five categories of arms control using as criteria assessments of the significance of the agreements for that category. In this way, it becomes clear that arms control by international organisation has been the most significant area of arms control in terms of widening. Prior to the emergence of the post-cold war period, it had proved extraordinarily difficult to create an international consensus strong enough to produce concerted action by international organisation. Of course, prior to 1919 the basic building blocks of such activity did not exist. Many earnest discussions took place within the League of Nations, but little disarmament action ensued. During the cold war, superpower spheres of interest and vetoes reduced the scope for United Nations activity. However, since the late 1980s, the actions of the United Nations in Iraq, Cambodia, Mozambique, Somalia and elsewhere have demonstrated the firm existence of a category of arms control activity which, previously, seemed to range from insignificant to non-existent. The disarmament activities of the United Nations have, therefore, clarified the status of a hitherto unclear category. This is not to suggest that the UN's activities have been generally successful for, as was seen in Chapter 6, many problems have been associated with the United Nation's arms control work in a number of countries. However, when considering the range of arms control activity, disarmament by international organisation must now be seen as an important and independent category for analysis.

If arms control by international organisation has been the most significant development in terms of widening, it is clear that arms control to create norms of behaviour has been the least significant in the post-cold war world. There have been no major attempts at the codification of the behaviour of states in violent circumstances similar to the efforts in the Hague and Geneva conferences in the last decade of the nineteenth century and the first decade of the twentieth, and the middle of the century, despite violence and atrocities in the former Yugoslavia, Angola, Sudan, Transcaucasia, and elsewhere. Few agreements were signed in the immediate post-cold war period directly concerned with creating and strengthening norms of behaviour, with only five agreements immediately apparent: the 1989 United States–Soviet Union Agreement on the Prevention of Dangerous Military Activities; the 1989 United States–Soviet Union Agreement on the Notification of Strategic Exercises; the 1992 Open Skies Treaty; the 1992 CFE 1A Agreement; and the Vienna Documents of the CSCE. None of these agreements had any connection with the traditional agenda, which related to prohibitions on certain types of weapons, to norms protecting and defining non-combatants, and to prohibitions on the resort to warfare in certain geographically defined areas. These agreements were concerned with the cold war innovation of confidence- and security-building measures. Although important, these agreements were very narrowly defined. Where pre-existing norms were challenged, as in Bosnia, little was done to support the laws of war.

The other three categories of arms control identified in this book – at the end of major conflicts, arms control to strengthen strategic stability, and proliferation control – were all areas in which major arms control activity took place. Such agreements included CFE, START I and II, the START I Protocol and the Chemical Weapons Convention.

What are the possible reasons why the pattern of arms control widening took the shape that it did in the post-cold war world? That there were major agreements in the category of arms control at the end of major conflicts was clearly expected by many policy-makers. CFE, START I and the unilateral nuclear cuts that followed were designed to shape the new world order by concluding the disputes of the old world. In the area that was at the heart of the cold war, relations between the superpowers and in Europe, events moved very quickly. Indeed, policy-makers in many countries made the calculation that the post-war settlements that had been arrived at in the 1990–1 period would not be adequate for ensuring strategic stability in the midst of such fast-moving events. Hence, Hungarians and Romanians moved to establish an Open Skies regime, and Americans and Russians to further nuclear stability through START II. Although not all regions in the world were tied into the cold war conflict, the end of the cold war had major implications for most. This was a logical period in which states sought to establish greater stability, whether that be in South Asia with the Indo-Pakistan agreement, or in South America with the Argentine–Brazilian agreement. The end of the cold war also had a significant effect upon efforts for proliferation control. It opened the way for the conclusion of the Chemical Weapons Convention, movement towards limits on nuclear testing, and led many to argue that, in the post-cold war order, there should be limitations placed on conventional weapons, since they were deemed by some to be an important cause of war – hence the P5 initiative, and the Arms Register.

The second important issue referred to the widening of arms control *within* categories. In the post-cold war period, this was particularly relevant in relation to managing the proliferation of weapons. With the development of international relations over the course of the twentieth century, arms control designed to create defensive proliferation management was much reduced. In the post-cold war world, only the document confirming the obligations of the new Germany and the attempts to re-orient the direction of the cold war institution, CoCom, could be identified with this approach. In addition, with the end of the cold war, regional proliferation agreements were increasingly designed not to create new regional arms control regimes, but rather to support existing ones, as was clear with both the START I Protocol and the unilateral nuclear disarmament by the South Africans. Most clearly, the globalisation of international relations has led to a widening into a greater emphasis on global proliferation management, with the examples of the Chemical Weapons Convention, the agreements over conventional weapons transfer restraints in the P5 talks, the United Nations' Arms Register, and the unilateral limits on nuclear testing. Thus, the nature of arms control to manage proliferation has widened, and the balance within that category has altered in the post-cold war world.

On the other hand, arms control to create norms of behaviour narrowed considerably during the post-cold war period. As already seen, those agreements had little connection with the traditional agenda and were concerned with the cold war innovation relating to confidence- and security-building measures (CSBMs). In addition, these agreements were narrow even in terms of CSBMs. During the development of CSBMs during the cold war, three distinct forms were identified, relating to greater openness, strengthening rules of conduct, and creating direct modes of communication. However, four of these agreements were concerned with CSBMs relating to greater openness.[1] One agreement alone (the 1989 United States–Soviet Union Agreement on the Prevention of Dangerous Military Activities) was related to CSBMs designed to create or strengthen rules of conduct. Finally, none of these agreements related to modes of direct communication. The narrowing of arms control in this category was, thus, marked: narrowing not only in terms of norms considered, but even narrowing within the confidence building measures sub-division.

Widening and narrowing within the categories of arms control should, perhaps, be expected over time. It has been argued in this book that policy-makers, historically, have frequently utilised the tool of arms control. However, this does not mean that they have had to use that tool equally. Recourse to particular tools may represent passing fashions or, more persuasively, may represent the nature of the political agenda in international relations which changes with the pattern of events, domestic pressures, the work of non-governmental organisations, the nature of national policies, and the influence of the media. One international reaction to the violence that has engulfed much of Africa, the former Yugoslavia and the former Soviet Union since the end of the cold war might be for states to attempt to strengthen the laws of war; or, it could be to try to limit the trade in small arms; or, perhaps, it might be not to use arms control at all. The point is that there are many forms of arms control that can be used at any point in time, but they should not all be seen to possess the same utility. Thus, a comprehensive, predictive, model of arms control would be extraordinarily difficult to develop.

The depth of arms control in the post-cold war world

The second thesis introduced in Chapter 1 was that arms control can be assessed on the basis of deepening. This concept of deepening, it will be recalled, refers to a process over time whereby arms control agreements may be said to have grown in relation to the level of detail provided in the terms of the agreement, the nature of the provisions for verification, and the provision for regime formation/continuation. How, then, can the depth of the arms control agreements of the post-cold war world be assessed?

In order to answer this question, three categories will be identified. The first category – *very deep* – refers to those agreements that were seen as path-breaking in terms of the depth of their provisions. These would be agreements that were longer, more detailed, more intrusive and increased the commitments of states more profoundly than hitherto. A second category – *moderately deep* – refers to those agreements that have fulfilled many of the basic criteria outlined above. Although not as profound in their implications as the first category, moderately deep agreements still demand significant commitments from states to implement the agreement and to maintain the agreement's requirements. The third category – *shallow* – relates to those agreements that comprise short documents, lacking detail and verification provisions.

Several very deep arms control agreements can be identified in the post-cold war world. This is particularly the case with both the CFE Treaty and the START I Treaty which, it has already been argued, reflected a pinnacle of cold war arms control practice. Since international suspicions were greatest during the cold war, naturally concern with creating detailed, verifiable agreements that would establish a strong compliance regime was very high.

However, the level of intrusiveness required to overcome such suspicions made very deep agreements difficult to reach during the cold war. The collapse of cold war suspicions in the late 1980s and early 1990s, therefore, made arriving at very deep agreements much more straightforward in the early post-cold war period. Both the CFE Treaty and the START I Treaty were extremely detailed documents, with extensive verification provisions, and both documents sought to explicitly create an arms control regime in, respectively, conventional and nuclear weapons. Other very deep agreements would include the Argentine–Brazilian Declaration and subsequent agreements, the Chemical Weapons Convention, and the United Nations' actions in Iraq, Mozambique and Somalia. The Open Skies Treaty, the Vienna Documents and the Hungarian–Romanian agreement were different from many of the other treaties in that they were concerned purely with verification and transparency; within those terms, however, they were also clearly very deep agreements.

A whole series of very deep agreements were therefore reached in the early post-cold war period, relating to many different forms of arms control and to different parts of the world. Such an outbreak of very deep arms control is completely without precedent in the history of arms control. Of course, depth is a relative concept. With the advance of arms control techniques and technology, greater depth should be expected in the final dozen years of the twentieth century compared with, for example, the final dozen years of the eighteenth century. However, if 'very deep' is defined in terms of the expectations and capabilities of the time, and not just in terms of technological possibilities, then the number and range of very deep arms control agreements reached at the beginning of the post-cold war period still may be said to be unprecedented.

The number of these very important agreements in many ways reduced the attention paid to other treaties concluded in the post-cold war period which could be described as moderately deep. Of particular significance in this regard would be the START I Protocol and the START II Treaty. In addition, other important arms control agreements that were moderately deep included the unilateral nuclear disarmament of South Africa and its accession to the Nuclear Non-Proliferation Treaty, and United Nations' actions over Cambodia, Haiti and Libya. A final example would be restraints on nuclear testing, which although taking the form of unilateral declarations (the United States, however, passed its moratorium into domestic law), were clear, probably verifiable through national technical means, and operated within a general global non-proliferation regime.

The final category relates to shallow agreements. These refer to those arrangements which either deliberately dispensed with detail verification and regime formation, or to those arrangements over which no such agreement proved possible. In the former category, examples would include the

CFE 1A Agreement, the limitations on conventional weapons transfers through the Permanent Five members of the Security Council, and the United Nations' Arms Register. Arrangements in which no agreement proved possible on creating any depth would include the attempt to extend the START regime through unilateral measures at the end of 1991, efforts which sacrificed both detail and verification to the desire to extend agreement on nuclear disarmament; the Indian–Pakistani agreement; and the United Nations' Resolutions with regard to Bosnia.[2]

The nature of post-cold war arms control

Applying the categories related to both the widening and deepening of arms control, a matrix can be generated to illustrate the nature of many of the agreements reached in the post-cold war world analysed in this book (Table C.1). In a categorisation of this sort, the general expectation would probably be that the agreements found in the column marked 'very deep' would be most effective, while those in the column marked 'shallow' would be ineffective as arms control agreements. However, this would not be entirely accurate, and is much too crude a way to use the concept of deepening. The India–Pakistan agreement, for example, although shallow, was the first significant agreement for many years between the two countries and initiated a new direction, albeit limited, for the two states in their security relations. On the other hand, the United Nations' disarmament activities in Somalia, although deep, were unsuccessfully implemented due to internal opposition in the country. It is, therefore, important to keep a focus upon the purpose and the possibilities of any arms control agreement, as well as its form and scope, rather than applying rigid formulae. There may well be circumstances in which a more shallow agreement is simply the most appropriate.

The analysis of this book has not sought to establish any criteria for assessing the success of arms control agreements. Very often, analysis of particular arms control agreements, or of arms control in general, focuses almost exclusively on this issue. This book has not addressed that question, for one of the central issues is that there has not been any general consensus on how 'arms control' should be defined in the post-cold war period. This book has, therefore, tried to present such definition. This has been attempted without imposing a deterministic tone onto the analysis. It is not argued that any arms control deal is 'better' than none, for the focus here is on typologies. Arms control agreements can fail in their own terms, can work to the disadvantage of individual states, and can be a focus of dissent and poorer relations between states. It is also perfectly possible for an arms control regime to be developed which may not be ideal for the enhancement of international security. The construction of the typology presented here

does not automatically imply that arms control is always universally beneficial.

Table C.1   *A matrix of post-cold war arms control agreements*

Category of Widening	Deepening		
	Very deep	*Moderately deep*	*Shallow*
End of conflict	● CFE ● START I		● Nuclear cuts, 1991
Strategic stability	● Brazil–Argentina ● Hungary–Romania	● START II	● India–Pakistan
Norms of behaviour	● Open skies ● Vienna document		● CFE 1A
Managing Proliferation	● CWC	● START Protocol ● South Africa	● P5 ● Arms register ● Nuclear testing
United Nations	● Iraq ● Somalia ● Mozambique	● Cambodia ● Haiti ● Libya	● Bosnia

During the cold war period, arms control was often compared and contrasted with disarmament. Briefly put, it was argued that arms control concerned agreed limitations on armaments in the interests of stability, which
could allow for increases as well as decreases in arsenals, and could encourage certain technological developments, if they were defined to be stabilising, while strictly controlling others. In contrast, proponents of
disarmament suggested that the concept was simply concerned with reductions in the levels of armaments, with advocates often arguing that arms
races led to war.[3]

Arms control, in this book, has been defined in a broader sense, one that
bears closer resemblance to its definition in historical terms, and one that
incorporates agreements over disarmament as well as other limitations on
armaments. Arms control must include broader normative restraints on
arms, on the use and possession of weapons. Further, agreements do not
have to be based on strict equality between the parties. One may argue that
this definition is too wide. If one is to include, for example, the *foedus inaequum*, should one not also include the destructive policies of, say, Genghis
Khan? The Mongol style of war was to terrorise opponents into submission

by the violence of their attack, often obliterating whole populations.[4] Could this, also, be seen as a form of arms control, in this broad sense? It could not, for arms control has to be about agreement between two polities. Leaders of Kievan Rus, or the Chin empire, did not agree to the elimination of their fighting capabilities by the Mongols. The Carthaginians, however, did agree to measures of deeply unequal disarmament in the Treaty of Zama with the Romans. One does not have to hold that two or more parties to a negotiation and agreement have to possess an equal hand; many of the examples examined in Chapter 1 illustrated that historically, this has not been the case. Arms control is not just about creating parity and equality in the interests of stability, although this is one form of the institution. It may also be about institutionalising inequality. This, and other, older, forms of arms control should not be ignored.

Perhaps a rather more pertinent criticism is that the analysis presented here is rather Euro-centric, or rather focuses too heavily on the developed world. Little has been uncovered about arms control activity in pre-colonial polities, such as in Asia or Africa. This problem of sources has meant that the focus on the developed world has been rather inevitable. There is clearly scope for further research in this area.

The assessment of the success or failure of arms control has not been a central part of this book, which has focused instead on producing a typology. Indeed, one could go further and argue that, in one sense, it does not really matter. International relations has, historically, been concerned with both competition and cooperation between polities. Some polities have, on many occasions, turned to arms control in order to manage these competitive–cooperative relations. The specifics of individual negotiations and agreements may have varied greatly, but the desire to turn to arms control has not. When polities try to establish new relations after a major conflict; seek to stabilise relations with actual or potential enemies; endeavour to create or develop norms of behaviour; attempt to manage the proliferation of weapons; or seek, on a collective and formal basis, to resolve regional conflict, it has been normal and natural to turn to the diplomatic tool known as arms control. There seems to be no reason to assume that this historical pattern will not be repeated often in the future.

What does this say about the future of arms control? At the end of this analysis, three issues seem clear. First, despite some expectations raised during the late 1980s and early 1990s that arms control was a tool of the past, this is unlikely to be the case, and arms control will continue to have a future. A tool which has been used by political entities for thousands of years to regulate relations between themselves is certain to offer new possibilities to leaders of states looking for ways to manage relations with putative, existing, former and perceived adversaries. Second, the widening of arms control is likely to continue, if not necessarily in creating new categories, then in forming new sub-divisions within existing categories. While emphasis in this conclusion has been placed on the arms control activities of the United Nations in suggesting a hierarchy for the five forms of arms control activity in the early part of the post-cold war period, different categories have risen and fallen in relative importance over time. It might be expected, for example, that arms control to create norms of behaviour may return to a more significant position in that hierarchy, as it did in the aftermaths of major confrontations and wars during the nineteenth and twentieth centuries. Third, although the concept and practice of deepening was greatly enhanced by the competition of the superpowers during the cold war, the development of arms control skills and the advance of technology in areas such as surveillance and communication may well, in themselves, further the process of deepening. However, it is the nature of international suspicions, the character of technical possibilities and their costs, and the scope for international cooperation taken together that are likely to be the key factors in determining the speed of the development of the deepening of arms control.

Arms control is a complicated phenomenon, one still not completely understood, although it has been in existence for so many years. Since arms control has been practised for so long, it is likely that it will have a future. Polities have utilised arms control with great frequency in the past. Given the difficulties in identifying fundamental differences in the nature of the competitive–cooperative character of international relations in the post-cold war period compared to that which has preceded it, it is not easy to explain why states should not continue to resort to the tool of arms control. What is so qualitatively different about the post-cold war world that could lead states not continue to respond to the complexity of competitive–cooperative relations with the tools that they have always used? Indeed, increases in international interactions through the further development of technology and communications may make recourse to arms control to ameliorate problems even more likely. Indeed, arms control techniques and approaches may be applied to areas such as environmental protection (for example, the protection of the ozone layer), or to ameliorate tensions between states over access to clean water.

One of the problems with the study of arms control in the post-cold war world is that it has been perceived through the prism of the arms control theory of the late 1950s and early 1960s. This book has not sought to undermine the intellectual basis of that body of theory. However, it has sought to argue that arms control is a much broader phenomenon than the one developed from those theoretical writings. What is called arms control theory is, in fact, only applicable to one of the five categories of arms control (arms control to strengthen strategic stability) and even then, essentially, only to nuclear arms control in that category. The study of arms control in the post-cold war period must be freed from these intellectual shackles in order to comprehend the breadth of arms control activity. This book stands as one contribution to that process.

Notes

1   The 1989 United States–Soviet Union Agreement on the Notification of Strategic Exercises; the 1992 Open Skies Treaty; the 1992 CFE 1A Agreement; and the Vienna Documents.

2   The mechanisms put in place to deepen UN action in Cambodia, Iraq and Somalia were not implemented in Bosnia which, therefore, reflected policy statements without follow-up. Bosnia, therefore, was the area of UN arms control which was the most shallow in this period.

3   See, for example, Philip Noel-Baker *The Arms Race: A Programme for World Disarmament* London: John Calder, 1958; and The Alternative Defence Commission *The Politics of Alternative Defence* London: Paladin, 1987.

4   On the nature of Mongol warfare and violence, see Francis W. Cleaves *The Secret History of the Mongols* in two volumes, Cambridge, MA; Harvard University Press, 1982; and Robert Marshall *Storm from the East: From Genghis Khan to Khubilai Khan* London: BBC Books, 1993.

Index

221